HEMINGWAY'S
FAITH

HEMINGWAY'S
FAITH

MARY CLAIRE KENDALL

Foreword by Maria Cooper Janis

ROWMAN & LITTLEFIELD
Lanham • Boulder • New York • London

Published by Rowman & Littlefield
An imprint of The Rowman & Littlefield Publishing Group, Inc.
4501 Forbes Boulevard, Suite 200, Lanham, Maryland 20706
www.rowman.com

86-90 Paul Street, London EC2A 4NE

British Library Cataloguing in Publication Information Available

Library of Congress Cataloging-in-Publication Data

Names: Kendall, Mary Claire, author.
Title: Hemingway's faith / Mary Claire Kendall.
Description: Lanham : Rowman & Littlefield, 2025. | Includes bibliographical
    references and index.
Identifiers: LCCN 2024025491 (print) | LCCN 2024025492 (ebook) |
    ISBN 9781538187913 (cloth) | ISBN 9781538187920 (ebook)
Subjects: LCSH: Hemingway, Ernest, 1899–1961—Religion. | Authors,
    American—20th century—Biography. | Catholic Church—Influence. |
    LCGFT: Biographies.
Classification: LCC PS3515.E37 Z6645 2025 (print) | LCC PS3515.E37 (ebook) |
    DDC 813/.52 [B]—dc23/eng/20240612
LC record available at https://lccn.loc.gov/2024025491
LC ebook record available at https://lccn.loc.gov/2024025492

♾™ The paper used in this publication meets the minimum requirements of
American National Standard for Information Sciences—Permanence of Paper for
Printed Library Materials, ANSI/NISO Z39.48-1992.

This book is dedicated to my father, Paul Albert Kendall, who would often say, with such joy in his heart, "Our Catholic Faith is so beautiful! We are so blessed!"

As I began to write this book, he told me, "All the gifts from God can be boiled down to one: Faith. Persevere to the end. Believe that God will take care of us until the end."

—PAUL A. KENDALL, SEPTEMBER 18, 2012,
PARAPHRASING ST. AUGUSTINE

"Politics and religion are two things I never discuss.
If my books don't make it clear how I feel about both,
then I've failed in my life's work."[1]
—ERNEST HEMINGWAY TO LEONARD LYONS, JULY 20, 1959

"And, when you are doing history, remember one of the things
we cannot do is to read into the past the prejudices
of the present. That's not history. That's journalism."[2]
—PROFESSOR EDWARD C. SMITH

1. Leonard Lyons, "The Lyon's Den," *New York Post* (July 21, 1959). Based on interview with Ernest Hemingway on the eve of his sixtieth birthday in Pamplona, Spain.

2. Mary Claire Kendall, "America Loses Pre-Eminent Civil War Historian; Professor Edward C. 'Eddie' Smith viewed history through a lens of truth and healing," *"Old Hollywood and Beyond," Substack* (April 13, 2023).

Contents

Foreword

When my father, Gary Cooper, met Ernest Hemingway eight years after playing Lt. Frederic Henry in Hollywood's film version of Hemingway's *A Farewell to Arms* (1932), the two immediately bonded.

It was at Sun Valley. The fall of 1940. The two icons were finally making each other's acquaintance. Hemingway had just finished writing *For Whom the Bell Tolls*, consciously modeling the protagonist on my father. And my father was filming *Sergeant York* (1941). They shared much over drinks by the fire in the Sun Valley Lodge. Their love of nature and the West and its indigenous peoples whom both had befriended in their youth. Their love of hunting and horseback riding. Their love of beautiful women. And so much more including tales of Hollywood.

Gradually they shared their love of the Catholic faith to which Hemingway had converted, then fallen away from for a few years, including, the second and final time, just before they met. A faith which my father, too, would find a religious home in, about which Mary Claire has poignantly written. "The best thing I ever did," he wanted his friend Hemingway to know as he lay dying.

My father would slip the surly bonds of earth just five weeks before his dear friend, on May 13, 1961. It was the toughest of blows for Hemingway, suffering intensely himself, albeit mostly from mental ailments due to a lethal combination of heredity and hard-living.

The facts about Hemingway's spiritual searching are artfully woven into this wonderful narrative in a deeper, more human and personal way, than the usual surface treatments of Hemingway's life.

As Hemingway said, "The best people possess a feeling for beauty, the courage to take risks, the discipline to tell the truth, the capacity for sacrifice."

All of this is evident in Mary Claire's book, though, candidly, it's hard to know the truth of Hemingway. Yet, as Mary Claire writes, "he was a complex man with a simple faith." So true. And my father loved him for it. "Poppa," as I called my father, did not suffer from the ailments that weighed down "Papa," and I think my father's stability helped Hemingway as much as Hemingway's wealth of knowledge enriched my father. Then, too, when they discussed faith, Hemingway shared doubts which my father helped dispel, no more dramatically than as he lay dying. That these great friends arrived in Heaven just about the same time makes perfect sense. And, they are, no doubt, cheering on *Hemingway's Faith* from their celestial perch. It's a gem!

—Maria Cooper Janis

Acknowledgments

I am deeply grateful for all those guardian angels helping me as I climbed what seemed like Mount Kilimanjaro. It would be impossible to name everyone, so let me offer this partial list of those who lit my path most brightly.

Charles Scribner III for providing the lodestar at the start of my journey in 2011, telling me that Hemingway considered himself a Catholic from that first moment being anointed on the battlefield in 1918; and, for staying with me throughout, offering sure guidance and key support.

Patrick Hemingway, for his keen insights into his father, and sharp Hemingway wit, starting with that July 2012 interview, "Hemingway on Hemingway and Hollywood," published in *Forbes*, among other memorable interviews and correspondence, notably his note, early on, in which he wrote, "I like your project about Hemingway's faith."

Redd Griffin, founding trustee of the Hemingway Foundation, who helped me understand Hemingway through the light of faith in many long conversations, 2011–2012; and Rev. Charles John ("C. J.") McCloskey, III, STD, for introducing me to Redd, among other acts of kindness.

H. R. "Stoney" Stoneback, the premier scholar of Hemingway's Catholicism, for crucial guidance and moral support as I worked to understand Hemingway in all his simplicity and complexity, notably for pointing me to the Robert Morgan Brown letters. In late 2021, Stoney passed from this life not long after our last conversation. I am grateful, too, to Matt Nickel, Stoney's protégé, for his crucial support and friendship; to Ed Renehan: I will never forget that time in Newport at the iconic Black Pearl, in August 2015, when he let me know, Stoney had given my work his full support. *That* was special; and to Joseph Pearce for publishing "Hemingway's Catholic Heart."

The many other Hemingway Society scholars, whom I have met along the way, whose insights and affirmations are so appreciated, including

Valerie Hemingway, Mary Dearborn, Hilary Justice, Scott Donaldson, Niklas Salmose—just the tip of the iceberg, if you will.

Maria Cooper Janis for giving me key insight into her father's relationship with Hemingway and for writing such a beautiful foreword.

The countless writers of biography and memoir, including family—Marcelline Hemingway Sanford, Madelaine "Sunny" Hemingway Mainland Miller, Leicester Hemingway, Elizabeth Hadley Richardson Hemingway (Mowrer) and Valerie Hemingway—and friends like A. E. Hotchner; and those who made it their life's work to piece together Hemingway's story, notably Carlos Baker and Michael Reynolds; those who have published Hemingway's letters—Fitzgerald's, too—including Baker and Sandra Spanier and Robert W. Trogdon—and Matthew Bruccoli. And the staff at the various Hemingway collections—bright lights all—who made my research smooth sailing, including those at the John F. Kennedy Presidential Library; Harry Ransom Center, University of Texas; Princeton University; and Oak Park Library, among others.

To all of them, named and unnamed, I express my sincerest gratitude.

My editors at Rowman and Littlefield, notably Richard Brown, for intuiting the importance of *Hemingway's Faith* in filling a void in the vast body of literature about this giant of American letters, helping me every step of the way, with counsel and wisdom, as I worked to bring this work to polished perfection; joined by his wonderfully deft Assistant Editor Victoria Shi who was such a delight to work with and so important to the final product.

Thomas D. Selz, who makes it all work from a business standpoint.

Last but not least, my parents, Paul Albert and Claire Yvonne Kendall, who kept me squarely focused on writing about what makes people tick—on biography—starting with that chance meeting, that summer of 1999, with that fellow in an upstate New York Olive Garden.

Preface

May 13, 2011, was the fiftieth anniversary of the death of Gary Cooper. That day, my feature about this iconic actor finally came out in *The National Catholic Register*.

Five weeks later, news of the fiftieth anniversary of the death of Ernest Hemingway by his own hand hit. He was Coop's close friend. I was intrigued. Suddenly this iconic writer was on my radar. I began reading *The Sun Also Rises*, a copy of which I had randomly picked up at a book fair at the Andrew Mellon Auditorium shortly after the end of the George H. W. Bush Administration in which I served, knowing it was a literary classic I must read. One day. Now, I was ready. My nerves were shot. I had struggled to gain a foothold as a writer of literary works for the better part of a decade. Reading *The Sun Also Rises* was so calming and put me to sleep each night, not because it was *boring* but because it was just so beautifully written. It was music to my ears and solace for my soul.

By Friday, September 9, I was watching A&E's *Ernest Hemingway: Wrestling with Life*, and felt as if "Hem" was putting his hand on my shoulder and whispering, "It's my turn." I really did feel his invisible presence and felt impelled to try and figure out what made *Hemingway* tick.

Three days later, I reached out to Charles Scribner III whom I had met at the CIC in Washington, DC, when he came to discuss and sign copies of his book *The Shadow of God: A Journey Through Memory, Art and Faith*. It was the Feast of the Most Holy Name of Mary. I was looking for a Hemingway angle, I wrote, and noted my recent feature about his close friend Cooper. Amazingly, he wrote back and told me that Hemingway considered himself a Catholic from the moment of that anointing on the battlefield along the Piave River outside of Venice. Now *that* was an eye-opener. His father and grandfather, particularly, were close to Hemingway, having published all of his works since *The Sun Also Rises*. *They* would know. I had my angle.

Then Fr. C. John McCloskey III, the former CIC director, introduced me to Redd Griffin of Oak Park, Illinois, whose mother had shared a room at Oak Park Hospital with Hemingway's sister, "Sunny," after she gave birth to Redd on December 3, 1938. Sunny had given birth the day before to her only child, Ernest Hemingway Maitland, and they all became great friends. Over Thanksgiving Redd and I spoke in one long session for *four hours* as I furiously scribbled away. Redd shared Sunny's great insight about the spiritual foundation of her brother's writing.

I was off to the races. Then after Redd tragically died a year later of a heart attack, I reached out to H. R. Stoneback, as noted, the premier scholar of Hemingway's Catholicism. He was very gracious and offered to help advance my research in any way he could and was very encouraging vis-à-vis my initial book proposal. Through the efforts of Stoney and his protégé, Matt Nickel, I was given the opportunity to write about Hemingway's Catholicism for *St. Austin Review* in a piece I titled "Hemingway's Catholic Heart," which I read as a paper at the international Hemingway conference in 2018 in Paris, chaired by Stoneback. After I began caring for my bed-bound father in late 2019, I kept advancing the project bit by bit and when Charles Scribner III read my article, he introduced me to his publisher, and herein are the fruits, all these years later, after that Friday in September when Hem touched my heart inviting me to try and understand *his heart*—his "Catholic heart."

Introduction

"To understand my brother's writing, you need to understand his spirituality. It was the foundation of everything he wrote."[1]
—MADELINE "SUNNY" HEMINGWAY MILLER

Ernest Hemingway belongs to the triumvirate of the three greatest writers from America's golden age of literature, also including F. Scott Fitzgerald and William Faulkner.

Known for *The Sun Also Rises, A Farewell to Arms, For Whom the Bell Tolls,* and *The Old Man and the Sea,* among other literary masterpieces, he is also remembered for his machismo and spirit of adventure: He was a big-game hunter, deep-sea fisher, boxer, avid swimmer and skier, outdoorsman and bullfighting aficionado, with a bevy of friends, including many well-known celebrities.

But what is less well known about Hemingway is that, in his writing, which he ranked his most important endeavor in life, he drew on his spirituality and faith, the wellspring of which, besides his strong Christian upbringing, was his Catholic faith to which he converted.

Previous biographers have either ignored this story or told it incompletely or inaccurately. For example, in his 564-page authorized biography, *Hemingway: A Life Story,* Carlos Baker mentions on page 44 that Don Giuseppe Bianchi befriended Hemingway when he was serving as an American Red Cross ambulance driver in Italy during World War I. After Hemingway sustained near-fatal injuries on the front, Baker writes, "The little priest from the Abruzzi came along the line of wounded men, murmuring the holy words, anointing each as he passed. He recognized Ernest and did the same for him." Then, without making any mention of any formal conversion in the intervening pages, Baker notes on page 126 that Hemingway was not

1

prepared to raise his first child, John Hadley Nicanor ("Bumby") Hemingway, Catholic, leaving the reader to wonder *why on earth* he would want to
raise him Catholic. Hemingway was, after all, raised in the Congregational
faith. When Baker does get down to defining Hemingway's faith, he calls
him a "nominal" Catholic. British writer Anthony Burgess, known for *A
Clockwork Orange*, and Catholic himself, superficially peppers his engaging
work about Hemingway some ten years later, with the "nominal" label, as
well.[2] Yet, as Hemingway's fourth wife Mary told the late H. R. Stoneback,
Distinguished Professor of English at the State University of New York,
New Paltz, who was the foremost scholar on Hemingway's Catholicism and
himself a convert, "Ernest was never anything in name only. When he said
he was a Catholic, he meant it."[3] Hemingway would later write to Robert
Morgan Brown that Baker reminded him of "someone touching religion very
carefully with a ten-foot pole."[4]

Jeffrey Meyers, writing nearly twenty years after Baker, is even more
dismissive, arguing that Hemingway's Catholicism was "bogus." His faith
is completely airbrushed out some thirty years later when Mary Dearborn
writes as if Hemingway's religious and spiritual life was nonexistent.

No wonder Hemingway was so leery of biographers. And, though, as
a classic "closet Catholic," he kept his faith to himself, a biographer should
look beyond the surface of Hemingway's reticence to discern the truth about
his conversion and his devotion. Otherwise, the portrait is incomplete. It's as
if, by analogy, a mirror in a portrait reflecting a beautiful painting is excised.
Let's say it's a portrait of Hemingway writing, and there's a magnificent
painting of Mary he looks up at when he takes a break from his writing. The
Marian painting would have been reflected in the excised mirror. But now,
all you see is a man writing, when the fuller reality is a man, writing, who is
in love with Mary.

The truth is, Hemingway was profoundly influenced by his Catholicism. As Charles Scribner III told me, "Hemingway called himself a Catholic, having been baptized by a Catholic priest in Italy during WWI."[5] Yes,
Scribner should know.

While biographers have failed to acknowledge this fact of Hemingway's
life, many scholars have recognized it quite clearly. Stoneback, for one, com-
menting on the observation by Reynolds Price, poet, dramatist, essayist, and
professor of English at Duke University, that "Hemingway's 'lifelong subject' was '*saintliness*;'" though, in Price's estimation, he did not consciously
know it.[6] Stoneback commended Price's "fine essay" (must reading for "all
students of Hemingway"), while advancing his key insight significantly.
"Hemingway," wrote Stoneback, "knew more than 'half the lesson of the

desert fathers' . . . Hemingway's subject, as I saw it, was saintliness, but he knew it, it was not secret from him but from his readers; it was his very own private secret that he kept mostly to himself and only revealed in his fiction."[7]

Imagine. "Hemingway's subject" was "saintliness." Who knew?

Certainly, the biblically inspired titles of so many of his works, including early on, *In Our Time* and *The Sun Also Rises*, hint at his spirituality. Yet, he was also extremely flawed, which, far from obscuring his spiritual sensibilities, only sheds more light.

He was a complex man with a simple faith—the hidden crucifixes, untrumpeted visits to cathedrals, and private celebrations of feast days as much a part of Hemingway as his big-game hunting, deep-sea fishing, boxing, and bullfighting—and writing, too—which, he enthused, in conversations with Ralph Withington Church, a philosopher and writer, and friend of Sherwood Anderson, in Paris in the 1920s, provided "actual grace."[8] So, in doing what he loved, he was storming heaven, grabbing buckets of grace that he cashed in later at moments when he showed great generosity of soul—sometimes even heroism. Or when his weakness threatened to overwhelm him.

Quite the opposite of the hedonistic image the intelligentsia and Hollywood revel in, regardless of the distortion. And the distortions are epic. As his son Patrick said, the depiction of his father in HBO Films' *Hemingway & Gellhorn* (2012) was "so ludicrous as to be beyond conception."[9] Far more accurate is the image of the disciplined writer, full of sin and in need of redemption, who infused his writing with a yearning for the very spirituality that he strived for, but often failed to achieve hobbled as he was by human frailties and circumstances that would challenge even the greatest saint.

Given this reality, it's an enigma why Hemingway's biographers have missed the mark, leaving such an empty, unexplored canvas of his life just waiting to be painted. As Stoneback writes: "Later in our exchange of letters Price lamented, among other things, Hemingway's disastrous luck in biographers and wondered why American academic biographers are simply unable to evoke the center of Hemingway's life. I, too, lament and wonder."[10]

This book seeks to fill the void and paint a portrait that reveals Hemingway *as he was*—flawed and in need of redemption, seeking grace especially through Mary, mediatrix of all grace—that wellspring of true healing—often without knowing it, just feeling it strongly. Which is what he wanted the effect of his writing to be. Writing, steeped in spirituality, helping us feel what is most deeply human, and divine—our humanity being the foundation of supernatural life.

❧❧❧

1

❧❧❧

Formed in the Protestant Heartland

Born as the Victorian era was breathing its last, Ernest Hemingway initially only knew the Protestant heartland of Oak Park, nine miles due west of Chicago, where it was said "the steeple churches began and the saloons ended."

Chicagoans had flocked to Oak Park after the Great Chicago Fire of 1871 when the Windy City outlawed building with wood—its predominantly wooden structures and sidewalks swallowed up in the epic conflagration triggered by Mrs. O'Leary's barn bursting into flames, the three-week late summer drought's high winds serving as an accelerant. The village of Oak Park, governed by the township of Cicero until 1902, welcomed wooden homes, while at the same time imposing strict prohibitions against enjoyment of certain worldly pleasures reflecting the prescriptive Congregational faith to which Hemingway's grandparents, on his father's side, adhered. His maternal grandfather, Ernest Miller Hall, hailing from across the pond, belonged to the more lenient Church of England, and blithefully ignored these Puritan rules, enjoying cigars and shots of whisky with friends in the elegant parlor of his new Queen Anne-style home, built of wood. He had met his wife Caroline in Dyersville, Iowa, where her widowed sea captain father had finally settled with his three motherless children, but not before taking them around the world on his cargo ship.

That was the world Ernest "Ernie" Miller Hemingway first opened his eyes onto in the summer of 1899—with its two fiercely competing visions of Christianity. Fittingly, for Hemingway—the disciplined, early morning writer—he was born at 8 o'clock on the morning of July 21. The setting was 439 North Oak Park Avenue, his Grandfather Hall's home, replete with reminders of the love of God, love of life, and love of country.

Hemingway was the second child of Dr. Clarence Edmonds "Ed" Hemingway and his wife Grace, née Hall, who had wed in 1896 after Grace's grand European vacation with her widower father. Grace was born on June 15, 1872, into a well-ordered Victorian world shaped by utopian ideals, while her husband, "Ed," born on September 4, 1871, was raised on Calvinist fire and brimstone. The couple had formally met in 1894, when Grace's mother was ailing from cancer and Ed, the family doctor's young assistant, offered Grace emotional solace as her mother's health deteriorated. They had surely passed each other in the hallways at Oak Park High School, where Grace graduated in 1891, the year after Ed, but only became acquainted during this intense period as Grace helplessly watched her mother's life slipping away. By the time her mother died on September 5, 1895, their friendship had blossomed into a full-blown romance and they were soon plighting their troth in holy matrimony.

On October 1, his parents' third wedding anniversary, the "little stranger,"[1] as Grace called her baby boy, was baptized shortly after noon at the First Congregational Church in Oak Park.[2] They had waited to baptize him until after their summer sojourn at "Windemere"—their new cottage on Bear (later Walloon) Lake in Northern Michigan, built on land they purchased the year prior. Migration from Detroit and Chicago, and their suburbs, to the "Northern Lower Peninsula" had begun some forty years earlier when the *New York Tribune* touted the climate as ideal for orchard farming. It was a veritable "Garden of Eden." Missionaries had flocked there even earlier.

"Abba," as his Grandfather Hall was known, passed onto his namesake a personal relationship with "his friend God." Abba and his beloved grandson played "walk-ride, a much stomping run," wrote Grace, who also wrote of how much Ernie loved the stories Abba told, especially the one about a pack of dogs. And, for the longest time, he insisted on being called Carlo, one of the dogs' names.[3] Then, too, Ernie loved Abba's stories of heroics on the battlefield during the Civil War, when, after emigrating from Sheffield England in 1860, he fought with the First Iowa's Voluntary Calvary's L Troop and was wounded in the thigh by a Confederate minié ball. But he refused the disability pension, instead moving to Chicago with his new bride where he started a wholesale cutlery business, enabling him to build his grand house on Oak Park Avenue, which he finished in 1890. With three extra bedrooms,

Hemingway family studio portrait, taken May 21, 1900. Grace with ten-month-old Ernest on her lap. Clarence, with two-year-old Marcelline on his lap. Unknown author. *Source:* Scrapbook. In the public domain. Scribner Archives.

it easily accommodated his daughter's growing family and became their home until his death in 1905.

Ernest's childhood was a well-ordered life complete with domestic staff assisting with the young family's many chores. The Hemingways grew their own fruits and vegetables, mostly in Michigan, and hunted and fished for their meals, then canned, smoked, and pickled everything for the winter months. What they did not grow, hunt, fish or raise, they bought from merchants ambling clickety-clack down the village streets in horse-drawn carriages or wagons in the case of milk and ice delivered for refrigeration.

GROWING UP WITH A GOD OF LOVE AND A GOD OF FEAR

In April 1901, when he was just twenty months old, young Ernie was part of the Wee Folks Band at First Congregational Church, down the street and around the corner from Grandfather Hall's home.[4] One night, about a year later, his mother sang "Onward Christian Soldiers" to Ernie, who responded, with his lisp, "Tweetie, oh Tweetie, ven I det to be a big boy I dont to be a onward tistian soldser.'"[5] About the same time, in April 1902, his sister Ursula was born, but it was not an entirely happy affair for her older brother. As Baker wrote, "He longed to have a baby brother and was deeply disappointed" when the new baby was a girl. "There was a tear in his eye." But he cheerily sloughed it off, saying, "I think maybe Jesus will send my baby brother tomorrow."[6]

The way little Ernie turned to God with such confidence reflects Abba's emphasis on God's love, counterbalancing his father's emphasis on God's wrath. "God," wrote his older sister Marcelline "was a person [Abba] knew intimately."[7] He attended Grace Episcopal Church at 924 Lake Street, a Gothic Revival church, completed in 1898, its architecture mirroring Catholic spirituality cast aside during the Protestant Reformation.[8] It was a few doors down from First Congregational Church, 848 Lake Street, where the Hemingway side of the family had their own pew.

Abba conducted "family prayers" in a booming voice after breakfast in the parlor, sitting at a "shiny varnished" center table on which rested his thick, gilt-edge *Daily Strength for Daily Needs*.[9] Marcelline wrote that Uncle Tyley would join in the prayer time and "(a)fter Abba had read the lesson for the day we would all rise, turn, and kneel down on the carpet in front of our chairs, resting our elbows on the black leather seats, while Abba knelt . . . But instead of closing his eyes or bowing his head as the rest of us did, he raised his head, his eyes upward, as though he was talking to God as he prayed . . . talking right to his friend God."[10] Family prayers, always led by

Abba, included grace before meals, and the cook, maid, and other household staff participated, as well.[11]

Abba also believed in progress, sending Grace to study voice in New York City shortly after her mother died. Her teacher, Louisa Cappiani, saw a budding opera star and arranged for Grace to give a concert at Madison Square Garden winning her a Metropolitan Opera contract. But Grace's sensitive eyes, weakened by a childhood illness, could not bear the bright foot lights and, instead, she chose to marry handsome, hardworking, and upstanding Dr. Hemingway, whose letters had warmed her heart.

Light, though, was a plus in the Hall household, Abba installing electricity in 1898, making theirs the first home to have electric lights just sixteen years after Edison had illumined Manhattan. All the better to keep a careful, loving watch on his namesake. "One day, after a particularly big exaggeration by Ernest—about how he had caught a runaway horse all by himself," Marcelline wrote, Abba told Grace, "Chumpy dear, this boy is going to be heard from one day. If he uses his imagination for good purposes, he'll be famous, but if he starts the wrong way, with all his energy, he'll end up in jail, and it's up to you which way he goes."[12]

"Abba and his little trio," Ernie, and his sisters Ursula (center) and Marcelline (right) © 1904 from Scrapbook, Volume II, 1901–1904. *Source:* In the public domain. Scribner Archives.

For now, he was going the right way, evidenced by his generous response, when Ed's brother, Willoughby, a missionary in Shanshi province, took up a collection while visiting Oak Park for his parallel work in India. Three-year-old Ernie was so moved, he got up to donate the gold coin his father had given him for his birthday. At first thinking the coin was lost, young Ernie "beckoned wildly" and the church attendant came back to Ernest, who, finding it, dropped the cherished gold coin on the collection plate.[13]

Ernie was busting to be a man. That same year, while spending the summer with his family at the Walloon Lake cottage, his mother wrote, little Ernie shouted, in response to her question, "fraid a nothing"[14] which some interpret as an overcompensating brave face—the same brave demeanor the legendary writer, famous for his machismo, would assume in adulthood. Sunny, though, observed her brother and saw not artifice, but genuine bravery.

Yet, without question, the dichotomy of fear and love in Hemingway's childhood, especially when it came to his relationship with God, was the dynamic shaping his personality, with love winning out, at least while Abba was living. He took this filial piety quite "seriously," his "A-men" at the end of grace at meals sounding just like a "Methodist revivalist," his mother wrote.[15] At four years and three months, during a long walk, he said to his mother, "Mama, I know why people die—it's to keep God company—He gets lonesome."[16]

God must have been lonesome on May 10, 1905—the day Abba, age sixty-five, died. He had suffered excruciatingly from cancer and almost killed himself to end his pain but, ironically, was saved by Ed, who hid the bullets from him. Five-year-old Ernie, going on six, had lost his best friend. Abba had just written him, "O comrade brave," in affectionate verse on Valentine's Day from Lake Windemere, where he was recuperating, telling him that the "squirrels" thought it "queer" he had left them "so long alone" and exhorted him to just ring them up on the "telephone."[17]

Now the only ones Ernie could call were his paternal grandparents, Anson and Adelaide, who lived across the street—on the Congregational side of Oak Park Avenue.

Born in 1844, Anson hailed from East Plymouth, moving with his family to burgeoning Chicago at age ten. His ancestor, Ralph Hemingway, had come to America with the "Great Migration" in April 1630.[18] Led by Puritan lawyer John Winthrop, they arrived in New England that June on the site of what would become modern-day Boston, establishing the Massachusetts Bay Colony. Descended from a long line of Puritan and Congregational ministers, Anson had a strict Puritanical fear of the Lord—no drinking, no smoking, no card playing, and *no dancing*. He served with the 72nd Illinois

Regiment then reenlisted with Company H, U.S. Colored 70th regiment as a first lieutenant, later working for the Freedman's Bureau in Natchez, Mississippi. After attending Wheaton College, he worked for super-evangelist D. L. Moody at the YMCA in Chicago before establishing a real estate business in Oak Park and marrying fellow Wheaton student, Adelaide Edmonds. The couple had four sons and two daughters, including Hemingway's father "Ed," and drummed into them their strict Christian beliefs that were, in turn, passed onto the grandchildren. The four "no's," along with Sunday school and church attendance and refraining from recreational activities on the Lord's Day, were sacrosanct.

In the summer of 1906, Ed and Grace and their children—Marcelline (age seven), Ernest (age six), Ursula (age three), and baby Madeleine ("Sunny")—moved into a new home at 600 Kenilworth Avenue. Grace had built it with her father's money, to specification, including the requisite number of bedrooms. Ed and Grace knew they wanted six children, their last two children, Carol and Leicester, arriving in 1911 and 1915, respectively. Otherwise, they slept in separate beds, wrote Sunny.[19]

The children were an important part of the family economy, tasked each summer with various chores including farming as soon as they arrived at the Walloon Lake retreat. But it was not all drudgery. "The excitement of being chased by a bull or a turkey gobbler," wrote Sunny, "and the enjoyment of seeing the fluffy baby chicks keeping warm in the farmhouse kitchen were a big part of our summer amusements."[20]

Likewise, when Grace delegated household management to Ed, he embraced the typically unmasculine role when he realized he could indulge his love of cooking, wrote Sunny. What he did not enjoy was singing, but he would humor Grace when she insisted, though his talent lay elsewhere. How he could do it all *and* be so devoted to the practice of medicine does boggle the mind. A graduate of Oberlin College (1893), Rush Medical College in Chicago (1894), and later New York Laying-In College in Obstetrics (1908), he tirelessly ministered to his patients and had to endure the soul-searing tragedy of losing some in childbirth.

Most importantly, he was a father, giving special attention to his endearing, sensitive young son, cultivating in him a love of nature and the great outdoors, while teaching him the "Agassiz" method of accurate observation of God's creation, which, as an official of the Agassiz Club, he was skilled in. This would serve as a critical foundation in Hemingway's ability to observe details, which he would remember point by point, weaving them masterfully into his writing. For her part, Grace, the formerly rising opera star, now a home-based music teacher, succeeded in inculcating a love of art and music in her children, insisting they attend concerts and operas. Ernie, though, preferred the more down-to-earth circus when it came to town. Animals intrigued him as he pondered their purpose in the order of things. Then, there was the woods and the wilds, which thoroughly captured his imagination as Ed taught him, from the time he was a toddler, to hunt and fish, the two going on many an expedition with gun or fishing rod intent on catching furry and piscatorial prizes of nature. Dr. Hemingway even bought his son a safari costume with a pith helmet after former president Theodore Roosevelt explored British East Africa (i.e., Kenya) in 1909, publicizing his adventures in a film released in April 1910.

Ed was fiercely patriotic and loved T. R.'s example and instilled in his children a love of country. When asked what he raised at Windemere, he said, "The best thing we raise is the flag."[21] It was straight line from Anson, a proud veteran, who had given Ernie his twenty-gauge Civil War shotgun for his tenth birthday, which he loved hunting with. Anson, like Abba before, would regale Ernie with his tales from the Civil War to his grandson's delight.

But it was not all sweetness and light. Doc Hemingway had a dark side. On top of his highly religious nature and strict disciplinarian ways, he could be extremely moody and prone to nervous exhaustion and depression. Over Thanksgiving 1903, he decided to take a two-week vacation in New Orleans away from the family to rest his nerves, frayed to the breaking point, which, he wrote Grace after the first of the year, had been a healing elixir.[22] His hereditary predispositions combined with his strict religious upbringing was a heavy psychological burden. Marcelline documented her father's good deeds and generous heart—including his invention of the spinal forceps, provision of medical care at the local orphanage, and practice of billing patients, without means, little or nothing. But she also wrote of his darker impulses:

> In our youth he would make no compromise between what he considered right and wrong. He believed in physical punishment. Even as a very small child, I remember that Ernest and I and the other children were soundly spanked when we had infringed some rule of conduct my father considered essential. He kept a razor strap in his closet, which he used on some occasions . . . My father's dimpled cheeks and charming smile could change in an instant to the stern, taut mouth and piercing look . . . Sometimes the change from being gay to being stern was so abrupt that we were not prepared for the shock that came.[23]

Marcelline's unpublished book manuscript provides a more unvarnished assessment of her father's harsh punishments. "At times, in our youth," she wrote, "it seemed we were spanked for almost anything and everything . . . If you yelled, 'I'll be good, I'll be good' and cried loudly the whipping was shorter, but if you didn't . . . the spanking continued and it became more violent until you did yell good and loud."[24]

Hemingway's mother, of the more tolerant Episcopal tradition, and a devotee of "spiritualism," also punished Hemingway, albeit with a hairbrush. And it is often claimed that she dressed Hemingway as a girl—as if the female twin of Marcelline—until about age six—which would have been psychologically wounding. Though, as Sunny wrote, the record does not support this. And, Doc Hemingway was *quite* the shutterbug. Yet it's clear Grace was attuned to gender fluidity, writing about Sunny, "She is game—and to be relied on in an emergency. As genuine a boy as ever inhabited a girl's personality."[25] Albeit, this may have simply been 1900-speak for calling Sunny a "tomboy," befitting her athleticism.

Yet Grace and Ed Hemingway's relationship, more than anything, shaped Hemingway's psyche. Early on, it was idyllic, radiating warmth in the life of the family, his father reading Alexandre Dumas novels, such as *The Three Musketeers*, to the children by candlelight in Michigan. That all stopped when Grace and Ed started having their "awful fights," which Hemingway recalled in his waning years.[26]

What were the fights about? Grace's spiritualism, with a touch of "Christian mysticism," rankled Ed, and surely sparked some arguments. Then, too, their seemingly less than fulsome conjugal life, evidenced by the separate beds, which, though not unusual in Victorian times, could, in part, explain the marital discord and, by extension, the harsh treatment of his children—Ed taking out his anger and frustration on them. Finances would be another obvious source of discord. After Ed died, Grace, pushing back on Ernest's financial dictates, said that when his father tried that, he "lived to regret it."[27] You can just hear the "awful fights" that ensued over finances. Dr. Hemingway, like his son, was, if anything, frugal, insisting Grace keep a careful record of expenses—to her chagrin. He traveled around in his horse and buggy until 1912, four years after Henry Ford rolled out his Model T, by which time he had retreated into his own world, quitting the Agassiz Club that same year. Coincident with these developments, his son, just thirteen, began "running scared," said four-time Fulbright recipient Earl Rovit. He honed a compensating tough guy image—a lifelong pattern, the seeds of which can be found in the loss of his affirming, engaged father, whose wife was increasingly incapable of sublimating her wants to her husband's needs.[28]

Grace taught music full-time, though the norm was for Victorian women to manage the household, men to bring home the proverbial bacon.

But "Grace Hall Hemingway" had a strong feminist streak, which only intensified after her father died. And the simple fact is, she did not like housework, albeit, she did like the finer things of life, like beaded dresses and feather-bedecked hats and had to work to afford these niceties; so she did, teaching students in her large performance room, the central feature of the home, while bringing in some 50 percent more income than her husband who toiled away in his small home office when not making house calls day and night. Grace also tended to many causes including women's rights, especially the right to vote, and developed her own talents including musical performance, and later painting and writing—even as her husband's needs often took a back seat, including on the day he died.

Helping make it all work, or not, was Ruth Arnold. Rejected by her family and, though possessing scant musical talent, she came to study with Grace and live with the Hemingways. She became Grace's helper and devoted lifelong companion. Given that Dr. Hemingway was, more and more, living in his own world, as correspondence between Marcelline and Grace reflects, it is understandable why Grace would seek an outside emotional attachment. But it makes it no less proper. Dr. Hemingway was emotionally fragile and needed the support of his wife—the kind of support he had given Grace when Mother Hall was dying. And, understandably, he resented Grace's emotional attachment to Ruth, especially when Ruth took Grace's side in matters that divided husband and wife.

"Like all men with a faculty that surpasses human requirement, his father was very nervous," Hemingway wrote in his art-imitating-life short story, "Fathers and Sons." "Then, too, he was sentimental, and, like most sentimental people, he was both cruel and abused. Also, he had much bad luck, and it was not all of it his own . . . All sentimental people are betrayed so many times."[29] He writes as Nick Adams, though he is writing of his own childhood and the hunting and fishing his father taught him and how idyllic everything was until it wasn't—as Grace pulled back, especially as she aged and suffered with arthritis, starting in her late forties. His father meted out cruel punishments to Hemingway as a child prompting him, at times, to go out to the shed, get his shotgun and set his father's head in his sights, albeit, feeling guilty later. Nick does the same thing. Clearly, Hemingway loved his father deeply, making the spiritual, emotional, and psychological wounds of Ed's abuse all the greater.

Dr. Hemingway's depression and mood swings had him spending increasingly more time away from the family. Besides the 1903 rest, after completing obstetrics courses in New York in 1908 when Hemingway was nine, he tacked on two weeks in New Orleans as he tried to rebalance himself. He spent much time alone in Oak Park in the summers, especially starting in 1911, staying behind to tend to the needs of his patients. But Doc Hemingway also needed time apart to heal, and would take another rest cure, in 1912, for "nerves," a routine that continued until his death.

Grace, too, like her husband, suffered severe headaches, and found it necessary to spend time away from the family—often fleeing to an artist's colony in Nantucket at 45 Pearl Street, where *she* calmed her nerves, taking her children with her, one by one. Ernest's first letter to Marcelline was received in Nantucket in June 1909 where he reported on his classroom's field day win, one fellow knocking out a classmate's two teeth, meriting "a licking" with "a rawhide strap" by the teacher."[30]

Late the following summer, Grace took Ernest to Nantucket and brought him to a women's suffrage meeting, where he promptly fell asleep.[31] Had he stayed awake, he would have gained insight into some of what was animating his parents' increasingly contentious relationship. The changing role of women was a tough pill for men to swallow given that their unique and irreplaceable nurturing role was gradually being supplanted, yielding bitter cultural fruits not fifteen years later in the "roaring twenties," "the time of great revolt in almost everything—in dress, morals, manners," George Plimpton said.[32] Which women traditionally upheld, the seeds of decay now subtly being planted. While these expanded roles often enhanced family development, when women lost sight of their unique nurturing role, chaos often ensued. But even at that, sweet fruits would follow, notably Hemingway's literary blossoming.

Through his parents' travails, Hemingway developed a sensitive conscience on display in his first letter, written to his father from Walloon Lake in early July 1907. Dr. Hemingway was in Oak Park tending to his patients and little Ernie wanted him to know that he had seen a "mother duck with seven little babies," while inquiring how tall his corn had grown. He was very much looking forward to going duck hunting with his "papa." Then, his conscience reminds him, "Ursula saw (the ducks) first." Closing, he cheerily reports, "We went strawberry piking [*sic*]"—gathering enough for "three short-cakes."[33] His father's response shows their warm relationship. "I received your card . . . keep very quiet about the wild ducks, so (we can hunt ducks together and) . . . have a glorious time."

In all his childhood letters, Ernest was always trying to please—his parents, minister, teachers, and, yes, God. In a May 1913 letter written to his father during a "missionary exposition" at the Chicago Coliseum the young people of Third Congregational Church of Oak Park participated in, he confessed, "My conduct at the Coliseum . . . was bad," as it was likewise in church that morning, but assured his father that his "conduct" would be "good" the next day. Grace wrote on the envelop, "To Daddy/ 'Confession.'"[34] The family had switched to the less prescriptive Third Congregational Church on South Kenilworth in Oak Park. (Grace, prioritizing her musical pursuits, preferred the choir director there.) Besides formal church services, the Hemingways required their children to participate in children's and youth church programs, such as the one at the Coliseum, and were urged to read *Youth's Companion* and other church magazines scattered all over the house.

Yet undergirding their religious formation was a rigid moral outlook that did not always fully capture the richness of Christianity. As Saint Pope John Paul II told university students several decades later, "It is only in God—in Jesus, God made man—that you will fully understand what you are. He will unveil to you the true greatness of yourselves: that you are redeemed by him and taken up in his love; that you are made truly free in him who said about himself: 'If the son frees you, you will be free indeed' (*Jn* 8:36)."[35]

In contrast, as Hemingway's brother Leicester wrote, "Our parents ran their lives and those of their children on the basis of Victorian morality . . . There were rules that could not be broken, and expectations which absolutely had to be met. The individual and his special needs and circumstances were secondary."[36] Apropos of which, in her unpublished manuscript, Marcella recounts the time her father demanded she leave the school immediately after her caught her dancing.[37] Never mind that she was a young girl in need of social life—not worrying about sinning, knowing that she would be forgiven if she succumbed to temptation, strengthened through sacramental grace, won through Christ's sacrifice on the cross. But then, she did not know the grace of the sacramental confession, one of the seven sacraments of the Catholic Church, and her father understandably wanted to keep her unscathed.

Ironically, in 1907, in spite of Oak Park's limited tolerance of Roman Catholicism, St. Edmond's Catholic Church at 188 S. Oak Park Avenue, was completed amid great celebration and hoopla.[38] That millionaire banker John W. Farson had opened his sprawling Prairie School–style mansion on the corner of Home Avenue and Pleasant Street to help raise funds for this Catholic ecclesial home could not have escaped the Hemingways' notice in a town where social happenings were much commented upon, especially when spiced with gossip.

Farson cut quite a figure in turn-of-the-century Oak Park, where he tooled around in the most up-to-date conveyance, wearing "immaculate white flannel suits, red cravats and ties, and top hats" with "a vast circle of friends who shared his interests in everything modern," his ever-shifting passions going from "horses to automobiles to roller skating"[39]—and now a new Catholic parish church. How tongues must have wagged when he opened his home to Catholics.

Arriving in Chicago at age sixteen after the Great Fire with $25 to his name, ten years later the now wealthy young man married Mamie Ashworth of Rockford, Illinois. Members of the First Methodist Church of Oak Park, the couple supported the local Horse Show Association and belonged to all the elite social clubs. Dubbed "prince of entertainers" by the local paper, *Oak Leaves*, he built his mansion, starting in 1892, adding adjacent properties to create a lavish Italian garden, the perfect thematic backdrop for his Catholic fundraising project. Before the land was developed, he entertained all of Oak Park with band concerts. After the estate was finally completed in 1906, the Catholic benefit was quite the party. But he was not long for this world. In 1910, at age fifty-five, Farson suddenly died of "heart disease." Three years before his death, St. Edmond's Catholic Church was dedicated with "imposing ceremonies," including Catholic rites performed by His Grace, the Most Reverend Archbishop James Edward Quigley, according to the *Oak Leaves* account of the June 1, 1907, solemnities. Young Ernie must have wondered about the new kids on the block.

HIGH SCHOOL "CONFESSIONS"

When Ernie entered high school in the fall of 1913, he was determined to give it his best shot. The Hemingway children were held to high academic standards, particularly by Grace, who pushed them to achieve and excel. But any illusions Hemingway had of gaining a scholarship were dashed freshman year.

"First Year Latin" at Oak Park and River Forest Township High School, was an "awful struggle," Ernest wrote in "Confessions," his senior year essay, in 1917. His Latin teacher, he wrote, was "under the opinion that I was brilliant but lazy."[40] He was "expelled from class" almost every day and was "only to be admitted to class again the next day on a promise of good behavior." "Some of the causes of expulsion," he wrote "were eating oranges in class, 4 boys using identically the same theme, dropping a little glass gobule [*sic*] containing a vile liquid, and shooting craps with Paul Haase."[41]

"Freshman English" he wrote, "was the only class I look back on with any warm glow." English was required during each of the four years, covering English I through English IV and the fundamentals of language. First-year English students read H. A. Guerber's *Myths of Greece and Rome*, supplemented by Rhodes's *Old Testament Narratives* and *One Hundred Narrative Poems.* "That's how I learned to write, by reading the Bible," mainly the Old Testament, Hemingway later said. Fiction read aloud during class included novels such as *Ivanhoe.* Outside of class, students read popular but banned novels by H. G. Wells and Owen Wister.[42]

Nor was he material for an athletic scholarship—finishing next to last in cross country, his first athletic foray, ahead of a friend who was "equally bushed." "I wore my cross country run bob proudly all spring until one day I attempted to see if I could hit it with a rifle and was successful." And he was about as good at musical harmony as his father. "W. Otto Miessner," he wrote, "gave me a 'completed' when I heartily agreed with him that he and Mendolsen [*sic*] were the greatest composers."

His two aspirations in high school—gaining a varsity letter "monogram" and acting in a play—were both achieved and promptly forgotten "like the 'gall and wormwood' of the prophet." Hemingway also had aspirations for winning the girls' affections but, while he was "well liked" he was "very shy," granddaughter Mariel Hemingway said. "He opened his sister's mail to see what the dames thought of him. And although he helped decorate the school dances, he left alone before they began."[43]

The very conservative, yet very progressive Oak Park High School was just beginning to teach its students about sex. It did not happen in a vacuum but rather was encouraged by activist Margaret Sanger in her series of columns on sex education titled, "What Every Mother Should Know" (1911–1912) and "What Every Girl Should Know" (1912–1913) for the socialist magazine *New York Call.* People were outraged by her frank discussion of such a delicate topic though, given the growing movement for women's rights, she also earned her share of support, one summary review praising her for "a purer morality than whole libraries full of hypocritical cant about modesty."[44]

Hemingway, though, had no illusions about this supposed "purer morality" and needed no textbook—it was all in his father's medical library. He was very protective of his sisters when it came to guys "on the make." For instance, one time when a boy was about to start necking with ten-year-old Sunny, he quickly steered her away from the masher. But now Ernie was in the crosshairs of progressive educators, intent on teaching him and his classmates "how to" courses about what, in 1914, Sanger dubbed "birth control." The same year he had rescued Sunny.

His hero, Theodore Roosevelt, was having none of it. By the turn of the century, birth rates were plummeting, coinciding with the Industrial Revolution, given the introduction of new, more accessible forms of contraception, abortion already broadly accepted and utilized—one out of every five to six pregnancies terminated in the mid-1850s, on the eve of T. R.'s birth. Thus, while in 1800 each family averaged over seven children, that number plunged to fewer than four by century's end. In a 1917 debate with Sanger in *Metropolitan Magazine*, a year after her articles were published as a book, T. R. wrote, "The most pitiful showing is made by the graduates of the women's colleges." Each graduate was averaging 0.86 children. T. R. thought it the patriotic duty of every American woman to have at least four! Now they were teaching kids "how to" separate sex from procreation. This did not bode well for the procreation project and was accompanied by a coarsening of culture, into which Hemingway fell headlong, in time writing about it beautifully.

The change was dizzying. The year before Hemingway began high school, the Armory Show came to the Art Institute of Chicago, the second stop, sandwiched in between New York and Boston, for what was formally called the International Exhibition of Modern Art. The nudes, especially Matisse's "Blue Nude" and Duchamp's "Nude Descending Staircase, No. 2" (also an example of futurist "cubism"), shocked Victorian sensibilities. But then, that was the idea. Now that censorship laws, specifically the Payne-Aldrich Tariff Act, were lifted, this "new art" was being developed in Europe. T. R., in a review in *The Outlook* on March 29, 1913, titled "A Layman's View of an Art Exhibition," while looking somewhat favorably on the new American artists, did not mince words. "That's not art," he wrote.[45] While Hemingway's parents bought annual passes for the Art Institute exhibitions, they surely skipped this one. At any rate, Hemingway was more interested in other topics and activities.

He was busting out of his clothes as he developed into a young man and wrote to his pregnant mother at Lake Walloon that he was about to split his pant seams and drew her a picture showing his shirt sleeve had crawled up on his arm that had grown about ten inches longer. He needed "long pants" like every other kid in class including Lewis Clarahan, his closest high school friend.[46] That spring, in the second semester of his sophomore year, Ernie hiked to Illinois' Lake Zurich, some thirty-five miles northwest of Oak Park, with Lewis. He enjoyed their hikes together in the plains north of the Clarahan home, near the Des Plaines River, not far from the Hemingway home, hunting "pheasants, northern owls, ducks and weasels," said Clarahan.[47] Lake Zurich was as far as they ventured. While luxuriating in this nature preserve, Ernest found out, in a call home on April 1, 1915, that his mother, age forty-three, had given birth—this time to a baby boy, the brother, named Leicester, he had so desired when Ursula was born thirteen years earlier—the one who would be so fiercely protective of his brother's legacy.

Hemingway Family. Ernest Hemingway holding woodchuck he shot, summer 1914. *Source:* MHS347_0005_1263. The Early Years—Ernest and Marcelline Hemingway in Oak Park. Oak Park Public Library Special Collections, Oak Park, IL.

Around this time, Sunny, the sibling who hung out with Ernie the most at Lake Walloon and idolized her brother, who nicknamed her "Nunbones," struck a "deal" with him over a dead porcupine and his rightful claim, complete with a waiver he had Sunny sign, as follows: "I hear-by agree to give Ernest Hemingway all my alleged share in a certain porcupine killed by Alfred Couch and agree never to say I had or have a share in it. (signed) Sunny Hemingway."[48]

But while the outdoors beckoned, his love of writing was growing. In fact, at Windemere, wrote Sunny, Ernie would sleep in a tent next to a little cottage they called the Annex, reading late into the night in his private getaway. He was storing up creative chestnuts and, on May 5, 1915, wrote to his older sister Marcelline, whom he affectionately called, alternately, "Ivory," "Marc," "Marce," "Marse," "Mash," and, most often, "Masween." He was interested in her admission to the story club—and how she did it—and swore he could write a better story. Otherwise, it was "Purgatory" for him, he wrote, signing his letter, "Thine eternally," but not before congratulating her. Grace, no doubt rolling her eyes, scribbled a note in the margins calling her son "crazy nuts."[49] His high school friend Susan Lowrey Crist looked deeper, calling him "clever, mischievous, daring and imaginative."[50]

"I think Ernie started seriously to write soon after 1915," an upper class-man recalled. "He had a typewriter on the third floor of the old home, well away from his family. By that time he was writing for the fun of it and apparently felt that he was developing ability along that line. He would read to me some of the things he was writing and was quite enthusiastic."[51] Hemingway had known he wanted to be a writer from his earliest days, wrote Sunny, and got more serious in his junior year. "Falling under the influence of Miss Dixon," he wrote, "I began a career of study."[52]

In January 1916, he started doing reporting for the *Trapeze*. Then he tried his hand at writing fiction for the school literary magazine, the *Tabula*, on which Miss Margaret Dixon, as well as Miss Fannie Biggs, who taught upper class composition and public speaking, were advisers. "(T)hey were both very nice and especially nice to me because I had to try to be an athlete as well as try to learn to write English," said Hemingway.[53] He had bulked up and varsity squads beckoned, but he would rather be writing and Mlles. Dixon and Biggs helped him channel his energies into writing. He told tales of athletic prowess and heroics, involving death and suicide in his first published piece, "The Judgement of Manitou," that transformed his rather paltry showing into a tour de force—first in track, then in football, which his father had driven him to compete in. Likewise, his latest obsession, boxing—which he pursued at home and in Chicago gyms—inspired his second piece, "A Matter of Colour." At the time, boxing was amateur only in Chicago. It had thrived in the 1890s at Tattershalls, on the corner of 16th and Dearborn, only to be shut down for a quarter century in December 1900 after a match was rigged.

But he also buckled down academically and got good grades in zoology—a 90 percent, which was so good that Doc Hemingway "let myself and another equally shady character hike up through Michigan during the summer," he wrote, "and was forced to wire money to keep us from the clutches of the law . . . $14.75 and costs satisfied the justice of the peace and we learned that it is foolish to leave game shot out of season in an open boat. Since then, I have been very cautious and the calaboose has known me no more."[54] He spent a brief time in jail, which, he wrote, "gave me vast éclat with all the half breeds in our district and I went on many good trips and acquired as the result of the summer the following items free of charge. First. 1 Working knowledge of Ojibway. 2nd. 17 French cuss words. 3rd. 1 Ash paddle hand [made] carved. A gift from the whitest Indian that ever drank bad whiskey. 4th. 4 illegal ways of catching trout. 5th. Knowledge of the habits of every game warden in Charlevoix, Emmett and Sheboygan counties. 6th. A bunch of experiences I'd even take Latin over again rather than miss."

Hem and his "shady friend"—likely Clarahan—had shortened the trip up north, Marcella wrote, by taking a boat from Chicago to Michigan and then hitchhiking—the trip spanning well over three hundred miles. Once there, they could hunt and fish to their hearts' content.[55] And the game warden's dismay. But that all got straightened out and served as good material for a short story. All good, clean fun. "I never knew him to drink," said Clarahan.[56] But he did witness the dramatist in Hemingway while they enjoyed the Northern Lower Peninsula's treasures that summer. They had taken the boat up Lake Michigan to Frankfort, then hiked over to Petoskey and nearby Walloon Lake. "When we were walking along, Ernest made up startling stories and situations and shouted them up to the trees . . . I don't think he lied but he would exaggerate any little incident" in an effort to heighten the "excitement and action." Then, too, his insults, said Clarahan, were just joshing.[57] When the *SS Eastland* had capsized and sunk in the Chicago River the previous summer—on July 24, 1915—claiming the lives of some 844 souls, Ernie made sure he and Clarahan were there to witness one of the greatest maritime disasters in U.S. history, the sight of so many souls being whisked into eternity, no doubt making a deep impression, though they did not make it in time to see any dead bodies, Clarahan said.

Heaven and hell, and faith and spirituality were central in his life, albeit now with an independent, sometimes irreverent, streak. In notes passed back and forth during classes at Oak Park and River Forest High School in January 1916, an unknown friend, again, likely Clarahan, asked if another friend was at some "Catholicismistic school" and Ernest assures him he's at the Episcopal school (i.e., Howe Military School in Howe, Indiana). Then his friend calls time-out on the distracting notes, prompting Ernest to call out the "preserver of my soul" while noting that he has "preserved" his friend "from all iniquity and sin."[58]

In the fall of 1916, Ernest and Marcelline rejoined the First Congregational Church of their childhood, leaving the Third where their father taught Sunday School and their mother sang. The First had more youth activities and Pastor William E. Barton, sister of Red Cross founder, Clara Barton, had, since 1902, brought a spirit of unity to the badly divided church. And while Barton opposed movies on Sunday in theater houses and supported the ban of liquor sales in the Village, he was not strictly a Puritan, believing that Christians "should interpret Christ in the light of the twentieth century's experience."[59] He also emphasized "the making of character."

Through it all, as Redd Griffin said,[60] Ernest acquired the grounding necessary "to realize his literary desires and begin distilling his spiritual aspirations." But he still had some elbow grease to expend on the family project.

As he wrote in "Confessions," "I worked steadily on the farm until the rainbow trout in the lake began to bite. One of over 4 pounds weight was landed and 3 which together weighed a little over nine pounds also were brought to net one day. The family, while enjoying the fish, seriously questioned the abandonment of the farm and so the last part of the summer was again spent in agriculture." He hoped to travel "way up north," in his post-graduation summer, writing, "I'll be wielding the unromantic hoe on the still 'unromanticer' spuds but I intend to take a couple of days off to look up my Ojibway friends and maybe catch the great, big, record monster of a trout that got

The Hemingway family at their cabin on Walloon Lake in Michigan. Standing rear, left to right, Marcelline, Sunny, Ernest and Ursula. Seated: Dr. Hemingway with Carol, Grace holding baby Leicester. Unknown photographer. *Source:* In the public domain. Scribner Archives.

away last summer." He needed the break. While tending to the spuds, he was also nursing a headache, but as he wrote Grace, "Dr. Whitter's medicine has cleared up my headache and I am feeling good."[61]

Ms. Dixon, who often described Hemingway as "the most brilliant student she ever had,"[62] said she detected in his "interesting account" in "Confessions," "your old love of making yourself appear much worse than you are. Don't put your own estimate on yourself, even if it's a bad one—they will make their own value anyway. I've enjoyed having you for a pupil these two years immensely and shall always be intensely interested in your career. If it's the North Pole, I hope you'll reach it." While she might have had a political tin ear—she loathed T. R. and loved Woodrow Wilson—she knew talent when she saw it. Then, too, her liberal attitudes introduced Hemingway to a new point of view.

Then there was Fannie Biggs. "'She was a kind of genius,' according to the chairman of the English Department, a frail but wiry little woman, with a well-read mind, with exacting requirements, and with a fine sense of humor."[63] She was not unaware of the emotional load Hemingway carried, both from family tensions and the ordinary male adolescent growing pains and eased his burden, which helped him greatly. He felt free to express his troubles to her and stayed in touch with her.

LEAVING OAK PARK

Upon graduating from Oak Park High School, as he worked the land, he also surveyed the landscape abroad in the wake of America declaring war on Germany on April 6, 1917. His father's opposition to the war kept him from enlisting in the army. Beyond his moral objections, he needed Ernest's help that summer up in Michigan. Ernest gave his Grandfather Anson a picture of their operation, writing, "we have been putting in about 12 hours per day, haying and working on the farm."[64] He had not yet thanked him for the birthday presents, he wrote, because he was so busy farming, and they were having a dry spell and in danger of losing their potato crops. He wrote his mother Grace, who was in Oak Park resting, that he had been working nine days straight and that his father was "as fearful as ever."[65] Then, too, he feared his mother would mishandle his things and asked her to refrain from throwing away anything "you don't like the looks of" and he promised to do the same on his end. They had finished bringing in all the hay, giving him more time to fish. "I caught three rainbow trout . . . in Horton's Bay . . . (5-1/2, 3-1/2 and 2 pounds) the largest catch of trout . . . ever," he wrote his grandfather of one evening's catch. If not for "the mosquitos and the fish," he had written Miss Biggs, late spring, "I would go absolutely bats."[66]

Grandfather came to the rescue when he sent his grandson copies of the *Chicago Tribune* to read. Ernest was hoping to land a job at the paper since he would not be matriculating at the University of Illinois. Instead, that fall, he landed a job at the *Kansas City Star*, after his uncle, Alfred Tyler Hemingway, introduced him to the editor, Henry J. Haskell. He worked there for six months—from October 1917 to April 1918—and learned the best rules for writing, he said. "Use short sentences. Use short paragraphs. Use vigorous english. Be positive, not negative," the *Kansas City Star* "Copy Style" manual instructed.

He saw life raw and real during his brief stint with the paper and showed he was his father's son when he helped a smallpox victim at the Kansas City train station in 1917. He also acquired a whole new cadre of friends including Charles Hopkins, a *Star* city editor and Carl Edgar, his roommate. Then there was Theodore B. "Ted" Brumback, nicknamed "Brummy." Five years his senior, this son of judge and Cornell dropout sporting a glass eye from a golfing accident,[67] was now on staff at the *Star* after serving a stint as an ambulance driver in France.

Meanwhile his mother upbraided her son for his lack of Christian spirit, prompting him to write back that she should not be bothered by his "cheerful" Christianity, that he was a "good Christian." "I pray every night" albeit he admitted he was so busy that he missed Sunday church. He assured his mother that while he did not "rave about religion" he was "as sincere a Christian" as possible. He also defended his friends, including Bill Smith, saying it did not matter what church he attended and that both of them had a strong belief in Jesus Christ and his Father God with an eye to eternity but that "Creeds don't matter."[68] Thus began what H. R. Stoneback called a "period of bitter rejection of Protestantism."[69]

He had met Bill Smith and his sister Katy in the summer of 1916. Their mother Kate Merrill of Louisiana, Missouri, had wed Professor William Benjamin Smith, with whom she had four children. He was a brainiac in math but not so much in the spiritual realm, where he espoused theories debunking Jesus. And he was inattentive to his wife when she began ailing from tuberculosis in 1890, during which time she gave birth to her two youngest, Katharine Foster ("Katy") Smith and William Benjamin ("Bill") Smith Jr., in 1891 and 1895, respectively. Her sister Laura had wed widower Gilbert B. Foster, heir to his late wife's St. Louis National Stockyards fortune and, after he died in 1894, the wealth she inherited enabled her to care for her sister and her two young charges. The family summered at the palatial

"Cottages" along Lake Charlevoix, just over from smaller Walloon Lake, where "Mrs. Dr. W. B. Smith" died on June 7, 1899. In 1902, Aunt Laura wed Dr. Joseph Charles. The couple bought a farm in 1913 not far from the Hemingways' Longfield Farm near Horton Bay where they all congregated. The Smiths, who lived a wealthy world apart, became some of Hemingway's best friends.

As the Smiths and Hemingways were bonding, America was fighting "to make the world safe for democracy," a cause its youth were eager to serve in. By Christmas, Dr. Hemingway finally relented, allowing Ernest to sign up for the Missouri Home Guard (soon folded into the National Guard). But, rejected for Army service for defective eyesight—he was essentially blind in his left eye—he next signed up for the Red Cross Ambulance Corps at Brummy's urging.

When Hemingway answered the call to serve abroad in "the war to end all wars," he was boyishly exuberant, telling *The Oak Parker*, "My country needed me, and I went and did whatever I was told."[70] First, though, he craved one last fishing trip in Horton Bay with Brumback, Edgar and Hopkins. While in Chicago on the last day of April for a quick visit and party in Oak Park, Dr. Hemingway promised to let Brummy and Ernie know when the telegram with sailing orders arrived. (Edgar and Hopkins were navy and army bound, respectively.) No sooner had they reached the North Woods and got their feet wet fishing than they were told to report to New York on May 8.

While in New York for two weeks for a physical exam, training and sightseeing, Ernie wrote a Kansas friend, "Ha Ha Ha Ha Ha Ha! Tis none other than the greatest of the Hemingsteins that indicts this epistle."[71] He was having a love affair with Mae Marsh, star of D. W. Griffith's *The Birth of a Nation*, he wrote—so characteristic of the "charming, enthusiastic . . . outgoing" personality Clarahan and his other high school classmates had come to know and love. When his parents heard of the affair, though, they thought he was serious and could not sleep a wink, said Clarahan.[72] So Ernie dashed off a reassuring telegram to let them know he was just kidding. Given Hem's handsome manliness and clear complexion he was Right Guide to the First Platoon, right up front, and got a "fine look" at President Woodrow Wilson, he wrote, while parading down Fifth Avenue from 82nd to 8th with 75,000 other men and women for the Red Cross Fund Drive the president was in town to launch.

He would soon depart with Brummy and other Red Cross volunteers aboard the dignified old French steamship, fortified against U-boat attacks, fittingly named *Chicago*, that spirited them across the Atlantic's choppy waters. Not any choppier than Hemingway sometimes got, letting loose en route, drinking too much and becoming loud and boisterous. After brief stops in Bordeaux and Paris, they boarded a train for Italy. "Hemmy," as he was called, shared a compartment with five other volunteers, and one night it was quite the scene. "Everything about him showed he wanted to impress us with his toughness," fellow Red Cross volunteer John Miller said. After Hemingway called him a "Son of a Bitch," they nearly came to blows when Miller demanded he apologize to his mother. The next day, Hemingway was contrite, noting he was "drunker than hell last night," and offered his hand in a gesture of apology.[73]

That was Hemingway. He had huge flaws but an equally great heart, with wounds and scars he tried to salve with alcohol and deflect with his tough-guy routine. With that sharp mind and quick wit, and highly competitive nature, he would sometimes lash out, especially when alcohol darkened his mood. Afterward, he always felt badly.

William "Bill" Horne Jr. ("Horney"), another Red Cross volunteer, hailing from Yonkers, New York, Princeton Class of 1913, understood Hemingway's heart—and his bad eye, a defect they shared and over which they bonded. "Among the 120 drivers recruited from all over the country—mostly the halt, the half-blind like me, the too young and too old," Horne recalled years later, "was a handsome, 18-year-old giant named Ernest Hemingway . . . During the ten-day crossing, Ernie and I became good friends. We landed at Bordeaux the day the enemy was stopped at Belleau Wood, and all of us got high on the native product. Though honorary second lieutenants in the Italian Army, we were just kids, and getting half a bottle of wine into you was pretty serious business. We took the night train to Paris and were received as *persona grata*. We were even saluted by French generals!"[74]

Like his father, "a real charmer," when "not in one of his stern moods," wrote Marcelline, Hemingway had a special gift for friendship—and "an ability to be congenial with people of all ages and from all backgrounds."[75] It would serve him well, as he now discovered a world apart from Oak Park, a new world that would give him a deeper understanding of the meaning of life.

❧❧❧

2

꽃꽃꽃

Medieval Truths and
World War I Heroism

Just shy of his nineteenth birthday, while serving abroad, in what would be one of the most dramatic plot points of his life, Hemingway discovered the richness of Catholicism—with all five senses. He bathed in Mary's love and soaked up the redemptive reality of her son Jesus hanging on that wooden cross, writhing in pain, to his very sinews, the great European cathedrals he visited punctuating this reality.

He was just seventeen and the experience was transformative. And quite unexpected. He was in Europe to help fight a war, not to find God.

"The U.S. had entered the war in Europe but would have no troops ready for another month," said Horne, "so the Red Cross was sending ambulance sections, with huge American flags painted on the sides, as a way of telling the Allies, 'Boys, we're with you!'"[1]

After the war broke out in August 1914, the Red Cross Ambulance Corps was founded by Richard Norton, son of Harvard President Charles Eliot Norton, to free up the fighting French from ambulance duties. Motorized vehicles were, for the first time, utilized to transport wounded soldiers quickly to medical facilities where they received life-saving treatment. Initially part of the British Red Cross, by October 1914, the corps was fully independent, buttressed by wealthy Americans living in London, and operated fifteen vehicles in the French theater. Drivers, serving six-month tours of duty, hailed mostly from Ivy League schools, predominantly Harvard, and possessed the requisite qualifications—conversant in French, able to drive, and accustomed to and desirous of the leisure time the service provided.

The American Red Cross arrived in Italy on December 20, 1917, its ambulances driving into Milan that day, after clocking some 500 arduous miles en route from Paris over dirt and macadam roads, riddled with potholes the heavy, fast vehicles left in their wake. Major Guy Lowell assumed its supervision shortly thereafter on January 1, 1918, overseeing its five sections and 135 ambulance drivers operating a fleet of 104 ambulances and 125 other vehicles[2] that had already handled 70,224 cases the previous year.[3]

Hemingway left New York on May 23 and, after crossing the Atlantic, it was "Paris and red tape" followed by "temporary duty in Milano," he told fellow corpsman and Second Lieutenant Henry Villard.[4]

LIFE IN MILAN: SPIRITUAL AND CARNAL

Ernest Hemingway in Milan, June 1918.
Source: In the public domain.

On his first day in Milan, Hemingway was immediately thrust into the war's brutal reality: "Had my first baptism of fire," he wrote in a postcard to his former employer, the *Kansas City Star*. "We carried them in like at the General Hospital, Kansas City."[5] He later filled in the blanks in *Death in the Afternoon*:

I first saw inversion of the usual sex of the dead after the explosion of a munition factory which had been situated in the countryside near Milan, Italy. We drove to the scene of the disaster in trucks along poplar-shaded roads . . . and, I must admit, frankly, the shock it was to find those dead were women rather than men.[6]

Afterward, wrote Baker, he "strolled through the Galleria and into the vast dim cathedral."[7]

They arrived in Schio on June 10, 1918, "about 20 miles behind the mountain front," said Horne. "Our ambulances would fan out from the town . . . at the west end of the Italian-Austrian line, and we'd cover our sectors a little east of Lake Garda, bringing in the wounded. By great good fortune I was assigned with Hemingway, Fred Spiegel, Larry Barnett, Jerry Flaherty, and 'Little Fever' Jenkins to Section IV, which we came to call the 'Schio Country Club.'"[8] They became friends for life. Hemingway also met and befriended Harvard grad (1916), John Dos Passos, known as "Dos," and like Hem a Midwest boy (born in Chicago), who struck literary gold. Dos Passos was leaving as Hem was just getting started. Their section transported the wounded—first, from the front lines to distributing or dressing stations, called smistamento or sanita, this being the most hazardous duty. Next, they transported the wounded to the field hospitals behind the lines, and, finally, to army transport centers, where the wounded were sent by train to the various other hospitals.

A week after they arrived, the American Red Cross opened their headquarters and hospital in Milan "within sight of the Duomo (Milan Cathedral), that magnificent pinnacled and fretted showpiece of the Italian nation," Villard wrote.[9]

To provide comfort to the soldiers, the Red Cross established a network of emergency canteens along the entire front at a comfortable distance from forward listening posts. Each canteen facility was directed by a Red Cross lieutenant—the principal duties being to dispense coffee, chocolate, jam, soup, cigarettes, cigars, postcards, and the like. The canteens also provided a place for soldiers to rest and recreate by strumming guitars and mandolins or perhaps playing an accordion, when not listening to phonographs and records. A motion picture projector, housed at one of the canteens, also gave them the opportunity to enjoy the latest silent films such as Charlie Chaplin's *A Dog's Life* (1918). Given that Hemingway and the others found life in Schio, far from the action, boring, these canteens provided a welcome opportunity. When an officer came through during "a lull on our end of the front," said Horne, "recruiting men to go to the Piave River" where "the offensive was hot, and men were needed to run the canteens," everyone eagerly volunteered "and eight were chosen, including Ernie and me. I was dropped at the 68th Brigata Fanleria, San Pedro Novello, one of the little villages, and Ernie went to Fossalta."

It was on June 24, 1918, having clocked two weeks at the "Schio Country Club," that they arrived at their new assignment with the rolling canteens serving under the supervision of Captain James Gamble, Yale Class of 1904. A wealthy young man, whose family, the Voorhees of Williamsport, Pennsylvania, made their fortune in timber, he was respected by his young charges. One day, he gave them a short leave in Maestre and some of them visited the Italian officers' brothel, Villa Rosa. "Ernest was extremely shy, and blushed furiously when accosted by one of the whores," Jenkins told Baker.[10]

As second lieutenant, serving under an American lieutenant and a French liaison lieutenant, Hemingway, like Horne, had mess hall privileges. He rubbed elbows with Italian officers and also met Don Giuseppe Bianchi, a young priest from the Abruzzi region near Florence. Don Bianchi, wrote Baker, "wore a cross in dark red velvet above the left-hand pocket of his tunic and quickly befriended Ernest who treated him with sympathy and respect."[11]

All the while they lived in "a half-blown-apart house and no one brought us supplies to dole out," said Horne, where it was "nothing but silkworms gnawing and mosquitos stinging."[12] "Ernie grew restless," said Horne, "so he borrowed a bike and pedaled to the front" where he delivered goods on foot along the Piave River to the troops, engaged in routing the Austrians. It was a military campaign, just north of Venice, fraught with danger—right where Hemingway, possessing the soul of a reporter, wanted to be.

A week later, Horne, content to stay put, received news that Hemingway had been mortally wounded around midnight on July 8 at Fossalta di Piave along the Piave River's west bank. "The guns, the tear gas, the bloody soldiers, the stench of rotting horses and human flesh combined to make it a ghastly nightmare," recalled Miller.[13]

"He was at an advanced listening post—a hole in the ground—when the Austrians discovered it and sent over a *Minenwerfer*," said Horne. "It landed right smack on target. One man was killed, another badly hurt, and Ernie was hit by shell fragments."[14] It was shortly after midnight, Baker writes, that the Austrians "sent another of their projectiles hurtling across the river . . . about the size of a five-gallon tin . . . 420 caliber . . . filled with steel rod fragments and miscellaneous metal junk."[15]

Lt. Edward M. McKey, who had established the first rolling canteen in February 1918, within range of the Austrian mortars, was killed on June

16 just days before Hemingway's arrival in the same spot where he was wounded.[16] It was all so predictable. "To get these supplies to these points," Major Lowell wrote in his *Report of the Department of Military Affairs: January to July, 1918*, "it was necessary to travel over roads within the range of Austrian guns and climb slopes covered by numerous machine guns and cannon" and "during such a trip, E.M. Hemingway was wounded by the explosion of a shell which landed about three feet from him, killing a soldier who stood between him and the point of the explosion, and wounding others."[17]

Hemingway was "in No Man's Land with three other men," when he was wounded, he recalled seven months later. "It was night and the star shells were continually lighting up the place and just then there was a bright light and I felt as if I were falling through the air. I thought I was dead, but I soon came to and found the observation post was strewn all over the ground."[18]

They were huddled in the dugout of the listening post when the incoming trench mortar landed its direct hit and knocked him unconscious, shell fragments striking his thighs and hand, and grazing his scalp. "'I tried to breathe,' Ernest wrote afterwards, 'but my breath would not come . . . the ground was torn up and in front of my head there was a splintered beam of wood. In the jolt of my head, I heard somebody crying.'"[19] Of the two Italian soldiers between Hemingway and the site of impact, the one was killed; the other, the one who was crying, had lost both legs.

Hemingway, though gravely injured himself, immediately—instinctively—sprang into action, lifting this wounded soul, carrying him to the first aid dugout. As Brian tells it, he managed to get fifty yards, when enemy machine gun bullets ripped through right knee and foot, after which he blacked out. The next thing he knew, he was in the dugout, blood-soaked, having carried the wounded soldier, along with himself, the final 100 yards to safety, miraculously so.[20]

Not yet fully conscious in this compressed moment of self-sacrificing valor, he would be awarded the Italian Croce di Guerra for heroism as well as the French silver medal of honor, the equivalent of the Medaille Militaire of Legion of Honor of France.

It was not until an ambulance driver came along to the dugout surgical unit and identified Hemingway that "they took him to the front-line dressing station," said Horne. It was at a schoolhouse near Fornaci, converted into a temporary hospital, where he was treated with morphine and tetanus immune globulin to prevent lockjaw.

As he lay waiting to be carried to the train station for the trip to the hospital, unsure whether he would live or die, he was "really scared," he wrote years later to Thomas Welsh, father of his future wife, and had "Fear of death" and "Belief in *personal* salvation" and prayed "with almost tribal faith" for the intercession of "Our Lady and various saints."[21]

As if on cue, "(t)he little priest from the Abruzzi came along the line of wounded men, murmuring the holy words, anointing each as he passed," wrote Baker. "He recognized Ernest and did the same for him."[22] This priest, Don Giuseppe Bianchi, is the one who had befriended Hemingway at the officers' mess hall.

"Brummy" wrote to Dr. Hemingway on July 14 to give him more details of his son's injuries, cheerily assuring him that his son was rapidly recovering and that the doctor had assured him that he would regain "entire use of both legs" in no time. He had to write the letter, Sunny wrote, because Hem's hands were so badly injured. Of the 200 plus pieces of shell "lodged in him," Brummy wrote, "none of them are above the hip joint." Of the more serious wounds, he wrote, "Only a few of these pieces was large enough to cut deep; the most serious of these being two in the (right) knee and two in the right foot."[23]

WOUNDED "GIOVANE AMERICANO" FALLS IN LOVE

He made quite an impression on the Italian soldiers in the trenches who spoke of their "'giovane Americano,'" wrote Brumback[24]—a description that, ironically, means "gift from God," or "God is gracious."

A month later, on August 18, after his hands had healed, Hemingway was able, himself, to describe the scene in a letter to his family and how initially he felt no pain from the 227 trench mortar wounds except for a sensation akin to wearing rubber boots drenched in hot water. Also, his knee cap was "acting queer" and the bullet, he wrote, felt like a "sharp smack on my leg with an icy snow ball" and "it spilled me." Yet he managed to get up and get the wounded to the dugout then "kind of collapsed" and noticed blood all over his pants from the bleeding Italian. "Well, the Captain (of the dugout) who was a great pal of mine . . . said 'Poor Hem he'll be R.I.P. soon.'"[25] "They carried me on a stretcher," he continued, "three kilometers to a dressing station . . . My wounds were now hurting like 227 little devils driving nails into the raw."

Next, they drove him in an Italian ambulance a "couple of kilometers away" to a second dressing station—a converted schoolhouse—where he received the morphine and antitetanus. "They did a fine job bandaging me," he wrote, and "all shook hands with me and would have kissed me but I kidded them along."[26]

Major Lowell, writing in *The Red Cross Bulletin* on August 5, 1918, and in the Italian edition on December 7, 1918, verified the accounts of Hemingway's injuries (albeit 237 wounds were cited), as well as his heroics in carrying the wounded soldier to safety, and the fact that he was awarded the Silver Medal of Valor.[27]

But he had won more than earthly medals. Hemingway considered July 8, 1918, a day of spiritual rebirth. It was the day he had stared down death and was "anointed" and absolved of all his sins. Now he "called himself a Catholic," wrote Charles Scribner III, scion of the publishing family that would soon bring Hemingway, the literary lion, to the world.[28] Stoneback deconstructs this crucial event:

> [Hemingway biographer Jeffrey] Meyers mentions for the first time that event which is at the crux in all discussions of Hemingway's Catholicism . . . "A Florentine priest, Don Giuseppe Bianchi, *passed* by the wounded men, *murmuring* holy words and *anointing* them. There was no need for the priest to give Hemingway *extreme unction*; he was not in mortal danger and was recovering from his wounds. Bianchi's perfunctory ceremony was not (as Hemingway later *conveniently* claimed) a formal baptism into the Catholic Church." (*Hemingway: A Biography* p. 32; emphasis added). Aside from the patronizing tone of this passage . . . Meyers seems confused about the sacraments. If the priest did "anoint" Hemingway, what else could the sacrament have been but extreme unction? It is also, most likely, under battlefield circumstances, that obtained, that the priest would first speak the brief Trinitarian words of "conditional Baptism" and then administered the viaticum, the Holy Communion given to those in danger of death.[29]

Hemingway—a bloody mess, with over 200 pieces of shrapnel, along with bullets, lodged in his legs, knees, and feet—was holding on for dear life in that schoolhouse, where he received morphine and antitetanus *and* a Catholic "anointing."

Then he spent five days in a field hospital after which the army transported him to the train for the trip to Milan and its American Red Cross Hospital.

His next-door neighbor at the hospital was fellow ambulance driver, Villard from Section I, who was much taken with the giovane Americano— "a good-looking son-of-a-gun," wrote Villard, "lying there fresh-faced and clean-shaven on the white-painted iron bedstead, and good-natured, too," which Villard found impressive, "considering he appeared totally disabled. He had a strong jaw and a wide, boyish grin that revealed an even row of dazzling white teeth, and his jet-black hair and dark eyes contrasted starkly with the snowy pillows that propped up his dark shoulders as he reclined at full length, one leg in a plaster cast, the other swathed in bandages . . . Whatever the extent of his injuries, there was no question about his magnetism or his mental alertness. 'You'll like it here,' he said warmly, taking my hand in a vigorous clasp. 'They treat you royally.'"[30]

In truth, he was mortally afraid the doctors would want to amputate his leg, yet kept a stiff upper lip, refusing "to feel sorry for himself," wrote Scott Donaldson.[31] Red Cross officers, including Captain Gamble who had supervised him on the rolling canteen, were also impressed with his magnanimity and good spirits.

The nurses also took note, considering him "their special pet, a prize specimen of a wounded hero," wrote Villard. Statuesque Agnes Von Kurowsky of Washington, DC, a flirtatious live wire, intent on seeing the world, was particularly fond of Hemingway, her captive audience, and dazzled him with her shiny chestnut-brown hair and shimmering grey eyes. She had arrived just a few days earlier to the mansion-turned-hospital and was his guardian angel, he wrote his family, and gave him "a hot bath" that lulled him into his first real sleep since setting foot in Italy.[32] She was soon working the night shift just to be near him at that romantic time. By late August, Hemingway was "in love again," he wrote his mother.[33] "As their romance developed," wrote Donaldson, "Agnes and Ernest held hands more or less openly and wrote daily notes to each other during the hours when they were apart."[34] By fall, the relationship seemed headed for the altar, though she was officially engaged to a doctor in New York. Hemingway had morphed from this awkward teen into a handsome, charismatic young man, knowing little of mature love and was much taken with the worldly wise Agnes.

At the same time, his friendship with Don Bianchi continued while Hemingway convalesced at the hospital and had two surgeries. Interestingly, the unnamed priest in *A Farewell to Arms*, Hemingway's iconic World War I novel, exactly mirrors Don Bianchi down to "the cross in dark red velvet above the breast pocket of his gray tunic."[35] Besides dressing in the same exact manner, both priests were small in stature and hailed from the same place—Abruzzi (the plural name, when it consisted of several areas; now called Abruzzo). And both priests were deeply spiritual.

Lt. Frederic Henri, the protagonist, played by future friend—and future fellow Catholic—Gary Cooper in Hollywood's 1932 production of the novel, images Hemingway's experience. Besides being an American Red Cross ambulance driver, he sustains wounds inflicted by trench mortar shell identical to the ones Hemingway sustained, both along a northern Italian river near Venice and the Austrian front. And, like Hemingway, he did not smoke, but drank—with gusto. (Though, Hemingway did smoke for a short time during and after World War I.) Henri falls in love with his nurse Catherine Barkley as Hemingway would fall in love with Agnes Von Kurowsky. While respecting the spirit of Evelyn Waugh, who wrote in his author's note to *Brideshead Revisited*—"I am not I; thou are not he or she; they are not they."—it is, nonetheless easy to imagine the newly anointed Hemingway having a conversation with Don Giuseppe not unlike this one between the priest and Lt. Henry:

"In my country, it is understood that a man may love God. It is not a dirty joke."

"I understand."

He looked at me and smiled.

"You understand but you do not love God."

"No."

"You do not love Him at all?" he asked.

"I am afraid of Him in the night sometimes."

"You should love Him."

"I don't love much."

"Yes," he said. "You do."

"What you tell me about in the nights. That is not love. That is only passion and lust. When you love you wish to do things for. You wish to sacrifice for. You wish to serve."

"I don't love."

"You will. I know you will. Then you will be happy."

Hemingway went on holiday with John Miller, now a patient as well, on September 24 to Lake Maggiore in Stresa to fish, drink, play billiards, and lavish attention on a cute girl, the baby of the Bellia family. Then Agnes was transferred to Florence on October 15, to nurse a Spanish flu victim back to health, and by month's end Hemingway was off to the Monte Grappa Front.

While they were apart, Agnes wrote Hemingway from Florence, telling him that she "yearned for them to be together . . . so that she could nestle in that hollow space he made for her face and then go to sleep with his arm around her . . . 'I love you more and more and know what I'm going to bring you when I come home,' she promised." Evidently, to stay under the radar of Red Cross officials, intent on dousing the flames of romance, she addressed some of her letters to the Anglo-American Club in Milan in lieu of the Red Cross Hospital. "This is our war-sacrifice, bambino mio, to keep our secrets to ourselves," and then she went on at length about not worrying about what others thought.[36]

Meanwhile, Horne had returned to Schio when Piave calmed down, and stayed till the fall, when the Allies began their Vittorio Veneto offensive from Monte Grappa to the Adriatic end of Piave. "One night I drove our N.8 Fiat to Bassano to see Ernie, and we had a jolly time together." But Hem developed jaundice, recognizing the symptoms from what Villard, who suffered a bout, had told him. He was driven back to Milan by Gamble who then cared for him, while Horne "went to the front line atop Mt. Grappa and had a steady week of carrying wounded until the battle was over," and the armistice declared on November 3, bringing an end to the war on the Italian front. "Ernie remained behind in the Milan hospital," he said, for "muscular therapy."[37]

Hemingway had hoped to travel to Abruzzi with Italian officer Nick Neroni for "two weeks shooting and trout fishing," but their plans fizzled.[38] Instead he visited the now defunct war zone in December and stored away more literary chestnuts. Agnes had returned to Milan on Armistice Day and they spent time together until November 20, and solidified their marriage plans. When she was assigned to Treviso, soon thereafter, Hemingway visited her on December 9, staying for three days, as her letters reflect, then spent the Christmas holiday with Gamble at his villa in Taormina, Sicily, though he concocted an elaborate tale of a competing adventure.

While the lovers were apart, they corresponded daily, though only her letters to him remain because she destroyed his letters. Agnes would later maintain that she was keeping Ernest on the hook to get him back to America and away from Gamble, whom she believed was sexually interested in Hemingway, telling him, he would become "a bum . . . if he started traveling around with someone else paying the expenses."[39] That their marriage plans were made after Gamble proposed just such an arrangement for a year would seem to support this scenario. In her letter from Treviso, on the eve of Christmas, one of her most affectionate, she regrets her absence on Christmas. "If this hits you about Xmas time, just make believe you're getting a gift from me (as you will someday). And let me tell you I love you and wish we could be together for our first Christmas . . . I miss you more and more, and it makes me shiver to think of your going home without me . . ."[40] The age gap, though, intrudes. She is proud of her "bambino mio," her dear boy "when he resolves to give up hard liquor." Ironically, she feared he might abandon her, as she abandoned her fiancé. "I never imagined anyone else could be so dear and necessary to me," she wrote. "Don't let me gain you only to lose you. I love you, Ernie."[41]

Hemingway was thoroughly smitten, telling Horne that getting wounded was worth it just to meet Agnes. Though she minimized their relationship, insisting it had only entailed some petting. Never mind that the war-time hospital atmosphere cultivated relationships that progressed far beyond that and the American Red Cross Hospital in Milan, "an old-fashioned mansion . . . (where) in the half-light from a street lamp (it) belonged to an era of horse carriages and opera lovers, of prosperous Lombardy bankers and businessmen, genteel folk," was quite the romantic setting.[42] And, while her diary, which Villard published, supports her minimalist account, her letters to Ernie tell a different story, which Hemingway's "A Very Short Story" published seven years later as part of the *in our time* collection, tells beat for beat. The protagonist is unnamed because it goes without saying: It's Ernest.

Wounded in the war, his nurse "Luz," cared for him at the Padua hospital, he writes, and "stayed on night duty for three months" while carrying on a torrid affair with him and caring for just a few other patients "who all knew about it." "Before he went back to the front they went into the Duomo and prayed. It was dim and quiet, and there were other people praying. They wanted to get married, but there was not enough time for the banns, and neither of them had birth certificates. They felt as though they were married, but they wanted everyone to know about it, and to make it so they could not lose it."[43]

In real life, Hemingway would ask Agnes to join him at the Cathedral of Milan for prayer and Mass, which he attended regularly.[44]

In the art-reflecting-life story, Luz writes him copious letters though he does not receive them until after the armistice. "They were all about the hospital, and how much she loved him and how it was impossible to get along without him and how terrible it was missing him at night." As with Agnes and Hem, Luz and her patient/lover were making plans for life. He would go home and get a job after which she would join him. "It was understood he would not drink, and he did not want to see his friends or anyone in the States."[45]

In the *very long story*, Frederic is trying to convince Catherine to marry him and opines on the importance of religion. "You're my religion," she says. "You're all I got."

Hemingway wrestled with similar feelings, writing Horne the day he received a letter from Agnes ending the affair, "Bill I forgot all about religion and everything else—because I had Ag to worship."[46]

Well, not quite. Another woman, Mary, the mother of Jesus, had entered his life and would have a much more profound and lasting influence. Don Bianchi had surely told Hemingway about the special role of Mary in the life of the Church. Then, too, recent events in Fatima, Portugal, some 1,000 miles southwest of Milan, were doubtless a prime topic of discusssion.

Starting on May 13, 1917, the Blessed Virgin had appeared to three shepherd children at the Cova da Iria, and again on the thirteenth of each

successive month until October 13, 1917. "The Miracle of the Sun" that occurred on the day of her last appearance, in which the sun spun around and
hurtled close to earth, drying previously drenched throngs of pilgrims, was
still very much on everyone's mind. Mary had spoken during the Fatima apparitions of the ongoing world war and what was needed for peace—prayer,
reparation, and consecration to her Immaculate Heart, the latter requirement
fulfilled, some sixty-six years later, on March 25, 1984, by St. Pope John
Paul II.[47]

Hemingway considered Mary's apparitions incontrovertible evidence
that the Catholic Church was the one true faith, he would tell a friend years
later.[48]

Thus, it's axiomatic that Don Bianchi had spoken with Hemingway
about Fatima and Mary's other apparitions.

Pope Leo XIII had written in his papal encyclical on the Feast of Mary's
Birthday five years before Hemingway was born:

> The recourse we have to Mary in prayer follows upon the office she contin-
> uously fills by the side of the throne of God as Mediatrix of Divine grace;
> being by worthiness and by merit most acceptable to Him, and, therefore,
> surpassing in power all the angels and saints in Heaven.[49]

Hemingway pondered Mary in his heart and prayed through her intercession. We know that, based on what he said to an intimate years later
about praying "with almost tribal faith" to her. He could take it to the bank
that she had the power to help him and would do so, if he asked, and often
when not asked.

Quite clearly, the night he was mortally wounded, she saved his life.

That sealed the deal. Hemingway would turn to Mary throughout her
life.

It is the spiritual iceberg in his writings, in which he obliquely or not so
obliquely, references her.

Mary, in turn, would provide Hemingway—"running scared" since he
was thirteen—with comfort and aid as he tried to deal with his emotional
wounds made all the more acute given his artist's soul and manic depression—the two, intrinsically connected.

3

❧❧❧

Breaking Away
and Starting a New Life

Hemingway was discharged from the American Red Cross on January 4, 1919. A few days later, he set sail from Genoa with the understanding that Agnes would follow him to America to tie the knot. Their last meeting in Italy, though, was spoiled by a quarrel over just how soon. Ernest wanted her to come right away.[1]

"On the train from Padua to Milan they quarreled about her not being able to come home at once," Hemingway wrote in "A Very Short Story." "When they had to say goodbye at the station in Milan, they kissed goodbye but were not finished with the quarrel. He felt sick about saying goodbye like that."[2]

On January 21, as Hemingway hobbled down the gangplank of the *S.S. Giuseppe Verdi* at New York's Ellis Island, he was given a hero's welcome—"a darn dramatic sight," said Horne—"over six feet tall, wearing a Bersaglieri hat with great cock feathers, enormous officer's cape lined with red satin, a British-style tunic with ribbons of the Valor Medal and Italian War Cross, and a limp! The *New York Times* carried a front-page story and a picture headlined, 'Most Wounded Hero Returns Today.'"[3]

Once Hemingway got back to Oak Park, it was a different story. All the hoopla was over. He missed Italy immensely and now felt lonely and misunderstood. His adrenaline would start pumping again when, on February 7, he spoke at Oak Park High School, to the Hanna Club, "a male-only group that met to hear outside speakers tell about the world of men."[4] Over a "spiffy" dinner prepared by Mrs. Foster, he vividly recounted his time in Italy as an ambulance driver and war correspondent, making the over 200 in attendance—a club record—feel like they were living the experience.[5]

Five weeks later, on Friday, March 14, Hemingway returned to speak to an assembly of the entire high school about his "crowded hour," as T. R. dubbed such a moment—when the enemy "dropped a trench mortar shell . . . filled with explosives and slugs." And he thought to himself, "Gee! Stein, you're dead."[6] The Austrians alerted by the blast fallout started using their "star shells" and "trench searchlights . . . to locate us." As Hemingway moved to escape to "the trenches," realizing he was wounded, he said, he nonetheless carried the wounded soldier, with blown-off legs, to safety. Just then, "their searchlight spotted us and they turned a machine gun on us" and pierced "Stein's" thigh. "It felt just like a snowball," he said, "so hard" and "with such force that it knocked me down." He was about to jump into the trench when "another bullet hit me, this time in the foot. It tumbled me and my wounded man all in a heap in the trench." The next thing he knew he was in the dugout.

He was serving with the 69th Regiment Infantry at the advanced listening post that night, he said. As for this "service" with the 69th, he surely felt like an "embed." As he told the Hanna Club, he was serving as a war correspondent, journalism being his first calling. Then, when the Austrians attacked the post, he surely felt like he was "serving" in the 69th, given that he had suddenly gone from "embed" to saving lives, including his own.

Back home he continued dreaming of marrying Agnes. But, as he wrote in his fictional account, "the major of the battalion made love to Luz, and she had never known Italians before and finally wrote to the States that theirs had only been a boy and girl affair." Just so! After Agnes was transferred to Torre di Mosto, she fell in love with an Italian officer named Domenico Caracciolo and, after a "big think," decided to break up with Ernest, calling him "just a kid" in her letter of March 7, which he received on March 30, in Michigan, where he was doing some writing. While he might blithely dismiss Agnes' "big dump" six years later in his "Very Short Story," the truth is, it was a huge blow to his sensitive psyche from which he never fully recovered and, in part, explains his marital infidelities: He never wanted to be callously tossed aside again. His heart could not take it. So, he was always looking for the next "love," just in case.

TRANSFORMING WOUNDS INTO ART

As he recovered from his injuries—physical, mental, and psychological—he was becoming Ernest Hemingway, with a zest to write and to see the world on his own terms, guided by his new faith.

Wearing his full uniform for several months, the long boots supporting his legs weak from his injuries and black velvet Italian cape supporting his ego, fragile and bruised, he continued to develop his "war hero" narrative, real and imagined, emanating from and feeding his storytelling passion, while at the same time he began distancing himself from his family given that he was suffering not only the visible but also the hidden wounds of war—"shell shock," as it was called in World War I, which was not well understood at the time, certainly not by his family. Their tendency to pressure him to get on with his life myopically missed the central fact of his postwar self: He was suffering from his first traumatic brain injury (TBI) to say nothing of the psychological trauma inflicted by the blast.

As Hemingway healed through writing, he would drink, as well, a habit he picked up in Europe, which Sunny and Marcelline recount in their memoirs. As in the Milan hospital, he hid the alcohol from his parents. Ernest had "almost depressed intervals when he retired to his room away from the well-wishers and curiosity seekers," Marcelline wrote.[7] One day, when she was upset, Ernest asked her what was the matter, then offered her a drink and after she took a sip, said, "Don't be afraid . . . Drink it up, Sis, it can't hurt you. There's great comfort in that little bottle . . . not just for itself. But it relaxes you when the pain gets bad. Mazaween . . . don't be afraid to taste all the other things in life that aren't here in Oak Park . . . Taste everything, Sis . . . Don't be afraid to try new things just because they are new."

His family could not help but see how Ernie had changed, without realizing the etiology—and, even if known, not knowing the cure. Marcelline wondered if he would ever be happy again in Oak Park, and she and the rest of the family expressed their concern. As he wrote to Larry Barnett, "My family, God bless them as always, are wolfing at me to go to college . . . Frankly I don't know where the hell to go."[8] His brother Leicester, though, realized the hidden nature of his wounds—that the "psychic shock" was what ailed him. His resulting insomnia was only relieved by light, and he remembered him telling Guy Hickock that when the blast hit, "I felt my soul or something coming right out of my body like you'd pull a silk handkerchief out of a pocket by one corner. It flew around and then came back and went in again and I wasn't dead anymore."[9] In "Now I Lay Me," Nick Adams, Hemingway's literary alter ego, relives what Hemingway told Hickock, contrasting light with darkness, and the spirituality implicit in that: "I myself did not want to sleep because I had been living for a long time with the knowledge that if I ever shut my eyes in the dark and let myself go, my soul would go out of my body." Nick describes this ever-present feeling in the dark nights recalling how "I had been blown up at night and felt it go out of me and go off and then come back." He felt it was hard to get rid of the feeling except by "a very great effort." Sometimes he would go fishing in his mind. "But some nights," he wrote, "I could not fish, and on those nights I was cold awake and said my prayers over and over and tried to pray for all the people I had ever known . . . If you prayed for all of them, saying a Hail Mary and an Our Father for each one, it took a long time and finally it would be light, and then you could go to sleep, if you were in a place where you could sleep in the daylight . . . If I could have a light I was not afraid to sleep because I knew my soul would only go out of me if it were dark."[10] "In Another Country," another short story from the same collection, published in 1927, likewise enters the psyche of a wounded American soldier lying awake in Milan, "afraid to die and wondering how I would be when I went back to the front again."

Given his brother's "agitated state,"[11] all the pecking away about his future was counterproductive, reasoned five-year-old Leicester. Ernie simply retreated to his corner, while nursing hidden wounds and charting his future. "Though Mother implored Ernest's help and tried to talk to him about the family situation," wrote Marcelline, "he blithely ignored her appeals and managed to leave immediately after meals with his friends or go fishing when something needed to be done; he promised vaguely to help 'some other time.'" His parents, too, were concerned over his "lack of adult responsibility" and "his rudeness and his willingness to let both Mrs. Charles, Bill Smith's aunt, and our family go on providing for him."[12]

Hemingway's situation mirrored that of Harold Krebs, whom he brought to life in his 1925 short story, "Soldier's Home." Like Hemingway, Krebs returns home from the war, in his case, to smalltown Oklahoma, shellshocked, his inner thoughts revealing what it is like to be a returning veteran, mistreated and afraid. Then, too, there is the dialogue with his mother, not unlike Hemingway's mother, in which she contrasts his lack of achievement with the progress of his peers, ad nauseam. Krebs responds with few words, revealing the numbness, pain, and fear he is feeling.

Then, too, the war had messed with Krebs's feelings about girls and how he relates with them. He observes local girls who had "grown up," whom he feels he can never bond with. "He liked to look at them though . . . Most of them had their hair cut short. When he went away only little girls wore their hair like that or girls that were fast . . . He liked to look at them from the front porch as they walked on the other side of the street . . . he liked the round Dutch collars above their sweaters. He liked their silk stockings and flat shoes." Then, again, he comforted himself, "When you were really ripe for a girl you always got one." But it's different postwar and he rationalizes his changed perspective, writing: "Now he would have liked a girl if she had come to him and not wanted to talk. But here at home it was all too complicated. It was not worth the trouble. . . . He liked the look of them much better than the French girls or the German girls." But they inhabited a world apart from him.[13] His perceived inability to make a connection with the local girls makes him feel even more isolated and lonely. Not only that but, like Hemingway, Krebs abandons his Protestant faith, that is, Methodist, and the notion that, as his mother says, "'God has some work for everyone to do . . . There can be no idle hands in His Kingdom.'"[14] When she asks him to kneel and pray with her, Krebs says he can't, and tells his mother he does not love her, given intense family pressure to make something of himself. When she asks if he wants her to pray for him, he says "Yes." He's trying "to keep his life from becoming complicated" and "had felt sorry for his mother and she had made him lie." Krebs, like Hem, resolves to go to Kansas City to work and "she would feel alright about it."[15]

LAST SUMMER AT LAKE WALLOON, PARENTS' ERODING MARRIAGE

By summer, armed with a collection of short stories he had written, Ernest reached out to a fellow vacationing in Lake Walloon who gave him a publishing roadmap including *Saturday Evening Post*, *Everybody's Magazine*, *Popular Magazine*, *Red Book*, and *Blue Book*. After sending up a few trial balloons, he headed out for his final camping trip of the year to the deserted town of Seney in the Upper Peninsula of Michigan, just fifteen miles from Lake Superior's chill, as he had written in "Confessions" he wanted to do. Some four years later, that trip would inspire another shell-shocked soldier's tale, "Big Two-Hearted River," the story of Nick Adams, alone on a hunting and fishing trip, as he seeks to recover from war's wounds. Albeit, on his actual trip to Seney, Hemingway was joined by two companions, war buddies Fever Jenkins and another "Schio Country Club" pal. Between the three of them, they caught some 200 fish. As Baker writes, Hemingway "later recalled that he was still badly hurt in body, mind, spirit and morals . . . When he got off the train, at Seney, said he, the brakeman told the engineer . . . 'Hold her up . . . There's a cripple who needs time to get his stuff down.'" Hemingway was "shocked," having never considered himself "crippled" and in the aftermath, wrote Baker, "stopped being one in his mind."[16]

Meanwhile Grace was enjoying her dream cottage across the lake from Windemere which she had finally built for herself, where she lived with Ruth, against Dr. Hemingway's wishes. If there was nothing to the relationship, it certainly had a whiff of impropriety, especially from Ruth's point of view who expressed her "love"[17] for Grace. On August 4, 1919, after Ruth came back home from the cottage to Oak Park, Dr. Hemingway barred her from the house. While, officially, their father's behavior was perplexing, Leicester, Marcelline, and Sunny did not say word one about Ruth in their memoirs. Furthermore, after their father's untimely death, both Marcelline and Sunny expressed regret that they had not been there for him. Grace was the one he needed the most. An early adherent of the cause of women's rights, at times, she failed to find the proper balance and gave her husband short shrift when she should have devoted more of herself and her time to him, rather than living a lake away when he vacationed in the Northern Lower Peninsula.

Ernest took umbrage at Grace's cottage, believing she should have saved the money and spent it on college for himself and his siblings. Never mind that he was not college bound. More than anything, he longed for the days when his mother was young and beautiful and his father handsome and virile and the marriage was good and strong. Now Doc Hemingway spent more time in Oak Park in the summertime as Grace, having birthed six children, enjoyed her cottage across from Windemere. Truth be told, he was probably better off in Oak Park as the strictures he insisted govern the lives of his now mostly grown children were being violated with reckless abandon during those summers at Windemere as the Victorian Age gave way to the roaring twenties—underscoring another troubling aspect of Grace's cottage a lake away. Staying with her in the new cottage were Ruth and the two youngest children, Leicester and Carol, while the older children, now ages 14, 17, 20 and 21, stayed at Windemere without adult supervision and guidance.

In the fall of 1919, as his parents' marriage continued to erode, Hemingway returned to Petoskey to do more serious writing, while continuing to heal from his war wounds. He stayed at Potter's Rooming House, 602 State Street, a block and half away from St. Francis Xavier Catholic Church, at the corner of State and Howard Streets. Built in 1902, the church had a beautiful side altar dedicated to Mary and grand altar pieces dedicated to many great saints, including its namesake. Hemingway could not miss the morning and evening bells and, no doubt, ducked in now and then, as he had done in the glorious cathedrals of Europe, to ponder his life, if not his next short story, and to pray. Then, too, there was "The Annex," a few blocks from the church down Howard on East Lake Street, where he enjoyed playing billiards and watching boxing matches in the adjoining park. While cranking out stories such as "Wolves and Doughnuts,"

Hemingway was invited to speak about his war experiences at the Ladies Aide Society at the nearby Petoskey Library. "He wore his sweeping cloak with the silver clasp and his well-polished cordovan boots," wrote Baker, and "the audience sighed in sympathy when he spoke of lying wounded in the roofless stable" telling them, it seemed "'more reasonable to die than to live.'"[18] There, he met Harriet Gridley Conable whose son, lame from birth, needed accompaniment at their home in Canada, while she and her husband, head of the F. W. Woolworth Canadian branch, wintered in Florida. Hemingway gladly accepted—leaving in January 1920, just as Prohibition was kicking in. (The Volstead Act went into effect on January 17, 1920.) Once in Canada, he landed a job freelancing for *The Toronto Star*, which began a long-term association with the paper.

That Ernest was descended from Rev. William Edward Miller, grandfather of the "finest, purest, noblest" man Grace had ever known, was no small matter, which she grandly trumpeted in a letter that wended its way to him shortly after he arrived in Canada.[19] She had always held up Grandfather Hall as the model of chivalry and strength, while denigrating his weak, ingratiating father, which hurt, angered, and demoralized Ernest, and, is perhaps the central psychological fact of Hemingway's life. It was the final straw.

When he returned to Windemere in the summer of 1920—farming no longer part of the summer routine—family tensions simmered and reached the boiling point after a raucous midnight party. It was his twenty-first birthday. "Hemingstein" and his friends had rowed and paddled over to Ryan's Point, where they sang around the bonfire, as one friend played his mandolin. No doubt, they also enjoyed kissing the girls on the perimeter. That was the night, Sunny wrote, where "the famous incident took place." Ernest had showed up with a male friend and two young women, and Sunny and Ursula were also there with dates. The revelry and general merriment had continued until 4 a.m. and Mrs. Hemingway and others in the community were appalled at Ernest's behavior. But Sunny insisted it was an innocent gathering while offering no real details.

Grace soon informed Ernest in a carefully scripted letter: "You are born of a race of gentlemen . . . who were clean mouthed, chivalrous to all women, grateful and generous . . . See to it that you do not disgrace their memories."[20] Furthermore, she wrote, "Unless you, my son Ernest . . . cease your lazy loafing and pleasure seeking . . . (and) stop trading on your hansome [*sic*] face to fool little gullable [*sic*] girls, and neglecting your duties to God and your Savior, Jesus Christ; unless in other words, you come into your manhood, there is nothing before you but bankruptcy—you have overdrawn."[21]

With that, she banished him from the family nest.

Ernest had a different take. "Mother," he wrote in a letter to Grace Quinlan, was pleased to find a reason to banish him since "she has more or less hated me ever since I opposed her throwing two or three thousand seeds away to build a new cottage for herself." He goes on to discuss the family "skeletons," noting that, while all families have them, the "Steins" have "heaps."[22]

CHICAGO BY WAY OF CHARLEVOIX

With that, he went to live in another boarding house, this time in Boyne City, Michigan, just south of Walloon Lake, and continued writing and figuring out what to do with his life. "One day in the Catholic Church at Charlevoix," writes Baker, "he and Katy [Smith] burnt a votive candle while Ernest prayed, as he said, for all things he wanted and never expected to get."[23]

Charlevoix, named after the French Jesuit missionary, Fr. Francis Xavier de Charlevoix, was the site of Catholic missionary work. St. Mary of the Assumption Church was established there in August 1890, a church bell added four years later. Whereas Fr. Francis spurned "a life of suffering and deprivation for the conversion of Indian souls" given his "eager curiosity concerning life,"[24] the real missionary work was done by Bishop Frederic Baraga of Marquette, Michigan. A Slovenian Roman Catholic missionary and author of Catholic poetry and hymns in Ojibwe language, he established nine missions in Northern Michigan. He had arrived in America some five years before the Treaty of Washington (1836) was signed between the United States and representatives of the Ottawa and Chippewa nations of Native Americans that ceded nearly fourteen million acres in the northwestern Lower Peninsula and eastern Upper Peninsula, 37 percent of the state of Michigan, poised to enter the Union, i.e., on January 26, 1837. The treaty provided support for missionaries. Baraga was a graduate of the University of Vienna, where he studied law, was ordained a priest in 1823, and answered the call from Bishop Edward Fenwick of Cincinnati seven years later for priests to minister to his growing flock of European and French-Canadian emigrants, including a large mission territory. He first ministered to the Indians at La Pointe, Wisconsin, then founded a mission at L'Anse, Michigan, where he was called "The Snowshoe Priest," and died on January 19, 1868, after suffering a series of strokes. Franciscan missionaries nurtured his legacy, tending to the Catholic settlers in Northern Michigan, and, by 1888, with congregations overflowing homes and meeting halls, they purchased land and built the church at Charlevoix. By 1893, a monthly mass was held, until 1900 when the priest from the Petoskey mission began celebrating a weekly mass.

Hemingway had quite consciously entered a rich vein of Catholicism when he walked into St. Mary's at Charlevoix, traveling fifteen miles from his Boyne City boarding house after Grace kicked him out. That he walked up to the left side altar, dedicated to Mary, the Mother of Jesus—an altar that remains to this day, not the same statue but the same antique gold-leaf metal stand on which the candles sit—and lit a candle and prayed through Mary's intercession was all of a piece with the Hemingway, who had prayed "with almost tribal faith," to Our Lady the night of his wounding. He was returning to ask for Mary's help. He was a man on a mission.

On September 30, 1920, he wrote to Grace Quinlan of his visit to the church, reporting that "we came out in a very fine mood and shortly after . . . the Lord sent me Adventure with a touch of romance."[25] That fling, presumably with Katy, who loved Ernie, was just the start.

In the fall, he moved to Chicago, teaming with speakeasies and picture palaces starring such silent film standouts as Mary Pickford, the first film "star," and Chaplin. Then, there was Theda Bara, "the vamp," who was starring in the Broadway play *The Blue Flame*, playing in Chicago and elsewhere as it toured the country. Ripping the heart out of Victorian sensibilities, it featured a religious young woman who dies, only to be brought back to life by her scientist fiancé as a soulless femme fatale, who seduces men and entices them to commit crimes, including drug use and murder. Chicago's streets were now ruled by Italian gangsters as the price of keeping the city wet in the dry twenties and this film picked up the tempo, as did Hemingway, who wrote a feature for the *Toronto Star* in December titled "Plain and Fancy Killings, $400 Up," for which he evidently interviewed a "hired guns" on how they evaded Irish pols and police.[26]

Soon after arriving in town, Hemingway went to see Ethel Barrymore in *Déclassée* at the Powers, which further reflected the unraveling social fabric. The *Chicago Tribune* considered it a waste of her talent.[27] Her marriage was suffering and would soon end in divorce after her husband's public infidelity. Fittingly, the play was about a troubled marriage.

Hemingway had decamped from Horton Bay on Friday, October 15, with Bill and Katy Smith, joined by their Aunt Laura. He was going to stay rent-free at the new home of their brother Y. K. Kenley, a wealthy advertising executive, and his wife "Doodles," i.e., Genevieve, at 100 East Chicago Avenue—until he could find a job. Meantime, he would write his features and short stories and hang with friends, and take in the Chicago scene, not expecting much in the way of fireworks, so to speak, as he plotted his next move.

(L-R) Carl Edgar, Katy Smith, Marcelline Hemingway, Bill Horne, Ernest Hemingway, and Bill Smith. Michigan, Walloon Lake/Petoskey area, summer 1920. *Source:* In the public domain.

FALLING IN LOVE—AGAIN

No sooner had Bill bounded inside the house and run upstairs for that evening's rollicking house party, than he found Katy's twenty-eight-year-old friend, Elizabeth Hadley Richardson, also from St. Louis, standing in the bedroom. She had arrived in town early that morning on the overnight train. Her mother—whom she had been caring for at the St. Louis home of her married sister Fonnie, Mrs. Roland Usher—had just died on August 19 from Bright's Disease, and Katy had invited Hadley for an extended three-week stay as, like Ernest, she began a new life. She was about to celebrate her twenty-ninth birthday on November 9. After climbing the stairs, they all gazed at this tall, plain beauty, with auburn red hair, no makeup, complemented by her fashionable new blue serge dress with a smartly shorter hemline, just below the knee. No one was more surprised than Mrs. Charles to see Hadley, whom she knew quite well, from St. Louis.

Hadley came from wealth on both sides of her family and had grown up in an idyllic turn-of-the-century (twentieth) rural enclave just north of Forest Park on Cabanne Place in the fashionable West End of town—right up from "5135 Kensington Avenue," fictional home of the Smiths in *Meet Me in St. Louis* (1944). This classic MGM Christmas musical mirrored the scene at the Richardsons' music-filled home, also a Second Empire Victorian, with not one but two Steinways, set back from the street with a lush lawn and four children. But appearances can be deceptive. As with the film, starring Judy Garland, whose mother had prevailed upon her to procure an abortion so she could star in the Vincent Minelli production, trouble lurked under the surface of the Richardson home. Whereas, like the Hemingways, both of Hadley's parents had deep puritanical roots going back to the Massachusetts Bay Colony; unlike the Hemingways, religion was virtually absent from their home, though, like Grace, Florence was a devotee of spiritualism and hosted evening socials to discuss issues relating to philosophy, society, and religion, while forbidding the serving of liquor, "not even a glass of sherry."[28]

Hadley had graduated in 1910, a year late due to illness, from the Mary Institute, her mother's Alma Mater, that T. S. Elliot's grandfather had founded, after which she matriculated at Bryn Mawr in the fall of 1911. Though, after suffering a nervous breakdown with thoughts of suicide, her mother considered her "too delicate, both physically and emotionally,"[29] to continue her studies, and she left Bryn Mawr in May of 1912, seeking solace by reading literature and playing piano. Her sister Dorothea, eleven years her senior, whom Hadley resembled and whose friendship she cherished, had died in an apartment fire earlier in the year. The loss had a profound impact on Hadley. Then, too, her father, James Richardson Jr.—a hopeless alcoholic, engulfed by financial problems, who was the son of super-successful James Richardson Sr., founder of Richardson Drug Company—had committed suicide on February 8, 1905, a month after his fiftieth birthday. In the wake of his death, the family moved to a more modest home on Cates Avenue. The suicide left a scar on Hadley's psyche, even as she denied it.[30]

Hadley's mother, Florence Wyman-Richardson, like her husband, born in 1855, was the daughter of educator and strict disciplinarian, Edward Wyman, from New England, and had much in common with Grace Hall Hemingway beyond spiritualism. Like Grace, an accomplished musician and singer, she was also active in women's rights and suffrage movements, and had dominated her weak, hapless husband, disapproving of his weakness for liquor. Reputedly a victim of sexual abuse as a young toddler, she loathed sex, believing it was only for procreation, and the less the better; though after marrying James in 1878, she bore him six children, also including James Jr., born in 1880, and Florence Jr., born in 1889, along with two boys who died as infants. Florence also bossed around Hadley, the baby of the family, who, after falling out of a second-story window as a child, remained bedbound as she recuperated and regained her strength. But emotionally she never recovered, and her mother restricted physical and sporting activities like swimming. Failing to make it at Bryn Mawr, Hadley became a shy recluse, nursing her ailing mother as the decade ended. She had grown up with a sense of inferiority, never allowed to focus on fashion or beauty, and had no success with the boys and "just didn't like them at all," she said.[31] In fact, throughout her life some of her closest friends were lesbians, some quite radical, though she was very feminine and there's no record of any lesbian affairs.[32]

As Hadley stood there blushing awkwardly, Ernest, dressed in his Italian military cape, focused laser-like on this beautiful, unopened book, adorned in the colors he loved. Hadley, who had lived like a hermit the last eight years, felt an immediate infusion of energy in Hemingway's presence. Though she had not pursued classical piano professionally, especially after her mother denied her one chance, pre-college, to study in Germany, still it continued to give her a sense of dignity and self-worth. Yet, as the life had gradually drained from her mother that summer, Hadley had totally abandoned the piano while ministering to her mother's every need.

Meeting Ernest at the dawn of the twenties was liberating and, with so much in common, they fell in love. Hadley's "friendly, straightforward, down-to-earth style" with a "quick wit," as Brian described her,[33] had to be very appealing to Hemingway. Yet, like Agnes, Hadley was eight years Hemingway's senior, with little interest in religion. Florence had taken the girls out of Sunday school early on in favor of Theosophy, leaving Hadley with little Christian formation. And while the electricity between them was palpable, this critical incompatibility, along with the age difference, would come back to haunt them.

Even at the outset, many in Ernest's orbit, including notably Sunny, told him he was too young to get married. Translation: Hadley was too old. Her sister Florence, or "Fonnie," warned her about the age difference, as well. Furthermore, she warned Hadley not to tell him about her trust fund. But she dismissed the former, and waited to tell him about the latter, though the trappings of wealth were apparent—her demeanor, her grandfather's Richardson Drug Company, and her friendship with "Aunt Laura" surely made Hadley more interesting to Hemingway. And her maternal warmth was just what Hemingway needed, given that Grace's other pursuits often took precedence over mothering.

After their three-week romance, Ernest took Hadley back to the train station on Thursday, November 4, and, no sooner was the train chugging off than she was pining for "Wemedge." Meanwhile Ernest, not thrilled with the open "marriage" between Y. K. and Doodles, moved in with Horney, who had written to him "suggesting he let me grubstake him while he became a writer. I thought he had talent, though I had no idea how much," Horne said.[34] They rented an apartment at 1230 North State Street. Hemingway was not enthused at sponging off his friend, staying rent-free once again, and was down-spirited because he was still without a job, besides odd jobs and the occasional feature for the *Toronto Star*. They would eat at Kitso's, a Greek restaurant on Division Street, which Horne believes was the setting for Hemingway's "The Killers."

Hadley soon visited again, arriving on Saturday, December 4, staying a week for a round of parties, constantly spending time with Ernest, though never alone. She was thrilled to be with her new beaux, employed or not, and just came to life around him, spontaneously performing on Doodles' grand piano for a full house—half-formed code words punctuating the nonstop buzz of conversation. It was a rare treat. But when asked to perform in a formal setting, initially at Hemingway's urging, she could never quite muster the courage to go through with it, always pulling out at the last minute.

When she returned to St. Louis, she wrote Hem that she looked forward to his visit to St. Louis, but he kept putting her off as they danced the dance of courtship. For starters, "Ernesto" wrote "Hash," using the newfangled lingo in which everything and everyone had a nickname, he did not have the "seeds."[35] Then, after the first of the year, he wrote that he needed, first, to dispatch the invitation from wealthy Jim Gamble, his Red Cross boss, to come spend time with him in Italy. Unlike Agnes, Hadley said she liked the sound of him, perhaps reverse psychology as she tried to nudge him off the ledge of that relationship.

Then, too, Hemingway had to deal with all his girlfriends, not least of which Katy. Growing up with four doting sisters, he was used to having a klatch of adoring women around him, and had grown to rely emotionally on female support. But Katy was in love with him, so he needed to reassure Hadley she was his one and only. That he gravitated to older women, including Katy, born the same year as Hadley, surely related to his psychological wounds, both those sustained in the war and from childhood. That Hadley had suffered hidden wounds, as well, growing up a Richardson, only solidified their relationship. At the same time, given her own physical injury, she was more sensitive to how Hemingway's visible war wounds affected him.

"Stein," as he was also known, finally landed a $40-a-week job before Christmas with the magazine *Commonwealth Cooperative*, published by the Cooperative Society of America, a dubious enterprise promising farmers savings, which, along with his literary writing, kept him busy. The Christmas season in full swing, Bill and Ernie were invited to move in with Y.K., who had now rented a big flat at the old Belleview Hotel at 63 Division Street, around the corner from them, spacious enough for all his friends and parties, as Doodles was away pursuing her art, their open marriage never more obvious. "It was an exciting atmosphere," wrote Horne. "Kenley was an erudite advertising man, with lots of intellectual friends like Sherwood Anderson, who had been a copywriter in his firm. On winter evenings, we'd sit around the fireplace and Ernie would read his stories with Sherwood commenting. Anderson recognized Ernie's talent."[36]

Anderson was enjoying a head of steam from his acclaimed collection of short stories, *Winesburg, Ohio*, published in 1919. But given that he was soon to leave for Paris, like so much else in Hemingway's life, that he even met Anderson was Divine Providence.

Hemingway was so busy after he landed his new job that he did not have time to write to Hadley, who corresponded with him frequently, expressing great support for his writing. Then, like his father, Hemingway began penning letters almost daily. Between the two of them, they exchanged hundreds of letters, which helped them bond, albeit it also risked the possibility of hiding behind and falling in love with their literary selves.

On January 12, 1921, he asked Hadley if she would pray with him someday at the Milan Cathedral, as Agnes had not.[37] Hemingway "liked to pray in Catholic churches and cathedrals," Stoneback wrote.[38] What's more, given that he considered himself a Catholic, he recognized the "disparity of cult" could pose problems. Hadley, though Episcopalian, was so in love, that on April 22, she responded affirmatively, writing, "I am doing the best thing a woman can do for a man. Bringing you back to religion."[39]

Meanwhile Ernie and Horney would get together with their old war buddies, "feeling like kids who had been in the same high school class, then separated for a few years and reunited," said Horne. "We would eat at one of the Italian restaurants on the near North Side, and turn up our noses just a little at guys who hadn't been in Section IV and shared our great experience."[40] Neroni was one of the kids, and he gave Hemingway some great stories he would later use in his writing.

On March 11, Ernest finally traveled to St. Louis, to visit Hadley sporting a brand-new Brooks Brothers suit displacing his wartime cape. He stayed in her room and she warned him that she would be in and out for things she forgot, which was endearing. That weekend, he decided she was *the one*. Hadley wasn't so sure. After all, Stein told some pretty tall tales.

On her trip back to Chicago on Thursday, March 17 to Monday, March 21, for propriety's sake she stayed at the Plaza Hotel, 1553 North Clark Street, with a girlfriend, Ruth Bradfield, since Doodles was out of town. Then, too, she got a taste of bachelor life, and found it not entirely to her taste, especially when "Fever" showed up with prostitutes, to say nothing of the drunkenness. One night when Ernest pulled her close to him to impress the gang and "announced, posing majestically, that they were the prince and princess," while thoroughly enjoying it, Hadley was embarrassed.[41] Apart from that, it was a lovely weekend spent double dating with Katy Smith and Bill Horne at a favorite Italian restaurant, Hadley wearing her lovely black silk embroidered dress, while they kissed on the street and cuddled and petted on the roof. On Saturday night, Hemingway took Hadley to Oak Park to meet his parents and was surprised how animated his father was, even though, nearing fifty, he was suffering from angina, though he *was* about to escape to Sanibel Island in April for another solo vacation. Likewise, Hadley found his mother "perfectly wonderful," and a welcome change from her mother's formality. Then, too, she was about to be free of her husband's constant pecking.

By the end of March, Hadley had set aside her reservations and was sure, as well, that they would tie the knot. "Nobody was ever sweeter to anybody than you are to me," she wrote.[42] "Allah be praised that we are living at the same time and know each other." And she intuited that, while Mrs. Hemingway believed her son might mistreat his "sedate little bride," all he needed was love and moral support for his literary ventures, which became central to their relationship. And, she decided it was high time to tell Ernest that was an heiress with a trust fund of $50,000, paying $1,000 a year (1973 value), which would make it easier for him to write.

Part of their bonding was sharing many books with one another, and in April, she finally read *The Red Lily*, another Anderson recommendation, which Ernest had mentioned in Chicago. It was about a couple, Jacques and Therese, and how Jacques had ruined Therese's happiness; albeit Jacques is an elderly count who has little in common with his young wife and theirs is a marriage of convenience, leading Therese to pursue a relationship outside the troubled marriage. As illogical as it might seem, Hadley saw parallels in their own relationship but later reflected that Hemingway could not be like him and at any rate she was not like Therese since she would never take such abuse quietly. That she could see any resemblance did intimate trouble ahead. In May, when he shared with her one of Kipling's notable short stories, "The Brushwood Boy" (1898), about a wounded warrior who dreams of seeing an enchanted woman on the beach, only to see her come to life, she gained a greater appreciation for just how much the war had changed him and felt she was rescuing him. (Ironically, Agnes had called him her "Brushwood boy.")

One of the books he started pouring over in January 1921, also at Anderson's recommendation, was Havelock Ellis's *Studies in the Psychology of Sex*. In the "roaring twenties," with readily available birth control, sexual mores were rapidly changing and sex before marriage, or sex without marriage, was becoming more common. At the same time, Hemingway had absorbed Oak Park mores to his core, and was more traditional sexually, so that, if he was licentious, bedding a woman he was not married to—not yet—he would feel dutybound to marry the woman. Then, too, it was not an unpleasant duty. Hadley loved sex. But she did not *just* want to read about it and took a pass on Ellis' book. Though, she did not take a pass when a St. Louis sculptress by the name of Marguerite Schuyller asked her to pose nude for the three Graces statues she was working on, given Hadley's classic figure. Hadley was to image Grace in the middle "swishing around in some reeds holding up a big bowl" and she happily disrobed several times a week that spring so she could pose in her naked splendor as her friend developed her sculpture. Ernest objected to Hadley doing such a thing, reflecting his Victorian sensibilities. But Hadley insisted, saying she was doing it as a favor to her friend.[43]

That May over Memorial Day, Ernest surprised Hadley with a visit, joined by Horney, who had taken a liking to Hadley's friend Ruth, and it was a jam-packed weekend. "We had great fun," said Horne, "making gin by boiling the ether out of sweet spirits of nitre over an open-topped burner. It was a silly thing to do, as it was very explosive and we got only about two teaspoonfuls of liquor. By the time we left, Ernie and 'Hash' were certainly engaged."[44]

But while rowing on the Meramec River Hadley, carrying the ugly secondhand vintage purse with missing beads Hem had given her for Christmas, let it slip into the water, under the canoe. Years later she referred to this act as "quite wicked."[45] But they did not discuss it so as not to spoil their relationship. Still this passive-aggressiveness on Hadley's part would become a recurring motif in the relationship, in which Hemingway suffered emotional pain. Sure enough, he started plunging into a deep depression—he was sick, loathed his job, and missed Hadley and even wondered about the depth of her feeling—the tossed purse, no doubt, sticking in his craw. Then, too, there was the age difference. She had swatted away any age concerns he shared with her via his friends—and was irritated he would even bring it up. At any rate, again, he liked being mothered. And he surely liked Hadley's sensuous side and her fine character, which he had intuited the moment they met.

Yet when he missed the party hosted by Helen and George Breaker to announce the engagement, attended by thirty guests, Hadley's "heart pounding like mad" at the prospect of making the engagement public, she began to think "Oin" was getting cold feet.

"We're PARTNERS," she wrote back on July 3, to counter the gossip spread by "the whole Charles family, including Bill [Smith]," that his literary output had ceased. Au contraire; he would soar with her moral support, she wanted him to know. Furthermore, she had enough resources to support herself and by inference him so it didn't matter if he had dry spells. Before he received her letter, his letter in which he said he felt so downhearted, he was pondering suicide, arrived. "What is this,?" she wrote back. "Not truly so low as to crave mortage, are you?," which, she wrote, would "kill me." Truth be told she was also feeling blue and suggested a visit, sending him a telegram on Thursday, July 7, which delighted him.[46] The next day, Friday, July 8, the third anniversary of Ernest's wounding in Italy, she returned to Chicago and, once more, stayed with Kenley and Doodles and "all the tensions were relaxed" with both feeling "much revived after the visit." Soon thereafter she bought a Corona for Hemingway's twenty-second birthday "with her most tremendous tender and admiring love." He began writing divinely, including a poem about the Corona and one, "Desire," which she quoted in her July 24 letter back to him, writing, "And all the sweet pulsing aches . . . And gentle hurtings that were you . . ." Then, too, his two-page satirical story, "Divine Gesture," left her "completely under its power," she wrote him on July 26.[47]

Quite clearly the cloud of depression had lifted for both of them and now what he wrote, she considered her own. As she wrote on April 23, in addition to his "wonderful strange beautiful gifts," she had her "own peculiar endowment" and when they were melded into a "unit" and became "gifted," she wrote, "I can practically go out to anyone, 'No, I don't write novels and stories . . . but Ernest does, and that's practically'" the equivalent.[48]

They craved becoming a conjugal unit—and the sexual healing that would keep the cloud of depression at bay, if only for a time. And, so it was, on their last visit together in early August, Hadley came alone and they stayed at the elegant and posh Virginia Hotel, on the corner of Rush and Ohio Streets in Chicago—built by Leander James McCormick, inventor of the McCormick reaper, ironically the year Hadley was born, on the site of the former McCormick house, destroyed in the Great Chicago Fire of 1871.[49] And it was there, in that richly appointed hotel, that Hadley and Ernest consummated their union. A clue into this comes by way a conversation Hemingway had with F. Scott Fitzgerald, the day they met, recounted in *A Moveable Feast*. Scott asks Hem point-blank if he and Hadley had had premarital sex and Hem responds quite implausibly that he did not remember. Scott was not buying. Hadley said years later that she had truly gotten to know Ernest that weekend and was delighted they had engaged in sexual relations.[50] Not only that, the last night at the Virginia Hotel, Hadley suggested that they take turns being the passive one—"the little, small petted one," which planted the seed in Ernest's mind of transcending physicality and becoming identical equals on a spiritual plane he would later infuse his writing with.[51] But, alas, vive la différence would assert itself, and having failed to get to know each other first on *all the levels* that precede carnal knowledge, la différence later became a hot fire like the great conflagration of 1871.

For now it was all bliss. "Oh I had the most heavenly time," she wrote Ernest as she headed for Wisconsin to spend the month of August with the Breakers. She missed him deeply, noting she and Helen "aren't . . . in tune with the infinite yet"—alluding to the world Ernest occupied.[52] Even at that, it was ephemeral "heaven," circumscribed by their failure to understand why reserving the marital embrace until after the wedding—making the sacrifice to forego the immense physical pleasure thereby getting to know more about the non-physical aspects of each other—might have given them a better chance at a lasting union built on a solid spiritual foundation. But it was the libertine twenties and Hadley was decidedly sensual, with not much of a spiritual core. So, it's understandable that they bought into the logic that they were getting to know each other better that weekend.

What they did not know as they luxuriated and enjoyed physical intimacy is how difficult marriage could get and when the going gets tough, it takes a strong spiritual commitment to the marital bond. When breached, even with your intended, it makes it more difficult to say "no" to another sexual bonding outside of marriage. In short, their commitment to the marital bond was less than perfect. Hemingway admitted as much, writing to Grace Quinlan just after his twenty-second birthday, a month before their Virginia Hotel assignation: "Think marriage might be a terrible fine thing you know—Anyhow Hash and I are going to have a very fine try at it."[53] Such tentativeness is one of the first things that is explored when a marriage falls apart to see if there were any impediments.

Hemingway realized how much other bliss he would be giving up—the bliss of fishing in Upper Michigan with friends, which, that summer, he did for the last time. Deep down, he was not convinced the bargain was worth it—as his novels and short stories often reflect. "Once a man's married, he's absolutely bitched," he wrote in "The Three-Day Blow."[54] "He hasn't got anything more. Nothing. Not a damned thing. He's done for." Married guys, he continued, "get this sort of fat, married look." And they begin looking for the exits. Whereas unmarried love is more exciting but ultimately ends in destruction, as well, his writings also reflect. Yet in spite of it all, he cared deeply for Hadley. Now vacationing near State Line, Wisconsin, in a log cabin, she was ill with strep throat, and he wrote her that he was praying for her—though she made light of his prayers.[55] As she read Fitzgerald's *This Side of Paradise*, that summer's bestseller, all she could think about was living in wedded bliss with Ernest.

Meanwhile, the invitation list was now ballooning to over 400 guests—including Ernie's old flames, most notably Agnes Von Kurowsky. Hadley was not unaware of the affair and it frankly gnawed at her that he would have the gall to invite her. Good that Agnes did not show up. For Hadley was the mirror image of her. Same height, same age, same eye color, same dry wit—the very picture of Ernest on the rebound. No matter. Hadley was not about to give up her chance to wed before age thirty, and, more importantly, she loved "Oin," and wanted to support his writing—considering art the highest calling and a thing of beauty. In the midst of all the wedding preparations—invites, budgets, attire, honeymoon, "Ernest's work was still their primary interest"—as he wrote to her about the novel he was pondering. "It'll be *wonderful* to have you writing a novel," she wrote back.[56]

They wed in a lovely ceremony at Horton Bay on September 3, 1921, at the small Methodist Church a stone's throw from the even smaller town hall, where they took out the marriage license before George Breaker walked Hadley down the aisle. Their marriage "was registered in the Episcopal church files because an Episcopal minister performed the ceremony," wrote Sunny.[57] That night they honeymooned at Windemere, Grace cleaning it to spotless perfection and adding many inviting touches; though they failed to return the favor when they skedaddled, leaving everything strewn about. They were both under the weather, awaking with bad colds the day after their nuptials, given the plunging temperatures. Even so, Grace's hopes that Hadley would prove a civilizing influence on their eldest son were dashed when she saw the the place in such disarray.

The feeling of disappointment was somewhat mutual. During their stay Grace, never content to fade into the background, tickled the ivories at her cottage, the noise wafting across Walloon Lake. Meanwhile, Hemingway introduced Hadley to his old girlfriends, which she found off-putting, and, one day, when he went to pick up his old Italian uniform stored in Petoskey, he got drunk after running into an old bootlegger friend, no doubt, at his favorite watering hole, "The Annex." He later bought a four-pound steak and commandeered a friend's boat to get back home and, as he approached the shore at Windemere, the rough water made it difficult to steer so he yelled out to Hadley who came running out and he tossed the steak into her waiting arms. Then he parked the boat up the road, and came home dressed in the uniform, singing old Italian songs, completely drunk,[58] the wounds of war, if not the wounds of growing up Hemingway, now patently clear.

The newlyweds settled in Chicago for a time, living in a downscale Chicago apartment at 1239 North Dearborn, Hadley now sporting her new "bob" hairstyle like so many women in the twenties, though the fashionable short cut was never quite her style. She was terribly lonely and one day soon after moving into the ugly, cramped abode, Mrs. Hemingway came calling. Her purpose: To talk about "love"—not sex; *that* was taboo—but her intent was clear. She wanted to make sure her son's sexual appetites were well satiated. While her motive was pure, Hadley did not take kindly to her "tactless intrusion," and at the Hemingways' twenty-fifth wedding anniversary on October 1, Hadley showed up in her plainest garb while not long after she was the belle of the ball at a fireman's gala.[59]

Hadley's trust fund enabled them to look beyond the shores of America for a home—especially after the sudden infusion of $8,000 (1973 value) when her Uncle Arthur Wyman died. Then, too, the favorable exchange rate eased their way.

Sherwood Anderson had just come back from a summer in Paris with his wife Tennessee, and soon invited the Hemingways for dinner, making an impassioned case for why Paris was the place to be. While the "dolce vita" of Italy was alluring, Paris was where writers and painters of renown were doing "serious work."[60] So, having spent considerable time preparing to move to Italy, where Hemingway hoped to reconnect with his newfound faith, and buying a huge stash of lire, by the end of November he had lined up a freelance gig with the *Toronto Star* as their European correspondent, and Hadley and Hem were Paris-bound.

As a parting gift, Anderson also gave Hemingway the blueprint for how a writer lived. First, he must read the literary greats, both American contemporary writers like Van Wyck Brooks, who had recently authored *The Ordeal of Mark Twain* (1920), and classic writers, too, ranging from Dostoyevsky and Tolstoy to Turgenev and Chekhov to D. H. Lawrence and T. S. Eliot. Second, he must have separate writing quarters. Third, he must cultivate book reviewers and magazine editors. Fourth, he must *never* write gratis.

Hemingway began pouring over the *Dial*, flush with Scofield Thayer money, scion of a wealthy wool-manufacturing Massachusetts family, to expand his horizons beyond the *Saturday Evening Post*, *Red Book*, and *Cosmopolitan*, the latter three, to a one, having rejected his short story submissions. But the *Dial* rejected him, too. So, Anderson introduced him to a New Orleans magazine, the *Double Dealer*, which would be the first publication to give Hemingway's work a serious look.

Anderson also wrote beautiful letters of introduction for Hemingway to Gertrude Stein, Ezra Pound, Sylvia Beach, and Lewis Galantière, which ensured a nice entrée for the budding young writer into the elite Paris literary community. He had also, of course, introduced Hemingway to the new literary wave of sexual expression, normal and deviant, notably Ellis's supercharged sexual writings that captured the sexual liberation washing over American culture reinforced by Margaret Sanger's gospel of free love and reflected by *Blue Nude* and "The Blue Flame." Hemingway took note. And, though he shared T. R.'s sensibilities regarding human love, he realized it was important to reflect these new cultural beats. Yet another reason to leave the Midwest.

But, then, he had already made the psychological break during the war and was ready for Paris, where he would meet the premier artists of the day in the cafés of Montparnasse and observe sexual liberation in full bloom, among both strangers and his circle of friends, while also soaking in the city's centuries-old spirituality, steeped in true love, and taking critical first steps on the journey to becoming Ernest Hemingway, iconic writer—starting with "one true sentence."

Once Hadley and Ernest boarded their train at old Chicago Union Station, at the corner of Madison and Canal, bound for New York City, early in December 1921, it was then they felt their lives together were beginning, for real.

4

⧥⧥⧥

The City of Light

"One True Sentence"

On December 8, the Feast of the Immaculate Conception, the Hemingways set sail from New York Harbor, Le Havre bound, in the grimy old French liner, *Leopoldina*.

As they settled in for the two-week ocean passage, Ernest was feeling exuberant and Hadley, now thirty, uncomfortable, as pretty girls gravitated to her husband. Hadley was no match for these fresh lovelies, especially two in particular who would keep popping up. But Ernest, young, virile, and handsome, seemed unaware of their interest and Hadley consoled herself that she and Ernest were "all in all to each other," even as she discovered her husband's magnetic personality drew people in wherever he went.[1] His literary gift was all of a piece with his magnetism. So, too, was his compassion: While traversing the Atlantic, he arranged a boxing benefit for a young woman and her baby, whose American husband had abandoned them.[2] Hadley had gotten the whole package and loved her husband dearly even as she could see warning clouds on the horizon.

After crossing the Atlantic, their boat docked at Vigo, one hour south of Santiago de Compostela and, over a four-hour stop, they walked along Vigo's cobblestone streets, soaking in Spain as a couple for the first time. (Hemingway had glimpsed Algerica near Gibraltar when the *Giuseppe Verdi* stopped briefly there en route home from the war.) At the wharf, Ernest began teaching Hadley about fishing, as he would introduce her to so many of nature's treasures—fingering the king of the fish: the six-footer tuna!

HEMINGWAY'S PARIS

The Hemingways arrived in the City of Light on or about December 21, 1921, just as the cold, damp winter was settling in and, to mark the occasion, Ernest jotted off a letter to Anderson. Then they set about exploring the city from their home base at the Hotel Jacob (now Hotel a'Angleterre) at 44 rue Jacob, not far from the ancient Île de la Cité, Paris's first settlement. Hadley thought Ernest was "eager for the reality of the present"[3] served up at Parisian cafés he loved that defined the artistic scene of 1920s Paris. And he was. Then, too, he was mesmerized by Hilaire Belloc's *Paris* about the city's historic past, the first book he bought upon arriving in the French capital.

Belloc, a Catholic convert, was a kindred spirit. His writings had helped G. K. Chesterton "see the light" in converting to Catholicism[4] and had nudged C. S. Lewis away from atheism. No doubt, Hemingway drank in Belloc's *Paris* and the Catholicism he so artfully expressed, like a fine wine, as he recalled his own conversion during World War I.

"Paris in the Dark Ages," wrote Belloc, gave way to an "awakening Europe" in which "The Normans show first how true a kingdom, with peace and order and unity, may be established" and how "Rome did not die; it was transformed" and how "the philosophy of the Empire had been touched with mysticism" and "the shrine, the miracle, the unseen had replaced the clear and positive attitude, the speculative and cold intelligence, which had distinguished the philosophy of Rome." In its place was "Medieval religion, its legends, its marvels . . . the one good counterbalance that ultimately saved the world from barbarism."[5]

Then, there was the present, where, free of the constraints of Prohibition, living in free-spirited Paris, the couple imbibed copiously—a bottle of wine, each, at lunch, then more at dinner, usually at a café around the corner that medical students frequented, capped off, at home, by cordials and other hard liquor—Hemingway believing all those spirits would enhance his literary output. As he famously said, "All good writers are drinking writers, and drinking writers are good writers."[6] Then, too, he was self-medicating as he strove to forget the horrors of war and to sleep, not realizing the side effects of all that alcohol—dehydrating him and stripping him of vitamin B—was only worsening his insomnia and depression. The pattern of getting drunk each night extended through their entire married life. "We drank like fishes," said Hadley later on. "We'd get so tight, we'd throw up together."[7]

Mostly, though, Hemingway was yearning for spiritual healing—intimations of it soon reflected, like glistening spiritual gems, in his writing. After penning the final version of his first short story in Paris, "Up in Michigan," which he had begun writing in America, he wrote a feature for the *Toronto Star Weekly* about catching a giant tuna at Vigo—"a back-sickening, sinew-straining, man-sized job . . . But if you land a big tuna after a six-hour fight . . . and finally bring him alongside the boat, green-blue and silver in the lazy ocean, you will be purified and you will be able to enter unabashed into the presence of the very elder gods and they will make you welcome."[8]

And so it was that, on December 28, 1921, the literary gods smiling down, he ventured into Sylvia Beach's Shakespeare and Company at 12 rue de l'Odéon, and presented her with Sherwood Anderson's letter of introduction. Expat Americans seeking fame from their perch on Paris's Left Bank had no better friend than Princeton born-and-bred Beach, who gave them a mailing address, and a loan, if needed. A petite, refined, intelligent beauty, this wartime Red Cross nurse and daughter of a minister now nurtured literary talent, and "was kind, cheerful and interested, and loved to make jokes and gossip," wrote Hemingway. "No one that I ever knew was nicer to me."[9] She allowed him, before paying the subscription fee, to borrow books and periodicals, displayed on shelves and stacked on tables, some featured in the windows, including the banned *Ulysses* and magazines like *Birth Control Review* frowned upon in America.

Next, he visited fellow Chicagoan Lewis Galantière, Anderson letter in hand. An American translator at the International Chamber of Commerce, twenty-six-year-old Galantière had impeccable taste, refined manners, and a warm sense of humor. No sooner had he treated them to dinner at upscale Restaurant Michaud than he was helping find them housing in the Latin Quarter, 5th Arrondissement, where so many literary lights lived and wrote while soaking in the Sorbonne, Pantheon, and Gallo-Roman ruins. They signed the contract for their humble new fourth-floor, cold-water flat at 74, rue du Cardinal Lemoine, on January 7 and moved in on January 9th. And it *was* humble, accessed by a spiral staircase, every landing equipped with a faucet and French pissoir, while funny angles shaped the space, consisting of a bedroom, living room, and small kitchen—big enough for just one person. Though at least the furniture was elegant.

Hemingway also rented a small room for writing on the top floor of 39 rue Descartes, the building where, twenty-six years earlier, on January 8th, French poet Paul Verlaine, who late in life had returned to his Catholic faith, died. And it was there, in the shadow of Verlaine, that Hemingway would hammer out on his Corona "one true sentence" that he "could hang onto," Hadley said years later, "without hurting his conscience, his terrific artistic conscience" as he worked to distill and clarify his vision to perfection.[10]

One day, as that first story he wrote in Paris churned in his heart and soul, he walked in the cold, damp weather past the filth, human and spiritual, of the Café de Amateurs onto the cobblestone Place de la Contrescarpe around the corner from their home, soon realizing it was too wet and chilly to start a fire in his writing hideaway, as he reminisced almost forty years later in *A Moveable Feast.*[11] So he walked down past "the ancient church of St.-Étienne-du-Mont" on rue de la Montaigne St Genevieve and the "windswept Place du Panthéon" to the "lee side" of Boulevard St.-Michel down past Cluny and the Boulevard St.-Germain to "a good café that I knew on the Place St.-Michel"—right across from the Île de la Cité, the birthplace of Paris in 200 BC, on which sits Notre-Dame Cathedral, devoted to Mary, the Mother of Jesus, whom Hemingway had fallen in love with after she saved his life.

It was a delightful café, "warm and clean and friendly," and the young woman waiting in front he "wished" he could place in "the story, or anywhere," was looking away, focused, it seemed, on the imminent arrival of someone special. But no matter, she was "pretty with a face fresh as a newly minted coin," unlike the dirty, drunk women at the other café. And as he enjoyed the soothing drink, the story initially wrote itself, and "I kept on writing, feeling very well and feeling the good Martinique rum warm me all through my body and my spirit." Now he was writing the story. Then, as he finished it, he looked up, and saw the fresh-faced woman was gone. Then, feeling sad but happy, not unlike the feeling after making love, he ordered some "*portugaises*"—oysters—and white wine and felt all good again. Maybe away from Paris, he could write about Paris, he reflected, just as he was writing about Michigan in the City of Lights, featuring an explicit sexual romp, reflecting changing tastes and mores, as well as his deft way of making his writing real—no doubt, jazzed up and inspired by that fresh-faced woman. Then, he made a beeline the quickest way back up the "Montagne Ste. Geneviève" home to his wife where he suggested a ski vacation in Switzerland to relieve the dark, dank winter weather, good Martinique rum only going so far to change his mood. "'I think it would be wonderful, Tatie,' my wife said."

As Hemingway kept grinding away each day, working late, drinking heavy, trudging through the cold wet streets, getting sick, he dreamed of that vacation, and, on January 19, decamped with Hadley to Chamby, Switzerland, for a two-week respite, where, to save money, they stayed at an inexpensive chalet, the Pension Gangswisch. The spot, with its fresh white snow, was suggested by those two fresh-faced girls on the *Leopoldina.*[12] He saved money, too, by taking a hiatus from renting the room above Verlaine's old haunt. Crisp snow-covered mountains were nirvana for him, the invigorating setting lifting clouds of depression. Hadley, too, loved the pristine air, the peaks rising up in majestic beauty, all calm and still, while she luxuriated in the skiing, though she did not like the two lush girls hanging around her handsome husband, whose stiff leg made it difficult for him to ski, his libido, though, still very much intact.

Once he got back down to the workmanlike task of reporting, one of his first articles featured Pope Pius XI's election, reaching editor John Bone's desk, on February 2, the day they arrived home, and the day Beach published *Ulysses*. He continued, as well, to store up literary chestnuts, with an extremely disciplined work schedule, his lifelong pattern, starting early each morning, including over breakfast with Hadley—"please without speaking,"[13] he asked, so he could continue to concentrate on the literary world he was creating within himself—after which he would head to his writing room a two-minute walk away. Writing for Hemingway was like breathing and Hadley understood this well. At day's end, as Hadley recalled, while cuddling, Ernest would sometimes grab a newspaper to read as he soaked up more material, providing fuel for the next day's writing.[14]

Around the same time, in mid-February, Hemingway met Ezra Pound at Shakespeare and Company, introduced by Sylvia, and he was soon venturing over with Hadley to Pound's studio at rue Notre-Dame-des-Champs to join the poet and his wife Dorothy for tea. Pound, a great translator of great literary works, fourteen years Hemingway's senior, had arrived in Paris in 1920, shaping modernist literary style. "Make it new!," he said.

Hemingway would remember Pound as "kinder and more Christian about people than I was . . . so kind . . . that I always thought of him as a sort of saint." Even if he was "irascible," so, too, were "saints."[15] And even if he had never read the "Rooshians," wrote Hemingway, most notably Dostoyevsky who wrote about "wickedness and saintliness." As Evan Shipman summed up Dostoyevsky over drinks at Closerie de Lilas, "He was best on shits and saints. He makes wonderful saints."[16] Once Pound demystified people for him, wrote Hemingway, he was able to view them through Pound's compassionate lens, even if he did store up his own less-than-favorable impressions for caustic and humorous literary portraits later on.

By early March, Hemingway felt confident enough to bring his Anderson letter of introduction to Gertrude Stein. A failed medical student who had come to Paris in 1903, after a failed romance, Stein had moved in with her brother Leo, "possibly the most discerning connoisseur of 20th-century painting in the world," according to Alfred H. Barr, the Museum of Modern Art's first director. Though, in 1914, Leo moved out, considering his sister's lesbian lover, Alice B. Toklas, "a kind of abnormal vampire," opportunistically basking in the glory of Stein's fame.[17] In time, Gertrude reinvented herself, hosting a Saturday salon for artists in her spacious and charming living room at 27 rue de Fleurus, the walls draped with works of art by the likes of Matisse and Picasso, rivals and friends, who were frequent guests. Their manner was formal, vision expansive, just as the modernist art clashed with the Victorian furnishings. Gertrude immediately took the talented Mr. Hemingway under her wing. And while Hemingway was "uncomfortable with homosexuality, he maintained a professional friendship with Gertrude."[18] Good he did, for she encouraged his spare style, alive with "the moment," suggesting he study impressionist art for inspiration. She also reviewed his short stories and unfinished World War I novel and thought the novel needed distilling.

Meanwhile, Pound was a frequent guest at the Hemingways' Paris flat, telling Ernest to focus on his prose while opening doors for him. That spring, *The Little Review* published six of his miniature stories. Hemingway, in turn, taught Pound boxing, though his mentor's sparring talent was even more limited than Hemingway's poetry. Pound also introduced Hemingway to established writers, including, in March, James Joyce, whose *Ulysses* he famously serialized in the *Little Review* in 1918, four years after serializing *A Portrait of the Artist as a Young Man*. That Ernest and Hadley had sailed to Europe aboard the *Leopoldina* was, they thought, a sign of good things to come, Leopold "Poldy" Bloom being *Ulysses*'s protagonist. Joyce and Hemingway frequented the cafés together, the studly Hemingway serving as a bodyguard to the slight Joyce, who would push Hem forward to parry any unwelcome belligerence. It was after "Joyce would fall into a fight," said Hemingway of Joyce who "couldn't even see the man" given his bad eyesight. "'Deal with him, Hemingway! Deal with him!'" Joyce would plead.[19] The Joyce family, though, was standoffish, preventing the kind of bonding Pound and Hemingway shared, though they were close enough until his untimely death in 1941 due to botched surgery, and surely discussed matters of faith. Joyce had abandoned his Catholic faith when he attended University College Dublin, though "he had a Catholic priest with him when he died," according to Fr. Leonard, a Jesuit priest, and is buried in the Catholic cemetery in Zurich.[20]

Pound, literary correspondent for Chicago-based *Poetry Magazine*, published by Harriet Monroe, opened more doors for Hemingway after the *Double Dealer* published his first short story in May 1922. An opaque parable titled "A Divine Gesture," the one Hadley had read during their courtship, it was an *Alice-in-Wonderland*-like satire in which God and the Angel Gabriel show up in the Garden of Eden only to find Adam and Eve have flown the coop. A month later, June 1922, the magazine published Hemingway's poem "Ultimately," on the same page as another up-and-comer, William Faulkner.[21] Soon thereafter, Monroe greenlit six of his poems for *Poetry* as Hemingway got the poetry bug out of his system and Pound, intent on nurturing Hemingway's prose, catalyzed "an inquest into the state of contemporary English prose."[22] One of the series of books to be published by Bill Bird's *Three Mountains Press*, named for the three hills overlooking Paris—Montagne Sainte-Geneviève, Montmartre, and Montparnasse (on the Left, Right, and Left Banks, respectively)—would feature Ernest's writings. Monroe, poised to publish his poems, agreed to let Bird publish them, as well. Hemingway was on a roll.

But journalism kept intruding. In April, he was dispatched to Genoa for the postwar economic conference where he met a chap named Paul Mowrer, a reporter for the *Chicago Daily News*, who allowed him to charge the cables he sent to the *Daily News* to his account. Ernest wrote fifteen dispatches providing funds for another trip to Chamby in May. For as important as writing was, travel was essential.

This time they were joined by Eric Edward "Chink" Dorman-Smith— a friend of Hem since that first meeting at the Officers' Club in Milan on November 3, 1918, just as the armistice was signed between Austria and Germany. Dorman-Smith had been posted to the Italian Piave Front a year earlier. Somehow, as they bonded over German ale, the young British infantry officer got the distinct impression that the brash young Red Crosser, sitting across from him, was recovering from jaundice after leading Arditi troops on Mount Grappa. Now that he was back in Hem's life, Hadley was delighted. She liked the influence Chink had on her husband, given his deliberateness and maturity. "He takes care of us," she said.[23]

After another invigorating ski vacation, they hiked to Italy starting at Bourg St. Pierre, traversing St. Bernard pass, where they stayed overnight at a monastery. Each day they trudged thirty kilometers but Hadley's fashionable new Abercrombie and Fitch oxfords were no match for the deep snow. Somehow she managed to reach the Italian side at Aigle, where Hem enjoyed some fishing, before they headed to Aosta, 100 km away. Upon arriving, Hadley's feet were so blistered and battered that she needed days to recover before hiking the final 180 km. Once in Milan, they relaxed at Campari's, the Cova and Biffi's as Chink and Hem reminisced about the war—capping it all off by betting on the races at the San Siro racetrack where they hit the jackpot. Rising at dawn, he would pour over the "dope-sheet," Hemingway wrote Stein and Toklas, and, after racking his brains, "Mrs. Hemingway, with about three cocktails and an indelible pencil to aid her, picks winners as easy as cracking peanut shucks."[24]

Hemingway also managed to fit in an interview with Mussolini, filing three articles, one of which predicted the Fascist takeover of Italy. Bidding Chink farewell, the couple traveled to Schio and places seared in Hemingway's memory from the war including the bank of the Piave River where he was wounded not four years earlier. But it was not the same.

Back in Paris, he frequented Beach's Shakespeare and Company which had become a comfortable spot, not far from the Quais de la Seine, along which he enjoyed walks, night and day, often alone, as he glimpsed the Cathédrale Notre-Dame de Paris rising up majestically from the scene, and perused the paperbacks at "le bouquinistes," a stretch of painted green riverside bookstalls, where he would buy books rich American hotel guests had left behind. Hemingway also enjoyed fishermen 'baiting' the catch of the day.

"At the head of the Île de la Cité below the Pont Neuf," he wrote,[25] at the site of the Henri Quatre statue, the "island ended in a point like the sharp bow of a ship" and the little park at the edge of the water was graced with "fine chestnut trees, some huge and spreading, and in the currents and back waters . . . there were excellent places to fish." These expert fisherman would always catch fish—especially "goujon," and Hemingway could eat a whole plate, which was "delicious fried whole," and he enjoyed it with Hadley, along with "splendid white wine" at "La Pêche Miraculeuse"—"a place out of a Maupassant story." Then, too, "if the day was bright," he wrote, "I would buy a liter of wine and a piece of bread and some sausage and sit in the sun and read one of the books I had bought and watch the fishing."

He only fished in Spain, Germany, or Italy. Then, too, new sports he introduced Hadley to helped rejuvenate his creative juices. Besides skiing, there were boxing matches, in between which Hem shadow-boxed in their cramped quarters, and steeple-chasing, often at the Auteuil Hippodrome, an eighty-two-acre racecourse, six miles west of Paris, poised to host the 1924 Olympics. Auteuil, Hadley reminisced years later,[26] was unforgettable. After they journeyed there on a crowded bus, they studied the horses in the paddocks and placed their bets, then settled in on the lush lawn, eating a delicious picnic lunch, enjoying a relaxing nap and soaking in all the color and excitement, hoping they would not lose. All the while, her gorgeous and talented husband made her feel so alive. Hemingway captured scenes from a similar excursion one fine spring day, this time to Enghien, not seven miles north of Paris. After taking the Gard du Nord train "through the dirtiest and saddest part of town," they arrived at the "oasis of the track," he wrote, and luxuriated on the "fresh cropped grass bank" enjoying the food and wine and awe-inspiring view of the "old grandstand" and the track and betting as the "first horses" were escorted to the paddock.[27] After drinking more and studying the betting form, Hadley slept on her waterproof, the sun glistening on her face. Though poor, they felt rich in spirit.

After the races, unlike at Anteuil where, in fact, they lost big, they had a rich wallet, thanks to a tip from someone Hem knew from San Siro. In Paris later that day, they enjoyed a repaste at Pruniers then traversed Tuileries Garden near the Louvre, memories of this occasion flowing out of Hemingway's heart and soul so many years later. As they walked through the Louvre Hemingway pondered if the three arches—Arc du Carrousel, Arc du Triomphe, and Arc du Sermione in Milan—actually lined up, as legend has it, that third arch reminding him of their recent visit to Milan with Chink.

Coming out of the Louvre through its grand gateway they stood on the Pont Neuf, "leaning on the stone"[28] of this, the oldest stone bridge in Paris, resting on twelve arches and graced by countless decorative flourishes. Henri Quatre ordered its construction in 1578 to span the Seine from the Musée du Louvre, rue de Rivoli and the Tour Saint-Jacques on the Right Bank to the Île de la Cité, on which sits Cathédrale Notre-Dame de Paris and the Sainte-Chapelle, chapel of kings, to the Left Bank and its rue Dauphine, the Monnaie de Paris and Saint-Germain-des-Prés.

As they gazed out over the Seine, they continued to reminisce about that trip with Chink. Then, Hemingway pivots back: "We looked and there it was: our river and our city and the island of our city."[29] After walking the span of the bridge, they arrived on their side—the Left Bank—and realizing how hungry they were, headed for Michaud's. "So we walked up the rue des Saints Pères to the corner of rue Jacob" and then peered inside the windows waiting for people to finish up, reminiscing about Joyce and his family, and his chilly wife Nora and two children, who would eat there, Joyce reading the menu through "thick glasses." As Hemingway felt hungry again, he pondered if "what we had felt on the bridge . . . was just hunger . . . 'Memory is hunger.'"[30] Later on, back at their flat at rue du Cardinal Lemoine, satiated by Michaud's, "the feeling that had been like hunger when we were on the bridge was still there . . . Life had seemed so simple that morning . . . But Paris," he wrote, "was a very old city and we were young and nothing was simple there, not even poverty, nor sudden money, nor the moonlight, not right and wrong, nor the breathing of someone who lay beside you in the moonlight."[31]

Clearly, gnawing away at Hemingway was the memory of Milan and its great cathedral and praying fervently to Our Lady as his life drained out of him by the Piave, and the memory of Our Lady's splendor honored by Notre-Dame on the Île de la Cité, reached by the Pont Neuf, its glorious bells ringing out every evening, light of the setting sun streaming through its magnificent Rose Window, so rich in the spirituality he had read about in Belloc's *Paris*—now bejeweling his writing.

"ONE TRUE SENTENCE" AND LOVE OF MARY

In May, the month dedicated to Mary, Hemingway had set to work writing "one true sentence" in "a series of carefully pruned statements," titled *Paris 1922*, wrote Baker, "which he had worked out in his blue notebooks, mimicking Stein's habit of scribbling away in them, and then copied his writing in longhand on three telegraph blanks."[32] Of the ten, one powerfully and beautifully weaves in the famous cathedral dedicated to "Notre-Dame" ("Our Lady"): "I have stood on the crowded back platform of a seven o'clock Batignolles bus as it lurched along the wet lamp lit street while men who were going home to supper never looked up from their newspapers as we passed Notre-Dame grey and dripping in the rain."

Writing about Notre Dame was not random. After his life was preserved that fateful day, he never forgot what Our Lady had done for him. As noted, he had arrived in Europe not long after the apparitions of Our Lady of Fatima to the three shepherd children in Portugal at the Cova da Iria, which made a deep impression on him, reflected in what George Herter, a friend since the early 1920s, best known for his *Bull Cook and Authentic Historical Recipes and Practices*, told H. R. Stoneback over 50 years later:

> "Hemingway was a strong Catholic. His religion came mainly from the apparitions of the Virgin Mary. He told me several times that if there was no Bible, was no manmade Church laws, the apparitions proved beyond any doubt that the Catholic Church was the true church."[33]

It's easy to understand why Hemingway found Our Lady of Fatima and other Marian apparitions so compelling—because, quite simply, *they are*. "Hemingway," Herter wrote in earlier correspondence to Stoneback, "could not understand why the Catholic Church did not publicize (the apparitions) . . . I have heard him mention all of these (Lourdes, Fatima, etc.) and others at one time or another."

Hemingway reveled in the story about the day, January 2, 40 AD, that "Our Lady of Pillar" appeared to the Apostle, St. James in Zaragoza, Spain, not long after her Assumption into Heaven. St. James was tired and discouraged and she came standing atop a pillar made out of jaspar wood, so that the people of "Hispania" would have faith as sturdy as that pillar. To commemorate her visit, as Mary requested, the first Marian shrine—the Basilica of Our Lady of Pilar—was built around the pillar. During the Spanish Civil War, two aerial bombs were dropped on the shrine. Both failed to explode, and they now hang on the shrine wall.

Some eighteen hundred years later, "Our Lady of Lourdes" appeared to Bernadette Soubirous, a humble peasant girl, on February 11, 1858, in Lourdes, France, and, after several more apparitions, finally, on March 25, Feast of the Annunciation, revealed to her, "I am the Immaculate Conception," that is, conceived without sin. Once again, Mary requested that a shrine be built, this time atop the grassy knoll where she had appeared and where, as proof of her miraculous apparition, healing water flows from a nearby spring. Countless pilgrims with debilitating conditions, physical and spiritual, have been cured through the years, starting with the pilgrims who joined Bernadette during each apparition in spite of stiff resistance from authorities.

In between "Our Lady of Pilar" and "Our Lady of Lourdes" came "Our Lady of Guadalupe," who appeared to Juan Diego, a poor Mexican peasant, from December 9 to December 12, 1531. Among other miracles, she lavished him with Castilian Roses, not native to that region, in the middle of winter. That the local Bishop was from Castille, Spain, where these roses, also known as Damask Roses, flourish, shows Mary's thoughtfulness and class.

Yanked away from the hunger of memory, that first summer in Paris, the Hemingways entertained out-of-town guests, often taking them to the bal musette next door—a French dance hall with an accordion band. Hemingway, typically wearing his striped fishing shirt, danced "with anything he could get his hands on," said Hadley.[34] That August, the couple traveled to the Black Forest, both flying a biplane for the first time, Paris to Strausborg, where they enjoyed good trout fishing, joined by Bird (and wife Sally), Paris head of International News Service, poised to publish Hemingway's *in our time*. Hadley had never fished before but was soon fishing like a pro with Ernest's help. All the while Hemingway rejuvenated his creative juices.

Then journalism intruded again, when, in late September, he was dispatched to cover the Greco-Turkish War, raging since shortly after the end of the Great War. While Ernest and Hadley rarely quarreled, Hadley became incensed when he readied for Constantinople. She was drinking too much, as was Hemingway, and their relationship had hit some turbulence, as Hemingway's soul hungered for spiritual healing—writing and all that fine wine and liqueur and Hadley's love only going so far to heal him. And she could feel it. Though, when he came back on October 21—lice-infested, sick with malaria, and bearing gifts—rose oil, and two necklaces, one ivory, the other antique amber, sold to him by a Russian nobleman now waiting tables, which Hadley forever cherished—they patched things up, though not before Hemingway evidently visited the brothels while on assignment, a scenario he wrote about thirteen years later in "The Snows of Kilimanjaro," suggesting it may, in fact, be true. He was down in the dumps, feeling sorry for himself, as Hadley said he liked to do, on the way to recovering and being "on top of the wave, absolutely roistering with the most wonderful joyousness."[35]

Soon diving back into his real writing, this time his horseracing story, "My Old Man," he revealed a newly emergent and distinctive Hemingway style—writing about what he had experienced and knew, rather than what he had read about. But before long, the *Star* dispatched him once again, this time to Lausanne, Switzerland, to cover the peace conference now that the war was over and it was time to settle territorial disputes. He arrived on November 22, two days after the conference commenced, and met muckraking journalist Lincoln Steffans to whom, as luck would have it, he gave his copy of "My Old Man." Steffans promptly sent it off to *Cosmopolitan.*

TURNING POINT

Hemingway wired Hadley asking her to join him and telling her of his encounter with Steffans. They had planned another holiday skiing vacation in Chamby but she was still recovering from the flu. Before long, though, she was packing up, deciding to surprise Hem by bringing his writings—all of them, carbons included. When she got on the train at Gare de Lyon, the porter took the valise with Hemingway's writings and placed it on a shelf right above her seat. In another telling, Hadley placed it under her seat, while the porter parked the heavier luggage in the storage area. With time to kill, Hadley wandered through the splendid railway station, the most beautiful in the world complete with a large clock tower just like "Big Ben" (The Elizabeth Tower) at The Palace of Westminster, and high domed glass ceilings, and Le Train Bleu restaurant. She chatted up reporters and bought a paper and a drink. But, when she returned to her seat some thirty minutes later, the precious valise was gone. Hadley had lost most all of Ernest's writings—excluding *"Paris 1922,"* later found randomly tucked away; "My Old Man;" and "Up in Michigan," preserved because, after Stein called it "inaccrochable," Hemingway stashed it away in a drawer.

When Ernest met Hadley at Lausanne, she was deeply distraught and finally blurted out what had happened. To think she would be so careless with his precious writings does strain credulity. Hadley had encouraged Hemingway's writing during their courtship and, as newlyweds, helped him in that critical launch phase, critiquing the first draft of his first novel as he wrote it in Chicago, seeking to capture the emotion of the war's debacle through the eyes of Nick Adams. She could see he had great talent, and helped shape the female voice in his work and also, of course, gave him a measure of financial security via her trust fund, along with much-needed emotional security through her unconditional love. Hadley realized that Hemingway was extremely sensitive and insecure, so common for writers of great talent, and that he needed her support. But now she was taking second place. As passionate as their love was, nothing was more important to Ernest than his writing. He had brought her back to life and *she* felt like she played a role in birthing his writing. Now that symbiotic relationship was waning. He was off alone writing. Gertrude Stein, Ezra Pound, and Sylvia Beach had displaced Hadley in transforming his writing.

Just as she had so blithely tossed that ugly beaded purse he had gifted her into the Meramec River, the thought does occur, might she have somehow willed his early writings out of existence to see if he was more married to his writing than to her? In the same way she would later destroy nearly all of Ernest's voluminous love letters written from November 1920 to August 1921. Letters which he wrote nearly every day during their courtship, while Ernest kept all of Hadley's letters. Even Hemingway suggested as much in the posthumously published *The Garden of Eden*, in a scene in which the wife burns her author husband's writings. Was she now destroying, or otherwise accidentally on purpose "losing," his writings in a bid to save the marriage? If so, it was an ill-conceived plan. For, while Hemingway's literary work recovered, the marriage never did.

Hemingway's semi-fictional Paris memoir has him immediately going to Paris on December 6, to see if Hadley had left anything behind, crestfallen to discover everything was gone, a story which Baker corroborates, even noting he had lunch Gertrude and Alice the next day. But, as Donaldson writes in *The Paris Husband*, rather, he "asked a committee of three—Steffens, Hickok and Bird—to look through the lost property office at the Gare de Lyon and to explore the possibility of offering a reward."[36] Nothing turned up, they reported on December 9 in a letter to Ernest, and no reward was offered. (Both stories, of course, could be true.) On Sunday, December 11, Hadley wrote to Clarence and Grace from Hotel Beau-Sijour in Champéry, Switzerland, making no mention of the "lost" writings. They had skied at Chamby the day before as she frantically searched for "X-mas" cards. Meanwhile Ernest was finishing his wire service assignments. By week's end they were off to Chamby for two weeks of invigorating skiing (and passionate lovemaking), once again joined by "peerless" Chink Dorman-Smith along with a bevy of other friends including Mrs. Phalen and her pretty daughter Janet, the O'Neils and their three children—including 12-year-old Barbara who would famously play Mrs. O'Hara, mother of Scarlett, in *Gone with the Wind*—and his childhood friend, "Izzy Simmons."[37]

Hadley, who had remembered to bring every bit of writing she could lay her hands on, had blithely forgotten to bring her birth control to Chamby and became pregnant. Yet another surprise for her young, trusting husband. He would carefully track her cycle so they knew when pregnancy was unlikely and had an understanding that she would not get pregnant—not yet. Now, if the theory is correct, after she had destroyed what she helped create, she replaced it with a pro-creation far more important than writing.

After Chamby, they headed to Rapallo, Italy, to spend time with the Pounds. Hadley thought Italy, which Hem loved so, would help her pregnancy. They took "long walking excursions" with the Pounds, stopping for hillside repastes of "fresh Italian bread and figs and wine, and sometimes a sausage."[38] And they played tennis, at which, as with everything else, Hemingway was fiercely competitive.

While in Rapallo, he met Princeton grad, Henry "Mike" Strater, who was a guest of Pound, and the two became close friends. Both were the same weight class, shared a love of boxing; and both were artists—Strater doing oil paintings, Hemingway painting with words.

Strater could feel Hemingway's pain at the loss of his work, as he continued to ruminate over it. Hem asked Strater if he would have left those treasured writings unguarded while going to find something else to read—the answer obviously, "no." "He was very upset," said Strater, "because it showed how little she valued" his literary work.[39] And it reopened that inner wound from when Agnes dumped him. Hadley had shown a similar lack of understanding. He and his writing were one and the same. Or maybe she understood all too well. That had to gnaw at him and it would leach out into his writing over the years.

While in Rapallo, Hemingway fortuitously also met Edward O'Brien, editor of the annual edition of *The Best Short Stories*. He was living in a monastery above town, and, like Strater, was sympathetic to Hemingway's plight.

Hemingway's passport photo, January 1, 1923. *Source:* In the public domain.

He said he would read "My Old Man"—the *Cosmopolitan* copy, spared as it sat in the reject pile. It was just the encouragement Hem needed, as, gradually, he transformed the lost manuscripts into great literature. As he and Hadley ventured to Cortina d'Ampezzo, in the Dolomites, north of Venice, for more good skiing, he was turning over a story in his mind.

First, though, he slipped away for another reporting assignment in Germany to cover the French troops invading the country's premier industrial region, the Ruhr Basin, where coal and steel were mined. It required fancy footwork to get the necessary visas. But, with Sarah Bernhardt's death on Tuesday, March 26, Ruhr was knocked off the front pages and, by Good Friday, Bernhardt's funeral procession dominated and Hemingway was off to Germany for ten days, though Bone wanted a month.

Upon his return, Hemingway wrote "Out of Season." About a young expat married couple who hire a drunk gardener as their fishing guide, it highlights weak and powerless men, seeking refuge in sports, the outdoors and alcohol, creating tensions in the marital relationship. Another clear case of art reflecting life. As Hemingway would write to Scott Fitzgerald, it reflected the state of his marriage. Hadley, no doubt, took note.

Back in Paris, he turned down Bone's next assignment to cover Russia and the British threat to cut ties with the Bolsheviks, given their belligerence toward Britain. Hem needed to get serious about the "Inquest" book Pound proposed. And he was getting nervous. The creative well had been closed and he was now opening it unsure what would flow out, and writing for Bone was interfering. If he had only realized both came from the same place, he would have calmed down. Still, he needed to create, not report. Four months on the road had interrupted his rhythm. After writing a police-beat story, he started going to the well of his Italian war experience, writing this first draft of a story he titled "Religion":

> Oh Jesus Christ, I prayed, get me out of here. Dear Jesus, please get me out
> . . . If you'll only keep me from getting killed, I'll do anything you say. I
> believe in you and if you only take care of me, I'll tell everyone in the world
> that you are the only thing that matters. That was during a shelling in the
> line near Fossalta. The next day my leave came and that night I was drunk
> in the officer's whore house in Mestre.[40]

He scratched this vignette, for now, completing eleven by the end of May, then rewriting and including it later in the year as "Chapter 8," ending it, "The next night back at Mestre he did not tell the girl he went upstairs with at the Villa Rossa about Jesus."[41]

Soon, he headed to Spain with Bird, this time joined by Bob McAlmon, whom he had met at the Pounds'. He loved Spain and, that July, traveled with his very pregnant wife to Pamplona for its "Fiesta: Running of the Bulls," his first time enjoying this marquee event in Basque Country. Hemingway was much taken with the medieval country, and its countrymen, who "like their language, tell it like it is," his son John said.[42] Meanwhile, he filed his story, "Trout Fishing All Across Europe: Spain Has the Best, Then Germany," while Hadley knitted baby caps and booties, careful to avert her gaze from the grisly bullfighting scenes.

In the fall of 1923, the Hemingways moved to Toronto, given Hadley's dwindling trust fund and their need to save money. Ernest had landed a full-time job writing for the *Toronto Star*, though, his boss, Harry Hindmarsh, Hadley said, was "jealous," overloading him with piddling assignments. Hindmarsh, "a tyrant trying to break Hemingway's spirit," failed to "comprehend his talent," said Morley Callaghan, a *Star* copywriter.[43]

One day Callaghan was reading in the library and, when he looked up, there was Hemingway studying him, with that engaging personality of his—"a real sweetness in his smile and a wonderful availability," conveying an eager and deep "involvement in everything." Though Hemingway's outlook on Toronto had dimmed, "I could see," wrote Callaghan, "it wasn't only the job that was bothering him."[44]

Hemingway had sought out this junior staffer to see what he was writing and asked him to bring him something. Callaghan missed his Friday "appointment," after which Hemingway lashed out, saying he wanted to see if he was "another GD phony."[45] Message delivered. The next Wednesday, Callaghan brought his carefully edited draft and Hemingway brought him the proofs for the Paris edition of *in our time*. The two sat across from each other in the library and just read. "Sitting there," wrote Callaghan, "I knew I was getting a glimpse of the work of a great writer." Hemingway, for his part, rated Callaghan "a real writer" and the two became fast friends.

Hemingway would often come by the library to talk with Callaghan, offering such gems as: "A writer is like a priest. He has to have the same feeling about his work." Which not only gives insight into the seriousness with which Hemingway approached writing but also highlights the fact that he had seen priestly dedication up close, notably in the person of Don Bianchi. And, said Callaghan, he spoke with the authority of a bishop, as if what he was saying in whispered tones was ex-cathedra.

On October 10, while Hemingway was en route from New York where he had covered the arrival of British Prime Minister Lloyd George, his son, John Hadley Nicanor Hemingway—a.k.a. "Bumby"—was born. "He wept with strain and exhaustion when he arrived at the hospital," said Hadley.[46] As a counterbalance to the professional hardship he was enduring, O'Brien had just chosen "My Old Man" for *The Best Short Stories of 1923*, dedicating the entire issue to "Hemenway." And McAlmon's Contact Publishing had just published his first book, *Three Stories and Ten Poems*, also featuring "My Old Man," as well as "Up in Michigan" and his latest, "Out of Season." Hem broke this news of his publishing first to his sister "Ivory," now Mrs. John Sanford, in a letter mailed on October 14, swearing her to secrecy because it featured a "whangleberry"—"Up in Michigan"—that would be a total shocker. The book had sold out immediately, he said, but he would send her a copy, so long as she kept it from the wrong family members, who, if they read it, would want him dead and buried, as opposed to praising him for his "corking good story."[47]

The family, now joined by baby Bumby, sailed back to Europe aboard the *Antonia*, leaving Quebec on January 13 and docking at Cherbourg on January 30. No sooner had they arrived back in Paris than *in our time*, his small volume of vignettes and stories, written, in part, while he was in Spain falling in love with that country and its bullfighting—"corrida"—was published by Bird's *Three Mountains Press*. The title, suggested by Pound, came from the English Book of Common Prayer—"give us peace in our time, O Lord." This was "the Inquest into the state of contemporary English prose" that Pound had set in motion. Five of the stories focused on World War I (1, 4, 5, 7, 8), six on bullfighting (2; 12–16), and the longest one (10), the aforementioned "A Very Long Story," about a love affair with a Red Cross nurse during the war. The other six "vignettes" were based on news stories he had covered both in Kansas and Europe.[48] Though the book's distribution was limited, it landed in the right hands and was recognized for its unique new style, spare language, and circuitous way of describing a character's state of mind.

FORSAKING ALL ELSE FOR WRITING

While in Toronto, Hemingway, longing for Paris and the life of a writer, gave his boss notice. He had decided to ditch journalism, and just write and create. Gertrude Stein had urged him to take this step, saying this way he will "see things" as opposed to seeing just "words."[49] Early on, with funds tight, rather than renting a space for writing, as Anderson had counseled, he was now writing from his new second floor home at 113 rue Notre-Dame des Champs overlooking a sawmill and lumberyard. It was the same street Pound lived on, right behind Boulevard du Montparnasse in the 6th Arrondissement, and closer to the Luxembourg Gardens, Shakespeare and Company and Gertrude Stein's home. Then, too, he found nearby Closerie de Lilas a comfortable place for writing, especially when the sawmill got noisy, the Left Bank riff raff, not usually known to darken its door.

He also worked at the Qau d'Anjou offices of Ford Madox Ford's *transatlantic review*, at the back of Bird's publishing operation. He had met Ford at Pound's studio and, at Pound's urging, edited the magazine, unpaid, during its inaugural literary year of 1924, *transatlantic*'s sole year of life. Featuring works of Pound, Dos Passos, Stein, and others, it also showcased Hemingway's early stories, starting with "Indian Camp," where he introduced Nick Adams as a young boy, Hem's alter ego, witnessing his doctor father doing an emergency Caesarean section, and featuring his uncle—the two doubles for Dr. Hemingway and his brother George. So it was that Hemingway gave creative birth to the iconic character who would breathe life into his lost war story.

The summer of 1924, Nick Adams stories continued to flow from Hemingway's creative well, including "The Big Two-Hearted River," his longest work to date, which he luxuriated in writing, beginning smack dab in the middle of May, finishing three months later, on August 15, the Feast of the Mary's Assumption into Heaven. Enjoying a meal at Brasserie Lipp with money received from *Der Querschnitt* for five poems, he wrote years later, "I did not want to leave the river where I could see the trout in the pool."[50] Over beer and pommes a l'huile, he was writing about the return from war without mentioning the war—an observation he made in his Paris memoir some thirty years later after suffering, some three years earlier, multiple wounds in a plane crash in Africa. "But in the morning the river would be there . . . All I must do now was stay sound and good in my head until morning." And, as he added, then deleted, "In those days we never thought that any of that could be difficult."[51] After that plane crash, it *was* difficult, but it brought him such joy to relive Paris. A waiter at the Closerie de Lilas, he wrote, had urged him to give up boxing, where he made ten francs a round battling with champs, because of this waiter's prescient concern that the ensuing head injuries might impact his writing.[52] So, he paid Hem to help him weed a vegetable garden near the Porte d'Orléans transit hub. Though Hem kept boxing, too. He had to. George Breaker had swindled much of Hadley's inheritance and he was hungry.

Under Gertrude Stein's tutelage, Hemingway had studied impressionist painters, notably Cezanne, Degas, Manet, Renoir, and Monet, at the Louvre, and set to work achieving in writing what they did on the canvas. "I learned how to make a landscape from Mr. Paul Cézanne by walking through the Luxembourg Museum a thousand times with an empty gut," he said years later.[53] As he wrote to Stein the day he finished "Big Two-Hearted River," "I'm trying to do the country like Cezanne . . . It is about 100 pages long and nothing happens and the country is swell."[54]

While writing "Big Two-Hearted River," he pondered "pigeons . . . perched on the statues of the bishops"—and, reflecting on his empty stomach, thought, "Cezanne was probably hungry in a different way."[55] Always the iceberg, just the tip, hinting at the underlying spirituality. Yet he had real physical hunger, as well. Making it as a writer was a steep climb punctuated by "*all of the stories back in the mail that came in through a slit in the sawmill door,*" he wrote, "*with notes of rejection that would never call them stories, but always anecdotes, sketches, contes, etc. They did not want them, and we lived on poireaux and drank cahors and water.*"[56] The *Harper's Magazine* rejection of his story about a broken soldier returning from war hit particularly hard. "Ernest said, at times it hurt him so badly that he would throw things against the wall and break down crying. And, I said 'I never think of you as crying,'" A. E. Hotchner said. "And, he said, 'Let me tell you, man, when the hurt's bad enough you cry.'"[57]

Ah, but, like a coiled spring, Hemingway was poised for success all the while becoming a beloved presence in the Latin Quarter, attracting friends like moths to a flame in that "small, backbiting, gossipy little neighborhood."[58] Archibald MacLeish, for one, sought out Hemingway after spotting *in our time* at Shakespeare and Company. His younger brother Kenneth had been killed on October 14, 1918, while on a raid with the Royal Air Force, his body found in a Belgian field the following May—engendering in the rising legal eagle, a desire to write poetry in Paris. Beach told him he could find Hemingway at the Closerie des Lilas late afternoons. The two Midwesterners, wired much the same way—highly competitive, from middle class families, just outside Chicago—bonded immediately over boxing, bicycling, skiing, and writing. MacLeish, Ivy League educated, AB from Yale, JD from Harvard, seven years Hem's senior, had served in France for two years during and after World War I. The MacLeishes invited the Hemingways to dinner and, the next morning, Hem returned a corkscrew he had stuck in his pocket with a note asking for a list of any other missing items, while apologizing for arriving "in an advanced state of alcoholism" as well as for his talkativeness replete with "doubtfully authentic reminiscences and dull obscenities." In fact, the MacLeishes had thoroughly enjoyed the evening, sensing in Hemingway a big future.[59] He could just suck the oxygen out of a room, said MacLeish—a feeling that only one other person, Franklin Delano Roosevelt, gave him.

"An emotional man," said Archie's wife, Ada, noting Archie knew Hem best. "He was unexpected and temperamental, a loveable person who needed a great deal of understanding." Under all that toughness was great "sensitivity," she said.[60]

His friendship with the novelist Nathan Asch shed light on this essential aspect of his personality and psyche. As Asch observed some twenty years later in a letter to literary critic Malcolm Cowley, one night they had dinner and were comparing their writing talents. Later as they walked to Le Dôme for coffee, "Hemingway fell into a boxer's crouch and began feinting and jabbing." Asch "began shadowboxing" and "hit Hemingway," who then "hit back, knocking him down," after which Asch hobbled back to his hotel room. "Later that night, there was a knock at the door. It was Hemingway. 'I couldn't sleep until you forgave me,' he said." He also wanted him to know he, Asch, had "more of everything than any of us."[61]

Cowley had studied Hemingway closely in Paris and on a long ride with Stoneback through the Hudson Valley in the late seventies, described Hemingway as "the great star of Paris" and "the most charming person I ever met but also the most difficult," possessing an "essential mystery. . . . It was as if Paris belonged to him," said Cowley, and what he most desired was "to give Paris to you as a precious and personal gift."

Hemingway particularly enjoyed Dos Passos's company. They had, of course, met briefly in Italy in the summer of 1918. "Dos" vaguely remembers a dinner at Brasserie Lipp with Hem and Hadley in Paris before Bumby was born, but the memories of the spring of 1924 after *in our time* hit bookstores, are most vivid. "Hem and I would occasionally meet at the Closerie des Lilas at the corner of St. Michael and Montparnasse" over "vermouth cassis" while chewing over "the difficulty of putting things down on paper." Both were pouring over the Old Testament. "We read to each other choice passages. The song of Deborah and Chronicles and Kings were our favorite." That Hem based his "wiry short sentences on cablese and the King James Bible," were to Dos proof positive that "Hem would become the first great American stylist."[62] Around 5 p.m., they would take the leisurely three-minute walk back home to the sawmill, where they'd help Hadley give Bumby his bath, which their wee one found a delightful exercise, and, once the babysitter reported for duty, they'd go out to dinner.

"He had an evangelistic streak," wrote Dos Passos, "that made him work to convert his friends to whatever mania he was encouraging at the time."[63] This included horse racing—Hem luring Dos to the track despite his distaste of gambling. One time, after they plunked down their winnings at day's end on what looked like a sure bet, the horse wiped out and they lost it all. "We nearly died laughing. I went back to Paris with my convictions about the folly of gambling much fortified," wrote Dos Passos. "Next time we went to Henry's Bar Harold pretended not to see us."

For Hem, gambling had, in fact, become a real addiction as he struggled to make a living as a writer, gaining acclaim but not enough money to support his family. Hadley's diminished trust fund made for a particularly tight budget. For a time, he even gave up writing, women, and drink, wrote Dos Passos, to pursue this maniacal obsession, consoling himself, Hem wrote in his memoir, that he was, after all, writing about gambling. As Dos Passos wrote, "He lived a pathetic barfly life, eking out a living selling tips on the ponies to American tourists he picked up in the various ginmills he frequented."[64] He finally came to his senses and, one day, just gave it up and went to see his friend Mike Ward at Guaranty Trust to deposit the money and have lunch with him at Michaud's. Ward suggested bicycle racing. Then, he began betting on his "own life and work," Hemingway wrote.[65] But soon enough his fresh new mania became bicycle racing especially at "The Six Jours at the Vélo d'Hiver," with its "special comical air," wrote Dos Passos.

Dos would peel off from the indoor track, in the shadow of the Eiffel Tower, when he started dozing. But "poor Hadley" had to stick it out. "Right from the beginning Hem was hard on his women," wrote Dos Passos. "Yet I'm convinced that he was more of a builder upper than a breaker downer. He left them more able to cope with life than he found them."[66]

During the early years of marriage to Hadley, as Hemingway struggled to grow as a writer, all his sensory appetites were well fed, and his emotions stimulated and calmed. Meanwhile, he did not tend to his spiritual life sufficiently and without that spiritual firewall, the normal vicissitudes of marriage become more difficult to weather. His reaction to her pregnancy underscores the tentativeness with which he had approached the marriage. That "fine try" that he was going to give it had hit some turbulence. But, while initially downbeat, he embraced fatherhood and it gave the marriage new life. Ernest loved Bumby immensely, while keeping up his active life—now adding the Tour de France to his adventures with Hadley. Actual, prevenient grace was earned through sports, don't you know! But the actual practice of his faith was nonexistent. It was not Hemingway but Stein and Toklas who arranged for the baby's baptism—not at a Catholic Church but at St. Luke's Episcopal Church—six months after his birth. The two, along with Chink, served as the godparents, after which Hadley hosted a luncheon cooked by Marie Cocotte, their femme de ménage.

SPIRITUAL THIRST

Over Christmas 1924, the Hemingways vacationed in Schruns, Austria, a less expensive alternative to Chamby. It was a wonderfully peaceful time. Resources or not, living simply was, after all, who Hemingway was—more aesthetic, not a poseur, putting on airs. Meanwhile, Hadley dressed plainly because Stein had urged them not to waste money on such a frivolity, suggesting they spend it on artwork or vacations and sports. Sometimes, though, Sally Bird or Ada MacLeish would tactfully slip Hadley elegant hand-me-downs.

During the vacation in Schruns, Hemingway wrote his friend Harold Loeb that he found "good crucifixes"[67] everywhere he hiked, imaging his own crosses. Then, too, Loeb had suffered with the demise of his literary magazine *Broom*, launched on the eve of Hem's arrival in Paris, only to see it fold at the start of the year—precisely when Hem began exclusively pursuing the art of "one true sentence." They had met at Madox's Thursday literary teas, and Hem enjoyed playing tennis with him in spite of his war-injured knee, which caused him great pain. Then, too, there were all the emotional wounds. Kitty Cannell, Loeb's girlfriend, thought Hemingway's magnetic exterior cloaked a cruel and vicious nature.[68] The hidden wounds inflicted by his father were no less real than war's wounds and the cycle of Hemingway's anger—aiming his gun at his father from afar as his anger boiled only to feel guilty as he simmered down—played out in other relationships throughout his life.

All of which made his relationship with Mary in the wake of his wounding all the more important. As St. Josemaria Escrivá de Balaguer wrote in his spiritual classic, *The Way,* "The love of our Mother will be the breath that kindles into a living flame the embers of virtue that are hidden under the ashes of your indifference."[69] The embers of virtue were obvious in spite, or because of Hemingway's own evident defects. He had fallen away from his newfound faith and would do so later during the Spanish Civil War, when he considered himself irredeemable, not worth praying for.

For now, far less jaded, he satiated his spiritual thirst with the quest for crosses and cathedrals and Mary and her apparitions, discretely tucked away in his writing—*Paris 1922* and Notre-Dame "grey and dripping in the rain," the starting point for the Chemins de Saint-Jacques de Compostelle (Way of St. James), by way of the rue Saint-Jacques, the main axial road of medieval Paris, part of the north-south corridor—"cardo"—of Gallo-Roman Lutetia Parisiorum (capital of the Parisii, a tribe of ancient Gaul), leading south, across the Pyrenees into Spain to Galicia's Cathedral of Santiago de Compostela. There, legend has it, the remains of St. James—again, the first one to whom Mary appeared after her Assumption into Heaven—were transported by angels, after he was martyred in Jerusalem, for his burial, thus the cathedral's name: Santiago for St. James, and Compestela, meaning document certifying completion of the "Way of St. James," as well as "Field of Stars" ("campus stellae") reflecting the Middle Ages' legend that the Milky Way stars outline St. James and lead pilgrims to his tomb. Pretty cool!

With this spiritual world swirling around in Hemingway's creative imagination, little wonder that *The Sun Also Rises,* his first novel, features a protagonist, "Jake" Barnes, inspired by St. James and the rue Saint-Jacques, which Jake describes on the eve of the trip to Pamplona as "the rigid north and south of the rue Saint-Jacques."[70] A curious description, H. R. Stoneback thought, since there's nothing rigid about it, unless the underlying spirituality along this medieval main street is glimpsed. There's the famous Church of the Val-de-Grâce, meaning "vale of grace"—an architectural splendor Louis XIII's wife, Queen Anne of Austria, built to celebrate the birth of their son

Louis XIV ("The Sun King") after 23 years of infertility—and the adjoining monastery, later converted into a hospital for wounded soldiers, imaging Jake's war wounds and Hemingway's, too. Then, too, the Institut Royal Des Sourds-Muet stood on the site of a hospice for pilgrims to Santiago de Compostela. *Le long de la rue,* there's a plaque dedicated to Pamplona, a town along the Chemins pèlerinage. There, at the famous siege, "Loyola had been badly wounded—like Hemingway in the legs by artillery—the 'wound that made him think,'" as Hemingway described his transformation "from soldier to saint."[71]

In Pamplona, Jake reveals his hunger for God when he sees the cathedral and approaches it. "The first time I saw it I thought the façade was ugly but I liked it now. I went inside. It was dim and dark and the pillars went high up, and there were people praying, and it smelt of incense, and there were some wonderful big windows. I knelt and started to pray and prayed for everybody I thought of."[72]

That little "rigid north and south" street along the Chemins de Saint-Jacques fairly shouts mystical truths of "suffering and joy, expiation and renewal," wrote Stoneback, while also noting that Hemingway said his first novel was intended as a "tract against 'promiscuity.'" Like Hemingway, we are all weak. We fall, are dirty with sin, and our souls are cleansed through these "rigid north and south" mystical truths.

The very mysticism that Belloc had written about twenty-five years earlier in *Paris.*

In Hemingway's second novel, *A Farewell to Arms,* Lt. Frederic Henry, who, like Hemingway, spent five months recuperating from his war wounds in the shadow of the Duomo, observes from his hospital bed that "[o]utside, the sun was up over the roof and I could see the points of the cathedral with the sunlight on them. I was clean inside and outside and waiting for the doctor."[73]

Not only his body needed healing, so did his soul.

5

꧁꧂

F. Scott, Pauline, Hadley, and Bumby

"The Sun Also Rises"

As 1925 dawned, Hemingway might not have found that doctor for his soul quite yet. His writing, though, was a healing salve and he was getting noticed in just the right places thanks to people like Ernest Walsh, the expatriate Irish-American poet living beyond his means at Claridge's, Hemingway famously capturing his flamboyant lifestyle in his "marked for death"[1] sketch of the day they met at Ezra Pound's. Bailed out by various patrons—notably Monroe; (She carved out a $100 monthly allowance from his past earnings); Pound; and Scottish suffragette Ethel Moore—this engaging, dark-haired, twenty-four-year-old invalid, sick with tuberculosis that ended his service in the American air force, would die the year after he published Hemingway's "Big Two-Hearted River" in the spring 1925 inaugural edition of the small but influential Paris magazine *This Quarter* he co-edited and launched to spotlight an "artist's work while it is still fresh."[2]

THE LOST GENERATION: CLASH OF CULTURES

The sick and maimed of World War I were a daily reality of "Hemingway's Paris." Those with missing limbs, disfigured faces, glass eyes, damaged brains—all victims of chemical and artillery weapons—populated Hemingway's writing. For example, the one-armed poet Blaise Cendrars, his limb lost while fighting with the French foreign legion, now sporting a "broken boxer's face and pinned up empty sleeve." He was the "only poet" at Closerie des Lilas.³ But what a poet—his physical loss transformed into spiritual beauty as he worked alongside French modernist painter Fernand Léger and other greats.

Life's ephemeral nature, made so blindingly obvious by the war, inspired Hemingway to see deeper spiritual realities, including them iceberg-like under the character and color of the physical world he wrote about—a world which collided with the one he came from, a reality catalyzed and captured by the "lost generation." Hemingway felt the moment deeply, expressing the depth of his feeling in his writing—not unlike Fitzgerald, who wrote in *This Side of Paradise* (1920) of "a generation grown up to find all gods dead, all wars fought, all faiths in man shaken."

F. Scott and Zelda had only recently come to Paris in the wake of his failed play, *The Vegetable*. Tiring of drunken Long Island parties as he feverishly scribbled short stories to try and stay solvent, an exhausted Scott craved a new base from which to write his next novel. At the same time, Hemingway, a promising no-name writer, toiling away in the Parisian literary vineyards, had just started turning heads, albeit not those of his family. His father, though, in an early March letter, did praise "The Doctor and the Doctor's Wife" he had read in *transatlantic*. Hinting at what was to come, Hemingway wrote back to his father that in his stories he wanted to convey "actual life" as opposed to just depicting or criticizing it but to make it real, so that readers felt like they were living it. Which meant writing about "the bad and the ugly" and the "beautiful." Otherwise it was an artifice.⁴

In the midst of Jazz Age exuberance, *actual life* contained an underlying sadness brought on by death, carnage, and the loss of war, masked by excessive drinking and revelry, and the inevitable marital infidelities.

While personally, Hemingway *was* his parents' son—married to a wife with whom he lived monogamously, a rarity in the sea of Parisian infidelity, where sexual immorality was openly celebrated; his writing reflected another reality. As Pound wrote, "Good art cannot be immoral. By good art, I mean the art that bears true witness. I mean the art that is most precise."⁵ He was "most precise" in his final typescript of *The Sun Also Rises*, writing that the Latin Quarter wreaked of "abortions and rumors of abortions, doubts and speculations as to past and prospective infidelities of friends, dirty rumors, dirtier reports and dirtier suspicions."⁶ Which mattered little to the bohemians. "It was quite all right to be dirty, drunk, a pervert, or a thief or a whore, provided you had a lively and honest mind, and the courage of your instincts," wrote Stella Bowen, who lived in a ménage à trois with Ford and his mistress, the writer Jean Rhys. "What damned you was social snobbery, bourgeois ideology, smugness and carefulness."⁷

But would his parents ever understand why his writing had to be so "true"? Probably not. No, definitely not! Even old man Scribner, who did appreciate Hemingway's art, insisted that passage be excised from the manuscript.

This clash of cultures was the kiln that formed Hemingway's unique sense of humor. When combined with the "irony and pity" spilling from the pens of New York literati, which Hemingway used so skillfully, it enlivened his writing, revealing what Orson Welles presciently observed: Hemingway was "riotously funny."[8] And he just let loose in Europe—writing *and* drinking—along with his war-weary, wounded peers, huddled in Paris cafés, trying to find their creative voices. Like so many of the "lost generation," Hemingway drank with abandon—when not writing, the Victorian era's strong work ethic guiding him to erect a strict wall between the two activities. But when he let loose, he let loose—his Grandfather "Abba" Hall's permissive attitude toward alcohol making it a comfortable avenue for doing so. While serving as a lubricant for writing, it most definitely enhanced the social scene, which Hemingway soaked up in equal measure. In late March, he attended a cocktail party hosted by Cannell, who introduced him to fellow expat and fashion journalist, Pauline Pfeiffer. A devout Catholic, gifted with a lively sense of humor, Pauline was living in Paris and writing for *Vogue*, the French edition, edited by Main Rousseau Bocher, also known as Mainbocher. She had written for *Vogue* in New York and was determined to make a splash in this city of haute couture and lavish entertaining. Initially Pauline's younger sister Virginia, known as "Ginny," was the one who glommed onto Ernest, Pauline finding him unsophisticated. But then, Ginny, who was not too interested in men, began telling her sister all about Ernest, and it was just a matter of time before Pauline would take another look. But first she had to cover the grand opening of the *International Exposition of Modern Decorative and Industrial Arts (Exposition internationale des arts décoratifs et industriels modernes)* in April and write about the avant-garde styles, which, that Paris spring, were christened "Art Deco."[9]

F. SCOTT FITZGERALD'S FRIENDSHIP

Meanwhile, unbeknownst to Hemingway, F. Scott Fitzgerald, whose literary gift had made him the "it" novelist and short story writer of the "Jazz Age," a term he coined to describe the "liberated" twenties, was becoming Hem's biggest advocate. The critic Edmund Wilson, a Princeton classmate of Scott, had reviewed *in our time* for *The Dial* in October 1924, highlighting its "strikingly original" style.[10] "Hemingway's little book," he wrote, "has more artistic dignity than any other that has been written by an American about the period of the war." Scott took note and began urging his editor at Scribner's, Max Perkins, to look at this new writer, "Hemmenway," with "a brilliant future," who had become the darling of the Left Bank literati. "He's the real thing," he wrote. Once Perkins read *in our time*, he wrote Hemingway, "Whatever you are writing, we should be most interested to consider."[11] Hemingway was skiing in Austria and Boni and Liveright had beaten out Scribner's, agreeing to publish his short story collection in the States. Hemingway eagerly accepted, only to see Perkins' letter belatedly, writing to tell him the news. "What rotten luck—for me, I mean," Perkins wrote back to Hemingway.[12]

Scott, undeterred, showed up a few weeks later at Dingo American Bar properly attired in his Brooks Brothers finest, and ordered a champagne. It was April 24, 1925, two weeks after publication of *The Great Gatsby* and Hem, as usual, was holding court with his fellow expats. Besides scouting Hem for Scribner's, Scott hoped meeting the dynamic up-and-comer would help blur the memory of Zelda's affair with French pilot Edouard Jozan, the steamy liaison betiding while he was sequestered at Villa Marie in Valescure toiling away on *Gatsby*. After a few more champagnes, Scott, who was hypoglycemic, turned white as a sheet and began sweating profusely, soon passing out. Not a very auspicious start to their friendship—a friendship Zelda would come to rue. But once Hemingway read *Gatsby*, he was awestruck and knew he must try and climb the same literary heights.

The two became like brothers, whiling away the hours at the Dingo, Café du Dôme, and other Parisian cafés plotting their next novel or short story, while eyeing the beautiful women and interesting characters passing through. Scott was so charming and emotionally needy, he failed to understand he was the senior partner in this relationship that became a salve to his soul. He had just finished writing the greatest novel of the twentieth century, while Hem, still essentially struggling to write "one true sentence," somehow dominated, famously writing of their first meeting, "He had fair wavy hair, a high forehead, excited and friendly eyes and a delicate, long-lipped Irish mouth . . . the mouth worried you until you knew him and then it worried you more."[13]

They were, of course, very different. As Mike Strater put it, "Hemingway was big, roaring, very aggressive . . . Scott Fitzgerald was very quiet."[14]

Raised Catholic, Scott always felt like the outsider, no more so than when he arrived at Princeton in the fall of 1913—Catholic, from remote St. Paul, Minnesota, in sea of Protestants. He was swiftly cut from the football team he had hoped would brand him a winner, only to find the father of his aristocratic love, Ginevra King, considered him a loser, ill-suited to marry his daughter. On the rebound in Montgomery, Alabama, during stateside war service, he met and fell in love with Zelda Sayre, a judge's daughter. A high-spirited beauty, she drew Scott out of his shell. St. Paul society, though, found their antics, reflecting the rebellious postwar tempo, too much. William Fellows Peet, for one, who had shared many a drink with Scott before he met Zelda, essentially withdrew from the relationship and, at his wife's request, the invitations to the mansion ceased.[15] But it was "like water off a duck's back." Scott had his eyes on the "city that never sleeps" and, eager to marry Zelda, transformed, with monomaniacal focus, a banal novel he had penned, into the hit, *This Side of Paradise*, then moved to Manhattan where he and Zelda wed in the sacristy of St. Patrick's Cathedral in 1920, becoming the "it" couple, while chasing illusive dreams of success as Scott's faith atrophied. This son of an alcoholic father, a failed businessman, whose mother's Irish immigrant father was a cash-rich wholesale grocer, was more fascinated by the rich and their playgrounds than edifices of the spirit, and, unlike Hemingway, who understood at a fundamental level that work was sanctifying, never anchored his earthly appetites in eternal realities. The glittering debutante balls and chic horsey events fascinated him as he studied the social cues and trappings of wealth. Cap d'Antibes was the apex, where the Murphy's soon-to-open Villa America featured a parade of wealthy sophisticates well lubricated with spirits of the alcoholic variety.

Hemingway, macho and down-to-earth, thought battlefield valor the highest achievement, and would rather be hunting big game than pretty socialites. Two-time Pulitzer Prize-winning novelist Booth Tarkington, best known for *The Magnificent Ambersons* and *Alice Adams*, both made into films, thought Scott and Hem got along famously, though, like Strater, he also thought they were a bit of an odd couple. Fitzgerald possessed a refined Princeton pedigree, his father hailing from a line of "shabby-genteel" landed Maryland aristocrats, whereas Hem was like "a Kansas University football beef."[16]

At the same time, they had distinct similarities. Like Scott, Hem had great charm—"the most charming manners of anyone I know," said Zelda.[17] Albeit he was tight-lipped as he won over hearts, reflecting that "essential mystery" Cowley had intuited. Both drew from the same midwestern well, where they were on the outside looking in to wealthy salons, while having domineering mothers and weak fathers. They were both married with one child, and, of course, both were dedicated to the art of writing.

In the last week of May, Scott prevailed upon Hem to join him on a trip to Lyon, five hours southeast of Paris, to fetch his Renault abandoned en route from the French Riviera during a driving rainstorm because Zelda had lopped off the top and, predictably, they got drenched. It was "a slick drive through Burgundy" with its limestone cliffs, he wrote Gertrude Stein, and Ernest was "a peach of a fellow and absolutely first-rate." Scott, though, called himself "a very second-rate person compared to first-rate people—I have in-dignation—as well as most of the other major faults."[18] Hemingway, for his part, wrote Perkins, that the trip was "great."[19] No inferiority complex, he!

The day Tarkington met Hemingway, he said, "I rather liked him. Fitzgerald brought him up and was a little tight—(and) took him away because Hemingway was to have a [boxing] fight that afternoon at three o' clock, though I gathered they'd both been up all night."[20]

What a fast friendship they developed, Hemingway writing Scott from the Festival of San Fermin, "I am feeling better" than ever, drinking only "wine since I left Paris."[21] A not-so-subtle hint that abstaining from the hard stuff would be helpful as Scott began thinking about *his* next novel. And he enthuses about the "wonderful country," then refrains from doing so when he remembers Scott's aversion to rural settings.

Then pivoting to the spiritual, he opines about Scott's "idea of heaven" suggesting an enclave of "wealthy monogamists" who were gorgeous and belonged to the "best families" whereas "hell" would be an enclave "full of poor polygamists" without any "booze." Then, he gets down to *his idea*: Heaven would have a "big bull ring" and a "trout stream," secluded and ex-clusive. And he would have two beautiful houses—one where he would live monogamously with his wife and children; the other for whooping it up with nine mistresses, one on each floor, bathrooms stocked with improvised toilet paper made from the magazines that had rejected him, including *The Dial* and the *New Republic*. And, he continued, there would be a "fine church like in Pamplona where I could go and be confessed."

Like Scott, Hemingway had great defects and needed dollops of grace to overcome them, grace that he knew the Catholic Church offered in abun-dance, but that he did not avail himself of while married to Hadley. She was virulently anti-Catholic, refusing even to allow Bumby to darken the door of a Catholic Church.[22] Scott was in much the same situation, married to an Episcopalian. And, while the Hemingways were monogamous, he's dream-ing of straying. They lived at the sensual level, getting drunk every night and making fulsome love, with no real spiritual compass or nourishment, render-ing Hemingway's soul a desert. With this God void, came a thirst for illicit sexual pleasures, which he sought to quench, if only in his imagination. For no marriage can fully satisfy a man's carnal desires given that a man, as this writer's late father always taught her, is, by nature, promiscuous; so he needs grace to overcome the disordered drive to misuse what comes naturally.

These channels of *supernatural* grace, obtained through the sacraments, were not flowing, though Hemingway was obviously desirous of them.

Still, without that shield of grace, he started cozying up to Lady Duff Twysden. He was talking with her the day he met Scott at the Dingo Bar. Hadley was well aware of his dalliance with Duff Twysden, calling her "a wonderfully attractive Englishwoman, a woman of the world with no sexual inhibitions."[23] Yet, oddly, she did nothing to douse the flames, which, unwittingly or not, laid the groundwork for her husband's infidelity later that year. Meanwhile, Hemingway told friends like Sylvia Beach and F. Scott in Paris in the twenties that he had converted to Catholicism in Italy; it was when he was anointed on the battlefield, and baptized Catholic.[24] While Hemingway minimized his newfound faith, if he even shared it with Hadley, it was an instant source of bonding with Pauline.

PERSONAL UPHEAVAL, SPIRITUAL RENEWAL

On July 21, 1925, after wrapping up his third journey to Pamplona—this time joined by Princeton-educated Loeb; Duff Twysden (recently divorced), with whom Loeb had an affair; Lady Duff's lover/companion Pat Guthrie; boyhood friend Bill Smith; Donald Ogden Stewart; and Hadley—he went to work, starting on his twenty-sixth birthday, writing the first draft of his first novel. Starting in Valencia, he continued writing in Madrid, and finished in Paris on September 21.[25] As the month was ending, he traveled alone to Chartres, about fifty miles southwest of Paris, taking with him the draft manuscript, though he would do no real work on it until Christmas. There, he absorbed the awe-inspiring Notre-Dame de Chartres Cathedral, built in the twelfth and thirteenth centuries, with its great flying buttresses supporting outsized and still-intact stained glass windows in this ecclesial home to both the Black Madonna as well as the famous relic, the Sancta Camisa, which, legend has it, the Virgin Mary wore at the birth of Jesus.

He was turning the title of his novel over in his mind. That summer when the owner of auto repair shop bemoaned his young worker's failure to finish Miss Stein's car on time, calling his generation "lost," it struck a chord with her. "'That's what you are,' Miss Stein said. 'All of you young people who served in the war. You are a lost generation.'"[26] Her summation of the spirit of the age—its postwar youth going, café to café, having a grand time, with no real purpose in life—appealed to Hemingway as a possible title, along with others he scribbled down on the back page of his *cahiers*. Then, he happened upon the Book of Ecclesiastes and the phrase "The sun also rises," in a passage referring to "the seemingly meaningless coming and going of the sun, the tides and the winds." That was it. Back in Paris, he had to deal with Duff Twysden's plea for money. Whether or not he eased her financial burden, he had been keeping company with her and she was top of mind, as he scribbled away in his *cahiers* his sketch of Brett Ashley, a composite of Duff Twysden and other women he was meeting, including Pauline: "We can't do it. You can't hurt people. It's what we believe in in place of God."[27]

Meanwhile Scott helped engineer a change of publishers for Hemingway to the far more prestigious and supportive Charles Scribner's Sons. Scott knew that, after Boni and Liveright published *In Our Time* in September 1925, if they passed on his next manuscript, Hemingway was free to sign with Scribner's. The critics were now comparing Hemingway to Anderson, one of their prize authors. Striking a blow for independence, he wrote a biting satire, *The Torrents of Spring*, and, as predicted, they rejected it and he bolted. Hadley thought it was ghastly, considering it ill-advised to trash his mentor. But Pauline thought it was funny and encouraged Ernest to take it to Scribners, which helped solidify the Scribner's deal, while driving a wedge, if ever so small, between Hadley and Ernest.

It is understandable why Scribners wanted him. Hemingway wrote in a way that made his readers feel just as deeply as he did. He had honed and refined his stories for five years initially getting published in avant-garde coterie venues like *Little Review* (founded by a *Dial* exile), *transatlantic review* and *This Quarter*, before his big debut, *In Our Time*, showcasing the whole collection and its crisp, declarative sentences that breathed life into the tired short story genre. Critics and readers alike soaked up "The Doctor and the Doctor's Wife," thematically linked to "Indian Camp," as an older Nick confronts parental tension, choosing father over mother; "The End of Something," about Nick's breakup with his girlfriend; "The Three-Day Blow" where Nick and his friend, Bill, opine about life while getting drunk; followed by Nick hitting the rails in "The Batter" and meeting a prizefighter in this literary tour de force; and "A Very Short Story," mirroring his World War I romance; teeing up "Soldier's Home," set in Oklahoma, imaging Hem's worlds-colliding homecoming; then "The Revolutionist," an unnamed crusader with an unnamed cause, set in Italy; followed by a trio of unhappy marriage stories, "Mr. and Mrs. Elliot," "Cat in the Rain," and "Out of Season," contrasting with the Parisian *in our time* featuring *just one* unhappy marriage; followed by "Cross Country Snow" about happy skiing in Switzerland with friends; and "My Old Man" about the seamy side of horse-racing in Italy and Paris; and the grand finale, the two-part "Big Two-Hearted River," a celebration of trout fishing Hemingway had learned from his father, whose shadow looms large in this story.[28]

Yet the monomania that was Hemingway's strength, enabling him to write with such discipline and skill, was also his weakness, impelling him to toss friends and lovers aside with callous alacrity and frightening regularity, notably Scott, who did not always have the discipline of Hemingway; though when he focused, his was "an exacting rigid discipline," wrote Callaghan.[29] Yet so much pulled him away from his writing, especially the care of Zelda as she descended into madness. Hemingway would begin distancing himself as Scott's drinking inexorably interfered with his writing, and Zelda became more erratic—"crazy," Hemingway said. The "utilitarianism" bred into him as a child, one of the most powerful and persuasive approaches to normative ethics in the history of philosophy[30] and a hallmark of Protestantism, was surely at work here, whereby, as its founders, Jeremy Bentham and John Stuart Mill believed, good and pleasure are indistinguishable. Which may explain why Hemingway was attracted to the idea of "saintliness"—sanctity. He knew he was flawed—seeking his own pleasure as a good in itself—and needed grace to overcome these objectively cruel habits. But all too often, his subjective drive to succeed, along with other natural drives, took precedence over other objective good. Yes, he needed grace to overcome.

Arriving for another Christmas holiday in Schruns on December 12, Hemingway picked up his newly christened novel and began writing again. This time the family was joined by Pauline. As Ernest wrote and edited, he was so absorbed by his work that he paid little attention to Hadley. Pauline, though, was giving both Hemingway and his writing her careful, nurturing eye, assuming the role she would play for nearly fifteen years. Hem, without realizing it, was succumbing to her charms, while pivoting to reembrace Catholicism, without the constraint of a Protestant wife who did not approve. While finishing *The Sun Also Rises*, which is drenched in Catholicism, he wrote Ernest Walsh on January 2, 1926, from Schruns:

> If I am anything I am a Catholic. Had extreme unction administered to me as such in July 1918 and recovered. So guess I'm a super-Catholic . . . It is most certainly the most comfortable religion for anyone soldiering. Am not what is called a "good" Catholic. Think there is a lot of nonsense about the church . . . But cannot imagine taking any other religions at all seriously.[31]

On February 9, he left for New York to square away his publisher, as his planned week in Manhattan stretched out to three and once back in Paris, early March, rather than going straight to Schruns, he lingered for a day, grabbing lunch with Scott and Zelda, to catch up and thank him for helping him land Scribners as his new publishing house. The Fitzgeralds had kept up a frenetic pace since April—including London's social season in the spring, Côte d'Azur in the summer, Paris at Christmas, then the Western Pyrenees for Zelda's health. Now, repeating the cycle, they were bound once again for Juan-les Pins on the French Riviera and Scott urged Hemingway to join them, and, though preoccupied with finishing his novel, he was intrigued.

First, though he had a passionate reunion with Pauline, skipping the first three trains back to Schruns. It all felt so right, then came "black remorse" and "hatred of sin and no contrition."[32] "If you deceive and lie with one person against another you will eventually do it again," he wrote in an early draft of his Paris memoir, opting to strike the text since the coming breakup was more complicated than that. Yet, unquestionably, he was flawed and weak and needed to try and amend his ways with the help of grace—the competing dynamics perfectly reflected in *The Sun Also Rises*, serving up an oasis of faith in a desert of decadence. His marriage was crumbling even as his Catholic faith was rekindling. As Ralph Withington Church wrote in an unpublished memoir, Hemingway spoke of this, his first novel, as "a pilgrimage to Pamplona."[33]

From Paris to Pamplona, he weaves in rich spirituality. One night before leaving, Jake reflects how Brett (Lady Duff) "only wanted what she couldn't have" and that "The Catholic Church had an awfully good way of handling all of that. Good advice anyway . . . Try and take it sometime. Try and take it."[34] En route to Bayonne they run into a group of Dayton, Ohio, pilgrims, making their way from Rome to Biarritz, one talking about "the power of the Catholic Church."[35]

In Bayonne, when Jake, accompanied by Robert Cohn, sees the cathedral, he says, "It seemed like a nice cathedral, nice and dim, like Spanish cathedrals."[36] Then, as they approach Pamplona he glimpses "the great brown cathedral."[37] Once in Pamplona, "At the end of the street," down from the hotel and restaurant they gathered at, Jake says, "I saw the cathedral and walked up toward it." Inside, he says: "I was kneeling with my forehead on the wood in front of me, and was thinking of myself as praying. I was a little ashamed, and regretted I was such a rotten Catholic . . . and (that) . . . it was a grand religion, and I only wished I felt religious and maybe I would the next time."[38]

Traveling to Burguete to go fishing before the start of the fiesta, "away off on the shoulder of the first dark mountain was the gray metal-sheathed roof of the monastery of Roncesvalles." In their room, Jake and his friends discover "a big, framed steal engraving of Nuestra Senora de Roncesvalles."[39] In Burguette, they talk of God and our transitory earthly sojourn and Holy Cross, Fordham and Loyola. Asking Jake if he's "really a Catholic," he says, "Technically," and when asked what that means, replies, "I don't know."[40] Oh, what

Hemingway could have become in the hands of that great saint from Aragon, Josemaría Escrivá de Balaguer y Albás, a Spanish Roman Catholic priest, then working with the poor of Madrid, known as the "saint of ordinary work" and "one of the people in the Church's history who had received the most charisms and had corresponded to God's gifts with the greatest generosity."[41]

Then, the telegram from Brett and Mike—they are finally arriving! It's onward to the Fiesta de San Fermín and the Corrida, as the bulls gore the steers. Afterward, at the café, the boyfriend of the love interest, Brett, verbally gores Cohn. No mention of cathedrals or monasteries in this scene, albeit Jake does reflect on morality vs. immorality.[42] And he goes "to church a couple of times, once with Brett," who wants "to hear me go to confession."[43]

One day during the seven-day fiesta there's a big religious procession with the "smell of incense" and ceremonies inside the chapel attended by dignitaries.[44] Then, page after page, it's a spiritual desert. Now, as Jake observes, "Everybody behaves badly," if given "the proper chance." In real life, at a café in Pamplona during this 1925 Fiesta, on which the novel is based, Hemingway had called Loeb "a lousy bastard" and the two almost came to blows.

Then, once again, we glimpse the spiritual as Jake and Brett are walking, and "(b)ehind were the trees and the shadow of the cathedral, and the town silhouetted against the moon."[45] Arriving at the Chapel of San Fermín, as the festival winds down, they "go through the heavy leather door that moved very lightly. It was dark inside. Many people were praying." But Brett wants to leave and, outside, says, "Don't know why I get so nervy in church . . . Never does me any good." As she heads off, Brett expresses concern over her new love interest, the prize bullfighter Pedro Romero, and weather conditions. "You might pray" that the wind dies down, says Jake. "Never does me any good," she says. Asking if he prayed, he says, "Oh, yes . . . I'm pretty religious." "Oh rot, said Brett. "Don't go proselytizing today."[46]

Near the end, Jake tells Brett, "Some people have God . . . Quite a lot."[47] Hemingway, for one. Though, he would insist in a conversation with Loeb, who wanted to know "why he portrayed Cohn as a wimp," that he was not Barnes and therefore all that "rot" was not Hemingway talking. As to why Hemingway was upset with Loeb over his affair with Duff Twysden in San Sebastian, en route to Pamplona, Loeb surmised that "I'd outraged his puritanism . . . He'd been brought up in Oak Park and had a do-gooder uncle and a rather puritanical family."[48]

Hemingway, though, had moved beyond Protestantism. He was fascinated with prevenient grace which, in Catholic theology, precedes redemption and conversion, and asked Withington Church, an American doctoral student of philosophy at Oxford, as they talked at length over drinks at

Lipp's, if such grace could be given for sports. When he discovered the answer was yes, Hemingway was ecstatic. "Sport as redemptive ritual," writes Stoneback, "is central to Hemingway's life and work." As Withington Church wrote in his memoir, what came through crystal clear was "his conviction that Sport, and bull-fighting in particular, afforded a major way to the redemption of man."[49]

Withington Church, author of *The Essence of Catholicism* (1924), would go on to write *A Study in the Philosophy of Malebranche*, published in 1931, expounding on "the nature of grace." Hemingway was certainly getting much grace for conversion and he needed it. "I wished I had died before I had loved anyone but her," he wrote years later of the moment he saw Hadley and Bumby as he arrived back in Schruns that March.[50]

Soon Gerald and Sara Murphy, joined by John Dos Passos, would arrive, learning from the master how to ski, while taking the measure of Hadley and finding her wanting. They left mid-March and, by month's end, Hemingway finally resumed work on the final chapters of *The Sun Also Rises*. While living monogamously with his wife and feeling good about it, he finished the novel, with its taut and vivid prose and hidden gems of spirituality, mirroring what was going on in his own life:

"We crossed to the left bank of the Seine and stopped on the bridge and looked down the river at Notre Dame."[51] Again and again in his writing, he was going to Mary, the mediatrix of all grace, for help. He needed her help.

Back in Paris, he was hopelessly confused as to what he should do about his unresolved feelings: He had a full-blown romance going on with his new lover and future wife, the very sophisticated Pauline, in the presence of his current wife, who did not have Pauline's fashion sense or way with words. It was all very awkward. When Pauline and Ginny took Hadley to the French Loire Valley in early May, emotions were laid bare. When Hadley heard Ginny comment that Ernest and Pauline "were very fond of each other," it was a dagger to her heart.[52]

Hadley confronted Ernest and he became incensed that she would even bring up the subject, thinking they could just go on as usual. After all, Pound and Ford had mistresses. Why couldn't he? Almost immediately, Ernest pivoted emotionally and spiritually, writing to his father on May 23 from Madrid—where he had traveled, ten days earlier, on the ninth anniversary of Our Lady of Fatima's first apparition. He was there for bullfighting and writing and wanted his father to know that he was taking the family to Piggott where Pauline Pfeiffer lived and where he could write undisturbed. He ended his letter by writing, "Having been at mass this morning, I am now at the bullfight this afternoon. Wish you were along."[53]

So, after receiving sacramental grace in the morning he was receiving actual, or prevenient, grace in the afternoon.

His dyed-in-the-wool Congregational father must have wondered what had gotten into his son. "The Eucharist that Saves the World," no doubt, the theme of the First Eucharistic Congress in 1881 in Lille, France—the upcoming one taking place in Chicago about which Pauline had written in response to his query. She thought the Congress concerned "progress," and "'Whither are we drifting,' and shifts the sail to the leeward."[54] Her own sail needed to be shifted leeward as she became entangled with Ernest, a married man with a child. But he had drifted from Catholicism, which he had embraced seven years earlier, and was now reembracing it, and she was hooked.

That May, at the invitation of the Murphys, the Hemingways ended up joining the Fitzgeralds, after all, at Villa America, the Murphy's summer paradise on the French Riviera in Cap Antibes, where great artists and social doyennes luxuriated. When the Murphys visited their friend Cole Porter at his home on the Côte d'Azur, they fell in love and, by 1925, had bought and transformed a fourteen-bedroom estate with Art Deco splendor, decorating it in black and white, with glass mirror accents, a roof to sunbathe on, and a lawn adorned with palm trees and other flora sloping down to the Mediterranean Sea. Hadley and Bumby had arrived on May 16, and, while Hemingway was at San Isidro for bullfighting and writing, his family was suffering a quarantine because Bumby had whooping cough. Each night, the exquisitely attired guests would come over to shabbily shod Hadley, bringing drinks and food. Pauline arrived on May 26, just before Ernest, and lived with the Hemingways blissfully unbothered by Bumby's contagion and by the fact that she was impinging on Ernest and Hadley's marriage.

The night of May 28, Hemingway made his grand entrance at Villa America where the Murphys were hosting the perfect party to celebrate the release of *Torrents of Spring* that day. Dom Perignon champagne and caviar was jetted in from the Caspian Sea and their signature simple hors d'oeuvres were lavished on the guests, as Gerald, an Irish Catholic Bostonian, set everyone at ease with his charm and bonhomie, and Sara, who grew up in Manhattan and on a 600-acre Hamptons estate, wowed in her elegantly sophisticated flowing summer dress.

Meanwhile, everyone was drawn to gorgeous Hemingway, tanned from a month's bullfighting in Spain, as both Hadley and Pauline fawned over him. Sara, too, found him magnetic, leaving Scott in the dust. He anaesthetized his hurt feelings by drinking before, during and after the party, greeting guests by saying, "I'm Scott Fitzgerald and I'm an alcoholic."[55] No matter that he had written the great American novel and made Hemingway's success possible. He would soon critique the final typescript of *The Sun Also Rises*, helping transform it into a masterpiece by suggesting major cuts to the first three chapters, which Hemingway merely lopped off in their entirety. Now, perplexingly he was on the outs with a suddenness that stunned him. What gave? Culturally Catholic Scott was not schooled in the utilitarian arts of picking up and dropping off friends and lovers with abandon. Of course, Zelda's penchant for stripteases and yanking Scott away from the literary muse out of jealousy by getting him drunk did not help.

Still, what gave?

Hadley was probably asking herself the same thing after her "friend," Pauline, made herself a permanent fixture in their home as she and Hemingway fell in love right under her unsuspecting nose. Hadley's good-natured, trusting personality came with a certain naïveté. For, if you were married to someone like Hemingway, so handsome and virile, you would keep a rich, young lovely like Pauline away—to protect him and the marriage, and your future with the man you loved, and that, together, you had brought into the world. Pauline was younger and wealthier than Hadley, whose trust fund had shrunk in 1924, after George Breaker embezzled and whittled it down by two-thirds at the very moment Hemingway had ditched journalism for real writing—necessitating his full-court press to a Mr. Cummings in February, a Mr. White in March, the Breakers, Helen and George, in August, and two days later, just to George to make sure he knew exactly where to deposit the funds—*that he had swindled.* Six months later rich, savvy and Catholic Pauline entered the scene, pursuing Ernest with dizzying speed, without scruples.

It came as no surprise to Sunny, who upon telling Pauline that she was in love with a married man, received this advice. "'(G)o ahead and get him.' She had found who she wanted, she said, and had gotten him and was glad she had."[56] Pauline's attitude is so at variance with her Catholic faith that it is hard to fathom how she reconciled her actions with the tenets of her faith. You cannot receive the sacraments if you are in the state of mortal sin. Dating and having sexual relations with a married man is most certainly a mortal sin—*if* you have full knowledge. Evidently, her knowledge was skewed by her belief that Hemingway's marriage to Hadley was built on a flawed foundation and that, given the ironically named "Pauline privilege" from St. Paul's guidance in his First Epistle to the Corinthians, his marriage outside of the church gave his relationship with her an opening—enabling him to wipe the slate clean and marry her. Hadley had never been baptized, Hemingway told Callaghan, so "it was easy to get an annulment."[57]

Pauline had prayed to St. Joseph every night for a "good, kind, attractive Catholic husband."[58] She knew Hemingway's marriage was troubled and that he thirsted for the Catholic faith. He had begun attending mass again shortly after meeting her, and receiving communion and the other sacraments,[59] which his May 23 letter to his father is testament to.

Then, too, Hemingway's rising star and Pauline's own writing and editorial talent made them a dynamic literary duo. The six thousand dollars she received annually from her family trust was helpful, too, to say nothing of Uncle Gus' perks, as Hemingway worked to establish himself as a writer of distinction. Also, not to be underestimated, the sexual attraction was sizzling hot. Early on in their relationship, Pauline rationalized sex outside of marriage by saying how much in love she was with Hemingway, who just needed a good confession as, of course, she did, too.

Katy Smith thought Hadley had "failed Ernest."[60] On August 12, some five years after they had consummated their union at the Virginia Hotel, they traveled back from Antibes to Paris and began living separate lives, in separate abodes. A week later, Ernest invited Hadley out for drinks and they argued violently in the taxi cab afterwards. "Such is alcohol," Hadley wrote Ernest early the next morning, noting she had could not even remember the source of their "bitterness," while acknowledging his sweetness and nobility.[61] By early September, still living in a hotel, she confronted reality. It was time for "a clean break."[62] By mid-September, she moved to a flat not far from Gertrude, as, bit by bit, Ernest, walking through the neighborhood, wheeled her the items she requested including her fine furniture and china. The Murphys urged Hemingway to stay strong, also believing Hadley had let her husband down, for instance, by virtue of his bearing an outsized share of the household duties. But Hadley still had not made the emotional break and, as she pondered their lives apart, was unsure if he was truly in love given how emotionally "weak"[63] he could be when someone loved him, whether or not the feeling was mutual. So, she gave them 100 days to stay apart and if they were still in love, she would grant the divorce.

Ernest and Pauline considered this a test that would only make their love stronger but, to resist temptation, they would need to be an ocean apart. On September 23, the eve of Pauline's transatlantic crossing aboard the *Pennland*, they spent the night at the Hôtel Le Meurice in Boulogne. Over a dinner of sole, partridge and brandy, they developed a code to communicate via cable: "Started" signaled Hadley had agreed to the divorce. It was a painful separation. Hem lived in Gerald Murphy's studio and, suffering pangs of guilt over leaving Hadley and Bumby, poured it all into "The Killers," which *Scribner's Magazine* accepted in late September for publication, the first of Hemingway's stories to appear in their flagship magazine, followed later that fall by the poignant story, "In Another Country," in which a seasoned Italian major, having just lost his young wife to pneumonia, schools a young American that if you never want to lose a loved one, *do not marry*. He was afraid of losing Pauline whose devout Catholic mother disapproved vehemently of her daughter's adultery, and wrote Pauline of his early morning enveloping despair, rescued by his writing. But when not writing, he continued to obsess. If the matter was not resolved by Christmas, he wrote, he would kill himself—a twofer, which would prevent Pauline from sinning and relieve Hadley of the need to file for divorce.

Hadley and Ernest would still get together and one night in early October, Hadley let her emotion spill over. "This affair of yours had almost killed my love of Umpster," she told her estranged husband. Later, she wrote Ernest of her "terrible fear" that her outburst would be taken "literally" and she hoped he would tell Pauline how much she loved their child. Furthermore she was "quite terrified" once home, remembering how Ernest had told her Pauline could find ecclesial exoneration given Hadley's expressed views on marriage.[64] As if to reassure Hadley, when *The Sun Also Rises* was published on October 22 in New York, and five days later in Paris, he dedicated it to Hadley and their young son, giving them all the proceeds.

On October 11, on the eve of publication, Hemingway traveled to Zaragoza with Archie MacLeish, with whom, along with Ada, he was spending considerable time during this difficult period. While in Zaragoza Archie realized that Hem "could not bear to be left alone. Even at night, someone had to be within reach, or he'd be overcome by his 'horrors.'" (Hem's "rivalrous nature," preventing him from praising other prose writers, also became apparent to Archie during their trip.)[65] On October 12, the Feast of Our Lady of Pilar, they arrived "on the north bank of the Ebro River where they joined the throng crossing the ancient stone bridge into the whitewashed town of Zaragoza" where off to the right, coming into view, was "the massive Nuestra Senora de Pilar . . . its domes brightly tiled in yellow and purple, white and green."[66]

They were celebrating the great Feast of Our Lady of Pilar, commemorating Our Lady's first apparition when she consoled a discouraged St. James. It was the start of the bullfighting that week in Zaragoza and "Pilar" was his code name for Pauline. So many layers of meaning. No doubt Hemingway was praying "with almost tribal faith" that all would be well.

Prayers answered, things calmed down as Hadley came to realize that Ernest and Pauline truly loved each other, and, while visiting Chartres in early November with Winifred Mower, she decided, a month shy of the 100 days, to grant the divorce, much to Hemingway's relief and gratitude. Winifred was in a marriage of convenience with Paul Mowrer, who soon joined them and counseled Hadley, letting her know how fond he was of her, cushioning the blow of the divorce, which, initially, upset Hadley greatly, understandably so, leading her, impetuously, to burn all of Hemingway's love letters. In later years, though, she had the light and grace to see that Pauline was, in fact, a good mate for Hemingway. At the time, he was handsome and young, "full of that machismo and vim, vigor, for which he was known," said John Hemingway (a.k.a. "Bumby," later "Jack"), whereas Hadley had become "matronly,"[67] the eight-year age difference magnified as the months rolled by.

Meanwhile Hemingway had to deal with his family's reaction to his hit novel. "Surely you have other words in your vocabulary besides 'damn' and 'bitch,'" his mother wrote from faraway Oak Park.[68] But Hemingway was a world apart, starting a new chapter in his life, and their criticisms had perhaps less sting. On December 30, Pauline set sail for Europe aboard the *Cleveland*, arriving in Cherbourg ten days later, where Ernest met her, ecstatic to see a now less gaunt Pauline, while a now trimmer Ernest sporting a new moustache, greeted her. After hugging and kissing, they hightailed it to Gstaad to continue the ski vacation Ernest had begun with Archie and Ada joined by Pauline's sister Ginny.

Ada thought Hemingway had concocted the story that he was baptized Catholic on the battlefield just so he could be free in the eyes of the Church to end his union with Hadley and marry Pauline. But this is one story Hemingway did not make up. As Guy Hickok, head of the *Brooklyn Eagle*'s Paris bureau, relates, on March 20, 1927, Hemingway visited Don Giuseppe Bianchi, the priest who anointed him in Italy and nurtured his faith. Hickok drove Hemingway in his well-traveled Ford to Italy for a tour of the country, including Pisa and Florence, and it is near Rapallo that he met briefly with Don Giuseppe, stirring Hemingway's rekindled faith. Outside Spezia, when Hemingway saw a roadside shrine, he asked Guy to stop and he "knelt and prayed for what seemed a long time, returning to the car with tears on his cheeks."[69] Meantime, Pauline impatiently awaited Hem's return from his "Italian tour for the promotion of masculine society," as she described it. More than male bonding, Hem was making the psychological break from Hadley as he prepared to embark on a new life with Pauline. It was an emotional hurdle not only for himself but also for the family he was leaving and he was seeking spiritual strength and solace at this critical juncture.

A "canonical inquest" was conducted at the Archbishopric of Paris on April 25, 1927. As Stoneback writes, "although none of Hemingway's biographers seem to be aware" of this significant development, "(a)cccording to Acte no. 146 in the Registre des Actes de Mariage de la Paroisse Saint-Honore d'Eylau (dated May 10, 1927), at that canonical inquest 'toutes dispenses' were granted, all was reconciled, and Hemingway was a certified Catholic in good standing."

As he wrote to Father Vincent C. Donovan, a Dominican from Chicago, he had been a practicing Catholic for years but "fell away very badly," not receiving communion for almost a decade. But the last two years, he had definitively gotten his spiritual "house in order," attending mass regularly.[70] As for Fr. Donovan's hope, after learning of Hemingway's conversion, that he become a champion of the faith, he wrote that he had "more faith than intelligence" and was "a dumb Catholic" and not a very good example albeit he was trying to live a good life and be a good writer, noting the former was easier than the latter. Fr. Donovan had written to thank Hemingway for saving his friend Don Stewart's life in Pamplona in 1924.

One night when he was sauced, Hemingway told McAlmon, dining with Hadley at a bistro, that their nuptials had been invalid because they had wed outside the church.[71] While true, the marriage could have been straightened out, though admittedly Hadley had no taste for that, preferring the laxer Episcopalian Church, especially on matters of sexual morality. Hadley became Paul Mowrer's mistress in early 1927, while he was still married to Winifred, finally marrying him six years later in 1933. In short, the "disparity of cult" was *real*. But what was also true is that, as with Hadley, Ernest's marriage to Pauline became a steeper climb given that they, too, had indulged before marriage—though its survival was not impossible as long as they had that reservoir of grace to strengthen them in the face of marriage's inevitable vicissitudes.

Soon after the dispensation was granted, they finally wed, coincidentally, on the twenty-second anniversary of "Abba's" death, May 10, 1927, at Saint-Honoré d'Eylau at 9 Place Victor-Hugo in the 16th Arrondissement. Afterward the MacLeishes hosted a small lunch for the newlyweds, having skipped the wedding given their displeasure over Hemingway's remarriage, not believing it was rooted in a true religious conversion. Yet Ada confirmed for Baker in March 1965 that, indeed, Don Bianchi had baptized him after his wounding in Italy, so she knew of and accepted, perhaps only in time, Hemingway's fervent Catholicism.[72]

The next day, the couple headed to Le Grau-du-Roi in the south of France for their honeymoon, arriving by rail to the preserved crusader walled city, Aigues-Mortes, bicycles in tow, where they were spirited away by chauffer to the secluded Rhone River Delta for good loving and fishing, capped off, twelve days later, a twenty-five-mile bicycle ride away, by the festival of Saintes-Maries-de-la-Mer, honoring the three saints named Mary—Mary Magdalene, Mary Salome, and Mary of Clopas—believed to be the first witnesses to Christ's empty tomb after his resurrection from the dead. They arrived by boat to the village, initially named Notre-Dame-de-Ratis (Our

Lady of the Boat, i.e., *Râ*), later changed to Notre-Dame-de-la-Mer (Our Lady of the Sea). Mary's shadow loomed larger than ever as the Mediatrix of all grace infused their marriage with plenty of it, which they soaked up all through the month of May, before returning to Paris just after Memorial Day.

No sooner had they arrived back to their new apartment at 6 rue Férou, and began to catch their breath and enjoy their new home, complete with a writing hideaway for Hem, than they were off to Spain for the bullfights— Valencia, Madrid, La Coruña, and Bilbao all beckoning, along with Santiago de Compostela, where they spent two weeks in what Hemingway had called "the loveliest town in Spain"—replete with good food and wine and trout fishing in a nearby town, and the gorgeous Cathedral of Santiago de Compostela, right near their lodgings, the cathedral bells' tintinnabulation waking them each morning focusing their thoughts on the Divine, soon to be nourished at daily mass. Arriving at the cathedral, Hem enjoyed looking up at the top of the nave observing the hawks hunting in the shadows, and was delighted one day when a peasant woman came up to him asking "where to eat the body of Jesus."[73]

Their marriage was being set on a good spiritual foundation. Then, too, Hemingway was on a personal pilgrimage of sorts as he listened to his heart and soul. Arriving in Santiago de Compostela just after the celebration of the Feast of St. James on July 25, the dust settling on all the pageantry, he carefully reviewed the final galleys of his second collection of short stories, sending them back to Max Perkins on August 17. Then he turned his attention to the new novel he was writing—about a father and son and their relationship, the kind of relationship he wished he had with his father, but never did past childhood because of his father's nervous condition, because his parents had just the shell of marriage, because his mother was far more focused on her developing her talents than in tending to her husband's needs, Hem's father, who had retreated into his own world. Hemingway was trying to bring him alive in his novel, but was having difficulty.

So, he responded to his letters and pondered one from his father, who wrote expressing deep upset over what Sunny had told him, that his son had split from his wife and remarried, a sin he thought merited eternal damnation. He finally wrote back in a letter dated September 14 and confirmed for his father, three months after the fact, that he and Pauline had wed, noting he would have returned to Hadley even after the divorce, finally granted in April, had she wanted it. His love and care for Hadley and Bumby would be unwavering, he wrote, just as for Pauline who he was now married to. "I have now responsibility toward three people instead of one."[74] He expressed the hope that his parents would one day be "proud" of his writing, which, he wrote, "is more important to me than anything in the world except the happiness of three people." His pain upon receiving this parental cold shoulder was unfathomable, he wrote. His work was about to be showcased in this next collection of short stories, *Men Without Women*, on October 14, 1927. And while his parents shrugged, the *Chicago Tribune* in its Christmas review gave a thumbs-up to his fresh, new, un–O. Henry style, in which he writes "with a very masculine virility . . . the facts of outward happenings."[75]

In the continuing subplot of his life, the first nine months of his marriage to Pauline, while chipping away on his next novel that was going nowhere fast, Hem endured an anthrax infection, influenza, a bad toothache, hemorrhoids, ski injuries, and a corneal abrasion sustained when Bumby playfully poked his right eye. But that was just the warmup.

In the wee hours of March 5, 1928, just after arriving home from a night out drinking with Archie, Hem stepped inside the bathroom and, mistaking the skylight chain for the toilet chain, pulled down the skylight, its jagged glass edge crashing down on him. It seems Scott had messed with the whole configuration one night when *he* was drinking, and it was never fixed. As Sunny writes, on one of her visits, by invitation, "to the apartment at Numero 6, rue Férou . . . They showed me the skylight chain that *F. Scott Fitzgerald* [emphasis added] had pulled, mistaking it for the plumbing chain, causing Ernie to get his forehead cut badly by the broken glass."[76] When Ernest received a cable of concern for his "good health" from Max Perkins on March 17, he wrote back about the skylight accident noting "a friend" had pulled that cord instead of the toilet chain which cracked the skylight glass so when he went into the bathroom at 2 a.m., seeing it dangling, he tried to hook it up, and, he wrote, the "whole thing fell." They tried to staunch the bleeding with gobs of toilet paper and a kitchen towel, which served as a tourniquet, and kindling wood. The third time was the charm after which they were able get him to the American Hospital at Neuilly, where they stitched up the arteries, including nine stiches in all, three underneath, six "to close it. No after effects but a damned nuisance."[77]

The Fitzgeralds set sail for Paris aboard the steamship *Paris* on April 20, at midnight, blissfully unaware of the trouble Scott had caused his friend, while leaving behind Wilmington where they had lived unhappily on the west bank of the Delaware River in "Ellerslie," a grand mansion that close Princeton friend, John Biggs, had found. They moved right around the corner from the Hemingways, at 58 rue Vaugirard, on the corner of Luxembourg Gardens, and Scott made sure his seven-year-old daughter, Scottie, attended mass at The Church of Saint-Sulpice, second largest church in Paris, where the Hemingways also attended mass.[78] It was on the opposite end of their narrow street, which connected the two landmarks, spiritual and cultural. Scott, for his part, while always keenly "aware he was living in the shadow of the (church)," could not bring himself to set foot inside. "Don't ask me about it. It's personal," he told Callaghan. "The Irish-Catholic background and all that."[79]

As they built this solid spiritual foundation, they prepared to leave behind the Paris of the twenties, that unique and frenzied time when wealth and fame were imbued with seemingly eternal values. Scott and Zelda's prank at Cap Antibes, stealing all the guests' shoes and dunking them in water because they wanted the party to "last forever,"[80] epitomizes this illusive grasp for unending happiness through transitory joys. When, in fact, true happiness is only found through spiritual wealth: "treasures in heaven where neither moth nor rust destroys and where thieves cannot break in and steal." (Matthew 6:19–24). Heaven that no man or woman—nothing—can ever take away.

No, eternal happiness was not to be found on earth—not even in Paris— as Scott wrote about so poignantly not long before meeting Hemingway:

Gatsby believed in the green light, the orgastic future that year by year recedes before us. It eluded us then, but that's no matter—tomorrow we will run faster, stretch out our arms farther . . . And, one fine morning——
So we beat on, boats against the current, borne back ceaselessly into the past.[81]

Hemingway looked in dismay at his new neighbor and old friend, the celebrated author of *The Great Gatsby*, who risked ending up like Gatsby, as he now struggled to keep the flame from going out on his next novel, while his jealous wife, now twenty-eight, was determined to make her mark as a ballerina under the tutelage of Lubov Yegorova.

"It worked out beautifully didn't it," Scott wrote Zelda after she entered the Clinique. "But it was a more irritable Ernest, apprehensively telling me his whereabouts lest I come in on them tight and endanger his lease."[82]

In 1926/27, after he turned thirty, Scott had begun drinking himself to death, with no letup in sight—his drunken carelessness occasioning many early morning episodes outside the Hemingways' home, for example, peeing on the steps and waking the neighbors, and indirectly causing his friend the horrific skylight injury. Yet, in the marvelous way Providence works, this accident had a salutary effect on Hemingway's writing. Whereas he had reached an impasse on his father-son novel; after the unfixed skylight, with its jagged broken glass, came crashing down and gashed his forehead, causing him to bleed profusely, he gained clarity, as his thoughts rushed back to that

Hemingway, shortly before leaving Paris, 1928. Photo by Helen Breaker. *Source:* In the public domain. Scribner Archives.

life-changing night he was mortally wounded along the Piave. As he would tell the *New Yorker*'s Lillian Ross years later, "I can remember feeling so awful about the first war that I couldn't write about it for ten years. The wound combat makes in you, as a writer, is a slow-healing one."[83] Though, he said, he had written three short stories that warmed up to the topic—also including "A Way You'll Never Be." The half-written, half-baked war novel that Hadley lost was coming back into focus. "When the pain dulled to the opiate's control, he knew exactly what he should be writing. The story had been there all along, ever since the manuscripts had disappeared in the Gare de Lyon," wrote Michael Reynolds. "The story was the war, the wound, the woman."[84]

And so it was, that, just as F. Scott Fitzgerald had spurred Hemingway's first novel, *The Sun Also Rises*, he catalyzed Hemingway's second novel, *A Farewell to Arms*.

The rough draft Hadley had encouraged her new beaux, then fiancé, to write while he was living in Chicago was molded from stories his Italian army veteran friend Nick had told him and from his own limited war experience, brought to life by "Nick Adams."

Now that he was settling down to marriage with Pauline, he was ready to take another crack at the novel, and, this time, to relive his injury, blow by blow.

6

⨯⨯⨯

Key West, Restless Heart

"A Farewell to Arms"

On St. Patrick's Day, 1928, Ernest and a very pregnant Pauline, left the City of Light, its magic and mystery, and the spirit of the "lost generation" Hemingway had indelibly captured in *The Sun Also Rises*. At the suggestion of John Dos Passos, they were Key West bound, embarking from Marseilles aboard *The Orita*. After plying the seas to Havana, they traveled by ferry to the most remote Florida Key where they settled temporarily in a downtown apartment as they awaited Uncle Gus' wedding gift—a brand-new yellow Model A Ford Roadster, delayed in Miami on a production line.

RICH CATHOLICISM

As they ventured around town, they discovered their new parish church was one of the Miami Archdiocese's oldest. Spanish Jesuits had briefly established a mission in the Upper Matecumbe Key in the late sixteenth century after Ponce de León claimed the land for the Spanish crown, but their work was stymied by English raiders and Shell Indians. Some 250 years later, President James Monroe authorized an anti-pirate squadron, which was established on December 22, 1822.[1] Hat tip to Matthew C. Perry, legendary, hard-drinking Naval officer, married to U.S. Senator John Slidell's sister Jane, who planted the U.S. flag on Key West after arriving on his schooner *Shark*, earlier that year, coincidentally on March 25, Feast of the Annunciation. With the naval base humming by 1823, Catholics were not far behind. A visiting Havana priest offered the first mass in city hall on October 10, 1846. By 1851, Bishop

Francis X. Gartland of Savannah had dispatched Fr. John F. Kirby to Key West, where he established "St. Mary Star of the Sea" parish, dedicating the first Catholic Church on Key West at the corner of Duval and Eaton on February 26, 1852. In 1901, the church, by now ensconced on Windsor Lane, burned down, and in its place, was built a beautiful non-wooden American Victorian Gothic church, with elements of early Renaissance Revival style, featuring a rusticated exterior and two steeples—ocean and gulf breezes wafting into the interior space through rounded arched doors (traditional gothic) topped by halfmoon lunette colored-glass windows with louvered shutters, the vault ceiling decorated with pressed metal, round-headed arches buttressing it. Gracing the architectural splendor was a gorgeous stained-glass window behind the altar depicting the church's patroness.[2] A grotto to Our Lady of Lourdes, dedicated on May 25, 1922, became the vortex of prayer as hurricanes and tropical storms loomed. Sisters of the Holy Names of Jesus and Mary ran the school for 100 years after which their chapel was transformed into one offering perpetual adoration to the Blessed Sacrament. Pope Benedict XVI elevated the church to a minor basilica on February 11, 2012, the Feast of Our Lady of Lourdes.

Ernest and Pauline had chosen just the right spot to nurture their Catholic faith and, on Easter Sunday, April 8, they attended mass at St. Mary's, soaking in all its history and spirituality. Two days later, on Easter Tuesday, quite by chance, Hemingway's parents—arriving from Havana that morning, due to embark for St. Petersburg that evening—ran into their son as he was fishing. It was a poignant father-son reunion after a four-year hiatus. Now gray-haired, Dr. Hemingway was carefully and quietly measuring his sugar lest his diabetes worsen, while sagging under the weight of tax debt given his devalued Florida investment. Grace, as usual, was all wrapped up in herself—now her painting. After absorbing her news, Hem picked up Pauline and they toured the island, joined by Uncle Willoughby, back from mission work in China.

Life in Key West was remote and slow and Pauline and Hem were not sure this was the place for them. Then they met Charles Thompson, wealthy scion of Key West, and his wife Lorine, and started to feel at home. While Pauline was anxious to head out to Piggott to prepare for the birth of her baby, Hem was never happier.

Key West, with its wonderful salt water and salt air, bathing Hem's lungs, his heart and soul, was working its magic, as he fished tarpon with Charles by day and drank at various watering holes by night, while polishing off the first one hundred pages of his war novel before noon. The fishing was so good that he soon realized he needed more than an 18-footer and an afternoon in the shoal waters of Key West, and, with memories of summers past at Lake Walloon knocking at his heart, he sent SOS telegrams and letters to "the boys"—Strater, Dos, Waldo Peirce, an American painter Hem befriended in Paris, and Bill Smith, who arrived first, on April 24—and soon they were enjoying themselves capitally, including way out in the Gulf on Dry Tortugas.

Hem continued his routine, devoting mornings to writing, enabling him to finish another one hundred pages of his novel, all the while Paul Pfeiffer awaited the arrival of his very pregnant daughter. But, his patience wearing thin, one day he simply showed up in Key West. On May 20, he put his daughter on the homeward-bound train as the last of "the boys" left and Paul and Ernest bonded, following Pauline by car five days later.

Paul Pfeiffer had pulled up stakes from his family's St. Louis–based Pfeiffer Chemical Co. in 1911, to find a better place to invest his considerable wealth and make a difference. That place was godforsaken Piggott, Arkansas, which possessed rich soil and humble, hard-working, yet culturally backward cotton farmers. So he bought up great swaths of land, under the auspices of the Piggott Land Company, and, in 1913, moved his family there, including Ginny and younger brother Karl, while Pauline stayed behind in St. Louis to finish boarding school at the Academy of the Visitation, coincidentally on Cabanne Avenue, Hadley's old neighborhood, where Pauline matriculated in 1901, graduating in 1913, then earning a degree at the Missouri School of Journalism in 1918. Paul, who also owned the cotton gin, the feed store, and the bank, paid 50 percent of the cost of infrastructure improvements and, with no Catholic church in Piggott, Mary built a chapel inside their home atop Crowley's Ridge on Cherry Street. Mary was a devoted wife and mother, solely focused on hearth and home, and, unlike Grace Hall Hemingway, was deferential to her husband, and very much a mother to Hem, filling a real void in his life.[3]

Even so, Hem found Piggott deathly dull as he tried to write while waiting expectantly for their new baby. And, while Paul was unphased by his son-in-law's celebrity, Mary loved Hemingway's twinkly eyes, dimpled charm, engaging mind and magnetic personality—to say nothing of his literary prowess. Finally, after two weeks, the boredom was broken when they packed up and headed out in their Ford for a taxing two-day drive to Kansas City, Missouri, some 400 miles northwest of Piggott, where Pauline and Hem stayed with Ernest's cousins, the Lowrys—Malcolm and Ruth White—on comfortable Indian Lane, what with its well-stocked liquor cabinet and nearby country club. Finally, a week later, Pauline's contractions began and she was admitted to Research Hospital. There, after eighteen hours of labor and a Caesarean section Hemingway begrudgingly approved, she gave birth on June 28 at 7:30 p.m., to a healthy nine-pound baby boy,

Patrick Miller Hemingway, his proud Papa announcing his arrival to family and friends in a telegram, noting both mother and baby were doing well.

As their back-to-back birthdays approached, Pauline was strong enough to take the train back to Piggott on July 20, where they shared their bundle of joy with the family and celebrated their birthdays.[4] All the while Ernest was giving birth, as well, to his novel and, so, on July 25, he steamed aboard the train back to Kansas City, where he picked up his Ford runabout and his pal Horney. Just one week after marking his twenty-ninth, the two were driving west to Wyoming, where Ernest could calm his mind—trout fishing in the Bighorn River, the best medicine of all—and finish his novel. His father had wanted him to come Windemere to write but Hem assured him, until the book was done, he would be as agreeable as a "bear with carbuncles."[5]

Driving 1,000 miles a day, on July 30, they finally wheeled into Eleanor Donnelley's Folly Ranch, 7,000 feet above sea level. To get there, said Horne, "We drove across a corner of Nebraska, up the Platte into Wyoming, and bumped over rocks and ruts in the Red Grade Road, climbing the Big Horn Mountains. As we snaked around hair-pin turns with steep drop-offs, I kept saying. 'Look out, Ernie!' He endured it patiently and finally said, 'Do me a favor, Horney, when you get out, just close the door.' I didn't peep after that."[6]

The dude ranch, though it had "a swell cook; Folly the collie; and some active trout ponds," said Horne, was also teaming with sixteen Bryn Mayr undergrads including his future wife, and Hem needed quiet. Biding his time, he wrote in the mornings and fished in the afternoons. One night, he told stories and, "with his hands doing most of the talking, our author gave us the low-down on Dorothy Parker's and Scott Fitzgerald's burning inspirations." After that, said Horne, he got distracted by a bullfight taking place in faraway Spain. "I think he was the matador and the bull." After Horne left, one day Hem rose early, and slipped away to Sheridan and its inn, clocking nine pages a day. Five days later he returned to Eleanor Donnelly's quieter Lower Ranch, where he upped his output to seventeen pages a day. But at night, feeling lonely, he imbibed a bit too much bootlegged whiskey, which brought his work to a grinding halt the next day.

Hem was longing for Spain, having skipped the Pamplona Fiesta, along with the Feria Valencia for the first time since 1923. As Baker writes, his memory conjured up "the white-painted restaurants along the beach, and the black pans of seafood paella, and the trips back to town for ice-cold pitchers of beer and good meat melons."[7]

Then, too, the memories of the Italian front came gushing in, and, by the time Pauline arrived on August 18, as he cruised to the finish line, he was about to write the climactic scene where Catherine Barkley dies in childbirth after a C-section, a detail he left out in his conversations with Pauline, who was just regaining full strength, sporting a scar. Patrick, she reported, was a chunky twelve pounds, which delighted Hem, who looked forward to a relaxing, romantic Wyoming respite with Pauline, in advance of which she had Hem's nearly 500-page draft novel, securely hidden away in Piggot, delivered to their vacation home via registered mail, insuring it for $4,000![8]

They cherished their visit with a French family, Charles and Alice Moncini, who made great wine, and served them delicious food on the "vine-shaded back porch" with a view of "yellow grainfields" and "distant brown mountains" that Ernest intently studied, sipping home-brewed beer, soon using this wonderful memory to paint a vivid story.

Hemingway finished the first draft of the novel by the end of August, after which he and Pauline set out to explore Wyoming, perhaps guided by the recently issued "Map of the History and Romance of Wyoming." Their first stop was Spear-O-Wigwam dude ranch, down the valley a piece, at the bottom of the Bighorns, near the Crow Indian Reservation. Then, it was on to Lincoln County just south of Yellowstone Park at the edge of Idaho's border, followed by a trip to Shell for a visit with Owen Wister, then sixty-eight, Hem's teen literary idol and close friend of Hem's boyhood hero, "TR." Wister wrote *The Virginian* (1902), and greatly admired Hemingway's writing. Needless to say, Hemingway forever cherished the visit. Then it was on to the awe-inspiring Grand Tetons and Snake River, where they gave fishing a try, before heading to a dude ranch in Moose, near Jackson Hole, then northeast back to Sheridan.

By September 23, they were back in Kansas City attending Sunday Mass, the pages of his war novel, writes Baker, numbering six hundred, exactly the number of fish he and Pauline had caught. Then, it was onward to Piggott, where Hemingway wrote "Wine of Wyoming," about a French bootlegging couple in Wyoming who opine about religion in America and its copious churches, most non-Catholic, and Catholics shunned, reflecting the reality Hemingway was now living as a Catholic in America. "En Amérique, il ne faut pas être catholique. (It's not good to be catholique. It's like the dry law.)," the wife says. At the same time, "It's better to be catholique if you are." Then, too, they are curious about "Schmidt," that is, Al Smith, and whether he was Catholic and, hearing he is, express doubt that he can win.[9]

Hemingway soon realized he needed a more suitable setting to make revisions on his novel, so, come fall, they headed back to Key West. That is, by way of Oak Park to visit his parents and siblings; and Chicago to gaze, awestruck, at the Winslow Homer paintings at the Art Institute; and, just before leaving, to gaze, equally awestruck, at the Cathedral of the Holy Name, where they attended mass on All Saints Day. Then, it was on to Conway, Massachusetts, for a reunion with the Archie MacLeishes; and finally, New York, where he took in the prize fights and visited Max Perkins to discuss, among other matters, the *Scribner's Magazine* offer of $10,000 to serialize the novel in their magazine, sight unseen.

Life was good. Albeit, Pauline's doctor had just told her she should avoid another pregnancy for three years. Three years??!! How would Hemingway remain faithful that long given Catholic dogma: No procreative, no unitive, except outside of the most sexually pleasurable fertile periods. And, as Hem had discovered with Hadley, it can be a sticky wicket trying to dodge the fertile periods. He would have to think about *that one*.

Then, too, his father was increasingly losing his grip on reality, as his endocrine and cardiac systems ground down and his ever-smiling mother did not have clue one about how to deal with her husband's ailments. Scott, too, could not seem to get a grip. After the Princeton-Yale Game at Palmer Stadium on November 17, with Scott's old friend and Hem's new friend, Mike Strater, the inspiration for Burne Holliday in *This Side of Paradise*—the two, having watched the fights at Madison Square Garden the night before— Scott, as usual, acted up. Drinking had become his avocation in 1927 and 1928. His next novel, now in its fifth year of development, took a backseat. Leaving sober for the game, the four arrived drunk, then later at Ellerslie Mansion, Scott, unable to hold his liquor, was pie-eyed as Zelda stared at the guests, hawk-like, when not giving her impromptu ballet recital. The next day, as they headed for Chicago aboard the *Spirit of St. Louis*, Ernest penned a note to Max outside Harrisburg doubling down on his theory that Zelda was the source of Scott's problems. In his heart, as he pondered the scenic Pennsylvania mountains, he knew he was right.

By mid-November, after picking up baby Patrick and the car in Piggott, it was back to Key West for final revisions, joined by Sunny, twenty-four and unmarried, who decided to spend Thanksgiving with them while helping with babysitting and typing. Sunny came to understand the spirituality underlying her brother's writing, on full display as she typed the manuscript for *A Farewell to Arms*. "She was Ernest's ardent protector," said Redd Griffin, who spoke with her about this foundational spirituality,[10] and described her as "cheerful, high energy, extremely alert and alive, and deeply religious."[11]

They needed all the spiritual strength they could muster for the next chapter of family life. Starting in 1926, just as the real estate boom was losing steam, their father, with immensely bad timing, had invested in St. Petersburg, Clearwater, and Gulfport properties at the urging of "Babbitt" twin Uncle George, mortgaging their debt-free home in Oak Park to do so.

Dr. Hemingway, hoping to retire there, had completed his Florida State medical examinations. But after the Great Miami Hurricane of 1926 ripped through, leaving $100 million in damages, the good doctor's property was "under water," as well. All of his savings were gone.[12] After suffering years of insomnia, he began losing even more sleep because of his battle with angina and now diabetes, which, in the fall of 1928, intensified.

The first week of December was a damp, dismal time, and Clarence's mood turned dark—at the very moment Grace was preoccupied with Christmas preparations. The mortgage note he had signed with Uncle George was coming due. Possessing "a conscience of heroic size," his son Leicester wrote, he was worried he could not pay it, nor did his brother lighten the load. Financial stress had always plunged him into fits of worry and depression and now he could see no way out. So, on December 6, ironically the Feast of St. Nicholas, the saint who gave gold to poverty-stricken souls—as Grace was running around preparing for the Nineteenth Century Club holiday party, a group that, since 1891, had worked to enliven the community through education, charity, and civic involvement—Dr. Hemingway, fifty-seven years old, shot himself behind his ear with the Smith and Wesson .32 caliber revolver his father had carried while commanding troops in the Civil War.[13] At the inquest, Uncle George said his brother's ill health rendered him a "hopeless case," while dismissing finances and mental health as factors triggering his despair.[14]

When Hemingway received Carol's telegram announcing the tragic news—albeit, no cause of death was given—he was on the train with Bumby en route to Key West, having just left Trenton. Making quick arrangements for the porter to keep a careful eye on Bumby, he telegrammed Max Perkins, phoned Mike Strater, and finally dialed up Scott who immediately wired him money. As the train lumbered on to Chicago, Hem thought wistfully of the hunting trip to North Carolina's Smokey Mountains, his father, hankering to relive the summers of his youth, had wanted to take with him.

Friday night, the family met Ernest in the new ornate Grand Hall of Chicago Union Station, with its soaring, barrel-vaulted skylight. After the excitement of seeing their now famous brother abated, Ernest learned the awful truth: Clarence had killed himself. After Leicester, just thirteen, recovering at home from a cold, heard the sharp, abrupt noise that morning, Carol, seventeen, rushed right home from school, as investigators poured into the house. Sunny, down in Key West, rued the fact that she had not stayed behind in Oak Park over the holidays where she might have saved his life with good cheer. Marcelline, too, had regrets over holding back her good news—that she was pregnant—telling Ernest after the funeral in an evening chat, she was saving the news for Christmas. If only she had told him, it would have brought such joy into his life. "Don't torture yourself with that thought," said Ernie. "Dad was too sick to think about anything . . . He was too sick to know what he was doing."[15]

That heart-to-heart was preceded by a more rancorous conversation during the viewing at their home when Ernest said he was having a mass offered for their late father; he had signed up for a prayer fraternity to help Holy Souls in Purgatory at Holy Name in Chicago a month earlier.

The funeral was held on Saturday, December 8, 1928, at 2 p.m., at the First Congregational Church, followed by the burial near his parents at Forest Home Cemetery. (Coincidentally he was buried on the Feast of the Immaculate Conception: "I am the Immaculate Conception," Our Lady of Lourdes said.) Ernest, Marcelline wrote Grace ten years later, had told her that their father's death by his own hand was a "mortal sin," consigning him to "purgatory," which, evidently, to her, meant eternal damnation.[16] But in Catholic doctrine, it means no such thing. Purgatory, deriving from the word purgation, meaning "cleansing," is a place to prepare for Heaven, where, to enjoy the "beatific vision," the soul needs to be free from sin. Marcelline never reconciled with her brother and her son, John Sanford, born in 1930, never met his famous uncle, he told this author, while confirming the family history of depression and nervous disorders.[17] Marcelline wrote in her unpublished manuscript that "Ernest, who had joined the Catholic Church before his marriage to Pauline was most concerned about my father's death. He had prayers said for him, he had Masses said for his soul."[18] Marcelline's memoir over twenty years later, not long before her death, paints a more sympathetic portrait of her brother, who, she writes, believed their father's mental illness lessened his sin if not totally absolving him. Leicester clarified the matter in his memoir, writing that, as they were preparing for the funeral, Ernest said:

> I want no crying . . . not in our family. We're here to honor [our father] for the kind of life he lived, and the people he taught and helped. And, if you will, really pray as hard as you can, to help get his soul out of purgatory. There are plenty of heathens around here who should be ashamed of themselves. They think it's all over and what they don't seem able to understand is that things go right on from here. I'm going to give Marcelline a piece of my mind.[19]

Hemingway surely cried privately. He was very close to his father in his formative years, hunting and fishing and boating and exploring nature with him. He later, of course, infused this world into his Nick Adams stories. Nick (nicknamed "Wemedge," just like Hem) and his friend Bill (as in

Smith, the one to suggest the use of dialogue in his stories, a Hemingway literary trademark), enjoy a fall night in Michigan orchard country, where Hem spent his summers and Smith lived. While bonding over drinks, Nick comments that his doctor father, who did not drink, "missed a lot." When Bill tries to soften the reality, Nick affirms his father "says he's missed a lot himself."[20] And now his real-life teetotaling doctor father, who missed so much, was dead by his own hand. That Hem desired the relationship to continue beyond his early teens, to no avail, made his father's suicide doubly tragic and his own somewhat inevitable. As he told Sunny in Key West, "I'll probably go the same way." "The thought seemed most unlikely," wrote Sunny.[21] Except for the fact that, as Sunny recounted, he wrote the same thing to Mary Pfeiffer.[22] Doc Hemingway was the parent he most cared for, feeling sympathetic to his plight—how Grace did not put his needs first. Then, too, rich Uncle George "did more than anything to kill Dad," Ernest wrote Grace on March 11, 1929.[23]

Ernest asked Grace and Leicester to send the instrument of his father's death back to him—the gun his grandfather had given him as a boy. After all the necessary paperwork was filed with City Hall in Chicago at the County Sheriff's Office, where it was impounded as evidence, it was returned to Hemingway in March.

Meanwhile, Ernest and Pauline and baby Patrick became knitted into Key West, which was still reeling from the 1926 hurricane. With marvelous timing, Max Perkins began visiting regularly, starting in January 1929, for a fishing expedition, which would become an annual event, as he continued to nurture the friendship with his prize author. Hemingway needed this friendship in the wake of losing his father so suddenly and cruelly, and the friendship only warmed through the years.

On his first trip, Max eagerly poured through the pages of *A Farewell to Arms*. He loved what he read, though, like Scott later, and Wister, too, he had some reservations, including the use of the first person and the two distinct stories. In early May, Hem finally got a taste of Spain, escaping to Hendaye-Plage—just across the border in Nouvelle-Aquitaine, the southwest most point of France—to finish *A Farewell to Arms* at Hotel Barron, just as he had done with *The Sun Also Rises*. Pauline and the baby were recovering from the flu in Paris and Hem was deathly afraid of influenza in the wake of the 1918 pandemic.[24] When he arrived back in time for Pentecost Sunday, falling on May 19 that year, a dinner invite from Scott awaited. The dinner did not go well; nonetheless, Ernest gave Scott the manuscript for his review, which went even worse. "Our poor old friendship probably won't survive this but there you are—better me than some nobody in the Literary Review that doesn't care about you & your future," Scott wrote parenthetically in his four-page letter, slicing and dicing the manuscript, ending "A beautiful book it is!"[25] Hemingway sent the final galleys to New York in time for serialization of the first five "books" in *Scribner's Magazine*, from May to September, and then gave Scott the cold shoulder. That Scott had fallen away from his Catholic faith, though he nonetheless revered Catholicism, may have played a small role in their drifting apart.

Hemingway had become "very Catholic," the poet Alan Tate told Stoneback, recalling in Paris in the late twenties, he attended Mass and bicycle races with Hemingway and said that "Hemingway's attitude towards bicycle racing, perhaps toward all sport, was 'rooted in a religious sensibility.'"[26] *That actual grace* he had spoken to Withington Church about was very real for him. Callaghan, too, his friend from the *Toronto Star*, sensed in Paris that summer that "he really had been Catholic for some time—by temperament" and that, "in spite of his puritan family, he was in fact intended to be a Mediterranean Catholic."[27] And he wanted to raise Bumby Catholic. Asked if she objected, Hadley finally wrote back, ""I do mind." He was baptized in the Episcopal church and it was her hope he would grow up "free of judgement and full of faith." Furthermore, when he is eighteen, she wrote, Bumby could "be as many Catholics as he wants."[28]

The novel continued building that iceberg of spiritually rich themes, replete with the same tension he infused *The Sun Also Rises* with, between "behaving badly" and spiritual uplift, aridity of soul and belief in God.

To wit: Catherine, though irreligious, gives Lt. Henry a St. Anthony medal before he goes to the front and is grievously wounded. Once he arrives back in Milan, their romance soon resumes, Catherine believing they are essentially "married." At the outset, the priest's proselytization and Henry's responsiveness, shows how, Hemingway-like, he is torn between spiritual and carnal love, trying to reconcile the two. He becomes good friends with the priest as they discuss war and peace, life and love, and the priest tries to bring Henry closer to God, helping him distinguish between love and lust. After he deserts his military post, the priest vanishes from his life as he and Catherine travel to Stresa where Henry tells Count Greffi, regarding belief, "My own comes only at night." Which tells the count he is "in love"—since that to him is "religious feeling."[29] Henry is not so sure, having been well schooled by the priest and his own conscience, and promises to pray for the spiritually arid count.

Fittingly, too, Hemingway's "dignity of place" is ever-present, as Redd Griffin[30] described it. While recovering from his war wounds, Lt. Henry glimpses the magnificent Milan cathedral outside his window as he carries on the torrid affair with Catherine. Once he returns to the front, while on leave, they spend time in Milan, passing by the "very big" Duomo, its "stone . . . wet," while they observe one couple, their seeming double, who "have the cathedral" to escape to; but, Catherine, now pregnant, feeling like a cheap "whore," rejects the idea.[31] Instead, they check into a gaudy hotel. "'Vice is a wonderful thing,' Catherine said. 'The people who go in for it seem to have good taste about it. The red plush is really fine . . . And the mirrors are very attractive."[32] Once they arrive in Stresa, Catherine is no longer plagued with such thoughts and they live in harmony the last three months of her pregnancy, albeit without benefit of matrimony, as Henry shares his central insight, foreshadowing Catherine's demise: "If people bring so much courage to this world, the world has to kill them to break them, so of course it kills them. The world breaks every one and afterward many are strong at the broken places. But those it will not break it kills. It kills the very good and the very gentle and the very brave impartially."[33] At the end, as the baby's life hangs in the balance, Henry considers baptizing him, though he himself has "no religion."[34] Catherine, too, does not feel the need to see a priest as she nears death.

In spite of the novel's beauty, the love and war themes were too distinct for Perkins, Wister and Scott, too, who observed how "the war goes further + further out of sight" as the love story takes over.[35]

Callaghan was amazed how Scott enthused over the novel, notably the iconic "world has to kill them to break them" passage, yet the two writers seemed to have no relationship. Finally, Scott began to ask about Callaghan's boxing matches with Hemingway, hinting and hoping for an invite. It was the eve of the novel's publication when, invited to join them, Scott let a fight go on *four minutes* too long, allowing Callaghan to deck Hemingway, blood gushing from his lip, as he lay flattened on the floor of the American Club ring. The key moment, wrote Callaghan, was when Hemingway stormed off, blaming Scott for allegedly failing to end the match on time because he enjoyed seeing Hem "get the shit knocked out" of him, wrote Callaghan. Which, perhaps more than anything, signaled that the same paranoia that had infected his father's psyche was now starting to work on Hem as well.[36]

Before leaving Paris that summer, Hemingway had one last outing with Callaghan, including a visit to Chartres and was surprised that his friend did not genuflect while he "was genuflecting right and left at all the proper places."[37] Once outside, Ernest just stood there for the longest time, pondering this marvelous spiritual edifice, a testament to faith, while keeping his thoughts to himself.

God was preparing Hemingway for great things. Not only did he keenly observe and movingly articulate societal changes lifting him to the pinnacle of literary fame, but he benefited from the exploding means of communication. Notably "moving pictures," which had just begun "talking," bringing him an unimaginably large audience, starting with the film version of *A Farewell to Arms* (1932). Even the Broadway stage would dramatize the novel in a short-lived run. Just the start of theatrical gold. With it, of course, came great fame and great temptation he was not equal to resisting. But that, too, was in God's plan.

The Hemingways spent the summer together in Spain—starting with the Feria in Pamplona, where a *Spur Magazine* correspondent spotted the accident-prone writer sporting a makeshift wrap on his wounded foot.[38] Then it was on to Valencia and Santiago de Campostela, where Hem wrote Perkins about Scott's timekeeping failure, now growing to an *eight-minute* lapse in his ever-expanding tale of the "5 p.m. boxing date with Callaghan." It was after lunch with Scott and John Bishop at Pruniers where he ate mounds of food, washing it all down with "several bottles of white burgundy"—a recipe for conking out by five. "I couldn't see him hardly," wrote Hem, noting his two additional whiskeys en route.[39]

"NERVOUS BITTERNESS," SEARCH FOR HEALING

At the time, Scott chalked it all up to Ernest's "nervous bitterness" over the impending publication of his novel.[40] The final week, they wound up their Spanish vacation in Hendaye for some fishing and sunbathing as Hemingway continued to fret and overindulge in food and spirits, finding the ends of his fingers had literally ballooned. So he cut out meat and alcohol from his diet entirely, drinking only Vichy water.[41] Besides Pauline's concern over his drinking, he had to try and calm his "nervous bitterness" in time for the debut of *A Farewell to Arms*.

The Hemingways arrived back in Paris the first day of fall. One week later, the novel's publication on September 27, 1929, gave the author exactly one month before the stock market crash to ring up sales. It proved a crucial window, his tally rising to some 80,000 in the first four months alone. Thus did the novel, his second, make him financially independent, to say nothing of the critical acclaim it garnered.

As the new decade dawned, Scott was fading, Hem moving on. He was frustrated to see his friend throwing away his talent on drunken benders as Zelda went insane just as the market crashed. If only Hemingway had understood Scott's hypoglycemia—just one drink, he was two sheets to the wind—he might have had more understanding for his friend's weakness, a weakness he shared, though with the happy result, he could hold his liquor—until it, too, destroyed him, starting around the time Scott breathed his last. Hem had rescued so many others, including Pound when he went mad later in life. But, with Scott, it was different, perplexingly so. Making matters worse, Scott was far too willing to abase himself to curry favor with Hemingway.

Now the roles were reversed from the time they met at the Dingo not five years earlier. As Scott kept trying to write *Tender Is the Night*, Hem, having banked two novels since *Gatsby*, began work on his next book—this one about bullfighting—from his comfortable Key West perch. The now celebrated author began writing this latest work after spending Christmas in Switzerland with the Murphys, who were nursing their TB-stricken son back to health, joined by the whole Villa America crowd. But, having left Europe definitively behind, Hemingway now found Key West had far too many distractions what with all the visitors from Paris and the siren call of fishing. So after working on his new bullfighting book and putting finishing touches on "Wine of Wyoming," he returned West that summer and fall for more concentrated work. After trying out one dude ranch, and finding it unsuitable, Hem and Pauline, joined by six-year-old Jack, as Bumby was now often called, ended up at the L Bar T, just south of Cooke City, Montana, where they arrived on July 13, 13th anniversary of the third appearance of Our Lady of Fatima to the three shepherd children. It was the spot Hemingway had found on the map two years earlier on his first trip to Wyoming with Horne. "Ernie . . . pointed out a lonely looking stream that started in the north, went for miles along Yellowstone Park's wild eastern edge, looped down south through wilderness, and finally swung north to the Yellowstone River, hundreds of miles and two mountain ranges away. 'Horney,' he said, 'that's the place.'"[42]

Given his rising profile, which "Wine of Wyoming" published that August in *Scribner's Magazine* only enhanced, he wanted to get away from civilization and its prying eyes, and the L Bar T, a working cattle ranch, accessed by a plank bridge, was ideal. Beautiful and secluded, it had a sparkling new cabin with a breathtaking view of Pilot and Index Peaks that fronted the Clark's Fork River, teaming with fish, and accented by grouse, ducks and geese, with the mountains rising up from the river packed with deer, grizzly bears, and elk, a veritable writer's paradise bathed in clean, crisp air.

While Pauline cared for Bumby in the morning, Hemingway wrote on the porch after breakfast and went fishing in the afternoon and early evening—or sometimes in the morning, when the lure was too strong. Often, Pauline would join him. "My mother and father were both fly-fishermen . . . and fished together . . . they both enjoyed it," said Patrick. "It was very much an ingredient in that marriage."[43]

Ernest caught hundreds of rainbow trout, and also shot bears and went horseback riding across the fields and into the mountains. Then, of course, he invited "the boys." "This is the most beautiful country" ever, he wrote Strater.[44]

The Hornes (Bill and his new wife Frances "Bunny") also joined the Hemingways at the ranch, traveling there by train then bus to Cook City. "There the group met us on horseback," said Horne, "with mounts for us, and I can still see Ernie on that big steed. He rode straight-legged, Indian fashion, because of his gimpy knee, and he looked like the man who invented Montana." After that, it was a "nine-mile ride down the southerly valley, past [the peaks] . . . The land rose above the Fork's east bank into steep hills and hogbacks. There were narrow stretches of forest, green and yellow steps leading to the ridges of Beartooth Buttes, 15 miles away to the east."

It was a fishing paradise, too, although while it poured rain, "the trout hid behind rocks," said Horne, but when the rain stopped, "I've never seen anything like it . . . We were using mostly wet flies, usually a McGinty at the end of the leader and two droppers along its length. The fish were so hungry and profuse that many times we had two on at once, occasionally three."

Meanwhile,

> Ernie . . . had brought along bushels of Spanish bull-fighting periodicals. We were at a spot where the river was about to dive down into a canyon, fast beautiful water full of trout, the kind of thing an avid fisherman would sell his soul for. Yet morning after morning, Ernie sat in the sun in an old rocker, reading the latest on corridas . . . He was enjoying his fame then, and I remember him as dominant, exuberant, damned attractive, a stand-out in any group. But when he was with his friends, he was *with* them, not apart from them.[45]

Dos Passos finally showed up on October 21, for the last exuberant hunting trip. By the end of October, the weather turning wintry, a bad snowstorm threatening, it was time to go. The morning of October 31, out-fitted with a bottle of bourbon and their warmest clothes, they set off for Key West in their Ford Roadster, with Floyd Ellington sitting in the back, Dos and Hem in the front. Taking a break that night, they slept in Mammoth outside Yellow Stone Park, making steady progress the next day following the Yellowstone River en route to Billings where they planned to drop Dos off for the train back east.

As dusk approached, the driving along Route 90 in Montana, between Park City and Laurel, became treacherous, and suddenly an oncoming car with bright lights momentarily blinded Hem's weak eye, and he drove as far to the right as he could before plunging into the ditch. While he did not suffer any injuries to his head, the oblique spiral fracture of his right arm almost doomed his writing career, along with his other great loves, hunting and fishing.

It all happened on the Feast of All Saints, November 1, 1930, about twenty miles outside of Billings. Fortunately, Dr. Louis Allard, one of the outstanding orthopedic surgeons in the region, was in residence at nearby St. Vincent's where Hemingway was treated. Using a new and innovative procedure, Allard drilled holes in his broken arm and fused it back together with kangaroo tendons. His seven-week recuperation at St. Vincent's, three days of which he was completely immobilized, at first threatened to plunge him into a deep depression—all the more inevitable given all that was going on in the world, what with the country sinking into Depression; Spain starting to spill blood; and a writer he did not respect, Sinclair Lewis, winning the Nobel Prize. Then, he found healing, as he perked up to monitor the comings and goings in the room across the hall. Two souls, he learned, had been injured in a café, one of whom, Costello, Hemingway's neighbor, holding on for dear life, was close-lipped about his assailant. Out of this mystery was born "The Gambler, The Nun, and the Radio," first published in *Scribner's Magazine* in April 1933.

The nun in the story, Sr. Cecilia, was inspired by Irish-born Sr. Florence Cloonan, who, nursing a bad heart, was given the simple task of delivering the mail to the patients. She spent much time at the bedside of Hemingway—"Mr. Frazier" in the story—during his seven-week convalescence.[46] A passionate Notre Dame football fan, Sr. Florence believed prayer won games. One Saturday, "Mr. Frazier" encourages "Sr. Cecilia" to stay and listen to the football game on the radio, but she demurs. "'It's Notre Dame! Our Lady! No, I'll be in the chapel. For Our Lady. They're playing for Our Lady. I wish you'd write something sometime for Our Lady. You could do it. You know you could do it, Mr. Frazier.' 'I don't know anything about her that I can write. It's mostly been written already,' Mr. Frazier said. 'You wouldn't like the way I write. She wouldn't care for it either.' 'You'll write about her sometime,' Sr. said. 'I know you will. You must write about Our Lady.'"

So poignant. Mary had saved Hemingway's life some twelve years earlier, and she had saved him that November 1. Now he was foreshadowing one of his greatest works some twenty-two years hence when he would write about an "old man" praying to Our Lady. And, now Sr. Cecilia is praying to her.

Mr. Frazier keeps encouraging her to "come up and hear the game." But she demurs noting the excitement "would be too much for me." "No, I'll be in the chapel doing what I can." Just five minutes into the game, "a probationer" comes in to say, "Sr. Cecelia wants to know how the game is going." They've got "a touchdown," Frazier said. Once again, the man comes and goes away reassured. "A little later they rang the bell for the nurse who was on floor duty. 'Would you mind going down to the chapel or sending word down to Sr. Cecilia that Notre Dame has them 14 to nothing at the end of the first quarter and that it's alright. She can stop praying.'"

But she keeps praying since that lead "might not mean a thing." Mr. Frazier keeps assuring her till finally he sends down word that they have won.

The next morning, she says, "I knew they couldn't beat Our Lady . . . They couldn't." At the same time, Sr. Cecilia is also ministering to the wounded, including "poor Cayetano," the recovering gambler.

Like Hemingway, Frazier's "nerves had become tricky." Over five weeks of recovery, Frazier "disliked seeing people while he was in this condition." Sr. Cecilia, who came to deliver the mail, was the one exception. "She was very handsome and Mr. Frazier liked to see her and to hear her talk." The mail was uninteresting that morning so they chatted.

"'You look so much better,' she said. 'You'll be leaving us soon.' 'Yes,' Mr. Frazier said. 'You look very happy this morning.' 'Oh, I am. This morning I feel as though I might be a saint.'" This was a left curve for Mr. Frazier. "'Yes,' Sister Cecilia went on. 'That's what I want to be. A saint. Ever since I was a little girl, I've wanted to be saint." She goes on and on about her burning passion for sanctity, reflecting the real-life model, Sr. Florence, of whom a fellow nun said, "She would say that. She said, 'I want to be saint.'"[47]

God was watching over Hemingway. "In the designs of Providence, there are no mere coincidences," said St. John Paul II, referring to his being saved on May 13, 1981, the Feast of Our Lady of Fatima, when, upon leaning down to bless a child's Fatima image, the trajectory of the bullet, initially aimed for his heart, changed and missed his heart. In the same way, it was no accident that Hemingway ended up in that hospital on that All Saint's Day with Dr. Allard ministering to his body, Sr. Florence ministering to his soul.

Hemingway was discharged on December 21, in a cast, which he would ditch once he got back to Key West, much sooner than advisable. But fishing beckoned. Writing, too.

Meanwhile, Pauline was busy searching for a suitable permanent home in lieu of the rented homes they had lived in their first three years in Key West. She had pondered a ramshackle old house at 907 Whitehead Street, built in 1851, when the Catholic Church showed up, now in total disrepair. Finally understanding its great potential, given that it was the only suitable site, what with its 1.5-acre secluded lot and lovely design, on April 29, 1931, Uncle Gus purchased the property, for just $8,000, as a wedding present.

With the help of out-of-work "Conchs," they transformed the estate, including carving a study out of the second-story carriage house where Hemingway could write.

After working all morning each day, his lifelong habit, he was ready for some spirits from the basement wine cellar they built, or, more often than not, at "Sloppy Joe's," his favorite hangout, a short walk from their home, owned by fishing and drinking buddy "Josie Grunts" Russell. They were great friends. By day they would fish the Cuban coast, joined by other friends, including, notably, Carlos Gutierrez, the expert fisher he met in Dry Tortugas in 1929, under whose guidance he would win every fishing prize there was.

Then, too, early in the afternoon, said Josie's daughter, they would soak in the salt baths in bogs near Key West Golf Course on Stock Island, built in 1926, which, Josie surmised, is one of the reasons Hem was so balanced and productive during his Key West years, the lithium in the salt, helping balance the chemicals in his brain, no doubt also drawing out the toxins that built up from the excess drinking.[48] Michael Reynolds' "Map of Key West c. 1936" shows "Old Salt Ponds" on the Southern edge of Flagler Avenue, about two miles southwest of the golf course.

By night, they would smuggle rum for "Sloppy Joe's."

But as much fun as chasing marlin and running rum and soaking in salt baths was, Ernest needed to keep his eyes on the real prize and soon craved Spain to finish his bullfighting book amid the usual summer fare.

Nothing, though, was usual that summer of 1931. Madrid had erupted in violence in the wake of King Alfonso XIII fleeing the country and the Second Spanish Republic being proclaimed on April 14 after elections swept the monarchists from power. Madrid was now under martial law and the Church, which had a cozy relationship with landowners and royals, was now on the defensive as emotions ran high, all of which Hemingway observed with keen interest. He escaped for now to Hendaye to finish his bullfighting magnum opus, joined by Pauline, who was several months pregnant, then peeling off for a bit to attend the Pamplona fiesta with Bumby and Sidney Franklin, an American bullfighter. Soon he was back, enjoying Santiago de Compostela, its cool breezes and warm spirituality with Pauline, who left early for Paris to relax and oversee shipment of valuables like Joan Miro's *The Farm* to Key West.

Just as summer turned to fall, the Hemingways sailed from Cherbourg to New York on *Île de France*, arriving in Kansas a month before Pauline gave birth at Research Hospital on November 12 to their second baby—another boy, another C-section, another month of recuperation, another Thanksgiving in the hospital, after which her doctor insisted no more babies for

Pauline. "If the Church insists that I must put Pauline through what I have just seen her through am afraid must consider myself an outlyer [*sic*] from now on," Hem wrote Mother Pfeiffer.[49] In December, he exhaled from the whole experience, including giving birth himself to his bullfighting book, soon to be christened *Death in the Afternoon*, and enjoyed some quail hunting in Piggott. Though, he startled Charles Thompson over shots of whiskey when he said he may end up killing himself just like his father. Along with his weakening faith, the strain of it all was weighing him down, made all the worse by the manic depression gene he shared with his father.[50]

Back home in Key West, in time for Christmas, with Patrick and their new baby, christened Gregory on January 14, their new house was becoming a warm and inviting home.

Meanwhile, their spiritual home, St. Mary, Star of the Sea, was within walking distance—a short block down Whitehead, left on Division Street (renamed Truman Avenue in 1948), and few blocks to Windsor. And they were regulars. "I go to church every Sunday and am a good father to my family," he wrote his mother-in-law in early 1932.[51] Albeit he was writing in the context of all the distractions—dyspeptic infants, falling plaster, leaking roof—that kept him from writing as he fretted over whether he would turn out a polished manuscript, noting the publisher would *not* be swayed by his exemplary fatherhood and practice of his Catholic faith. But he *was* good. "Oh yes, he never misses Sunday Mass," Fr. Dougherty said. "Easter duty? Most assuredly. Lovely wife and children, all of them Catholics, good Catholics too."[52] Gregory, though, would later assert that "(his father) didn't really believe."[53] Which, given countervailing evidence, seems to reflect his own feelings. As Charles Scribner III said, "He was raised Catholic by his devout mother, Pauline, and clearly rejected it later in life. Projection."[54] As Hemingway's longtime assistant Toby Bruce, who spoke with Stoneback at length in Key West in January 1978, said: "(He) (a)lways went to Mass, especially when he was here, still with Pauline. And afterwards, too . . . He was a real Catholic, and I think he tried very hard to be a good Catholic . . . He raised his kids in the church and was proud of how they did at catechism; he always gave money to the church . . . he spoke to the Catholic Sunday school kids; he planned to donate a considerable sum toward the restoration of Mary Immaculate Convent." But, said Bruce, religion was "not something he would talk about."[55]

Sunny observed how sometimes her brother needed to be "fortified" with alcohol before going to confession.[56] Good that he did take a swig, if that's what it took to go confession and get it all out. For he was thereby fortified with was the grace of the sacraments and had the strength to fight.

And he surely needed the strength. He now faced twin challenges to his faith—centered on Pauline's inability to have more children, and his inability to embrace the sacrifice that entailed; and the tumult in Spain, where he was dismayed to see the church taking the side of the monarchists.

In April 1932, Hemingway joined Josie Russell on the *Anita* for two months of fishing in Havana and, in between reading proofs on *Death in the Afternoon* and working on some short stories, discovered marlin fishing, which, wrote Baker, was "utterly satisfying as a sport, a living, a spectacle, and a form of exercise."[57] Hem's "happiest days were chasing marlin," said his son John.[58] Soon he was plying the seas off Bimini, the Atlantic and Caribbean, as well. Pauline had traveled to Manhattan where she hired a new aide, Ada Stern, to help with the children and housework, rejoining Ernest in Old Havana for a week. He was staying at the Hotel Ambos Mundo in a comfortable $2-a-night room overlooking the harbor and the Cathedral de San Cristobol,[59] where, until 1898, Christopher Columbus was buried. The Republic, founded four years after Columbus' remains were spirited away to the cathedral in Seville, was thirty years old, and was also experiencing political unrest; Cuba was now under martial law.

From her lovely Ambos Mundos suite overlooking the water, Pauline immediately dialed up Jane Kendall Mason, twenty-two, a high-strung and beautiful socialite, former model for Ponds Cold Cream and wife of wealthy George Grant Mason Jr, whom Pauline had met three years earlier on *Île de France*. Before long the Hemingways and Grants, who had a loveless marriage, were out on the town, dancing under the palms at Jardines de la Tropical and other swank spots, Hemingway dazzled by Jane's beauty and charm.

Death in the Afternoon featuring the matador, Cayetano Ordóñez, was published on September 23, 1932. The *New York Herald Tribune* thought the book alive with possibility while the *New Yorker* thought it was the death of Hemingway. No matter. He was having too much fun, hunting and fishing in Wyoming once again from their base at the L Bar T, where the Hemingways had traveled mid-July, and where he would write "The Light of the World." And, while world events were dismal, Hemingway kept turning out masterpieces. That winter, he invited Max Perkins on a pre-Christmas duck hunt in Arkansas, giving him his next gem, "A Clean Well-Lighted Place."

As 1933 opened, while wrapping up his third and final collection of short stories, *Winner Take Nothing*, Hemingway was introduced to Arnold Gingrich and soon began penning columns for *Esquire*, while continuing to fish for marlin in Havana, starting mid-April, and writing about it. Then, too, as his fishing logbook reveals, in between snagging marlin, he was snagging graces, attending Sunday mass regularly, including on April 16, Easter

Sunday. He needed the grace. "Drank too much!" he wrote.[60] And, he was weakening sexually as his flirtation with Jane intensified, though not for long. On the eve of summer, May 27, she fell from her second story balcony at "Jaimanitas," their lavish estate thirty minutes west of Havana, and broke her back. It was just days after a serious accident with Jack and her two boys, which, though no one was injured, left her badly shaken. That July 6, Hemingway wrestled for two hours with a great marlin only to lose him. The next day, he got his consolation prize, but fearing his strength would fail him before he brought the marlin to gaffe, he "promised a hundred Hail Marys, a hundred Our Fathers, and $5 to the church."[61]

As Ernest and Pauline embarked on a European trip down memory lane, everyone was on strike in Havana. Miraculously, they set sail on August 7, arriving ten days later in Santander, amid Ernest's "nervous bitterness," as Scott aptly described his feelings on the eve of publication, along with a building paranoia that everyone was out to get him including Max; and many *were*, but *not Max*. Max had no reason to stint on advertising. When Pauline and Ginny left for Paris in October, he felt lonely but they exchanged letters regularly and were soon together again to embark on their African safari, financed by Uncle Gus, and joined by Charles Thompson.

When they finally set sail for Mombasa out of Marseilles aboard the *S.S. General Metzinger*, a grimy, old steamer, on November 22, Hem was ready, down to a specialty rifle with a telescope recommended by lion tamer Clyde Beatty. Once in Mombasa, they caught a train to Nairobi 300 miles west, where they were assigned to British white hunter Philip Percival, just then wrapping up another safari. Meanwhile Hemingway and his party stayed at the Percival ostrich farm at Potha Hill in Machakos, twenty miles southeast of Nairobi, as Percival's wife Vivian set up shooting excursions for them in the Kapiti Plain. Once Percival returned on December 20, they motored over to the Serengeti where Hemingway shot two lions, a kudu, and rhino— his first. Back at Potha Hill, he met Alfred Vanderbilt, another white hunter and friend of Jane Mason, who had shot two elephants and was joined by a big strapping polo player, Winston Guest, who would become one of Hemingway's good friends.

No sooner had he gotten into the swing of things than he came down with a bad case of dysentery and was flown to Nairobi Hospital. While en route, he soaked up majestic Mount Kilimanjaro, which planted in him the seed of his most celebrated short story. By January 21, back on safari, he hunted kudu with Thompson, the two competing for the biggest prize, while Hem killed eighty-four lions among dozens of other wild animals, including three kudus.[62] While he might not have taken top prize in game hunting, he was killing it in book sales, Max writing him he had sold 12,500 copies of *Winner Take Nothing*—all his worry, his "nervous bitterness," for naught.

In the midst of big-game hunting, Hemingway wrote a column for *Esquire* at each stop, which, after they docked in New York Harbor in April 1934 aboard *Île de France*, enabled him to buy a thirty-eight-foot fishing boat, his new love, for $7,495, from Brooklyn's Wheeler Shipyard, retrofitted to his specifications. He secured the down-payment from Gingrich and, on May 11, he showed up in Miami, accompanied by his friend Captain Edward "Bra" Saunders and, together, they took the maiden voyage, sailing his new fishing boat, named the *Pilar*, in honor of Our Lady of Pilar, back to Key West. As they arrived into port, they were greeted by an entourage of friends and family at the Navy Yard, where he was given permission to dock.

Scott's book *Tender Is the Night*, an eight-year labor of love, had just come out, a month earlier, on April 11. Of course, Scott was anxious to know if his old friend liked it. Hem did not mince words. The writing was overdone, while the characters were underdeveloped, and without a crazy wife undercutting his work, it might have been great. Though, upon further reflection, he realized it was much better than, at first blush, he had thought.

His new boat docked, Hemingway began writing *The Green Hills of Africa*, his account of the Kenyan safari, a T.R.-inspired boyhood dream come true, that he finished in six months, portraying Pauline as the supportive wife and Percival as the unforgettable "Pop." When the book was published on October 25, 1935, the *New York Times* called it "the best trophy any writer has brought out of the big-game country in many years." While "Africa is thoroughly in the book," writes C. G. Poore, "the writing is the thing; the way he has of getting down with beautiful precision the exact way things look, feel, smell, taste, sound." Meanwhile, "Some of his sentences . . . would make Henry James take a breath. There's one that starts on page 148, swings the length of 149 and lands on 150, forty lines or so from tip to top."[63] Hemingway had abandoned the four-word sentences, all four letters, writes Poore, to the classics of his early writing. His post-boat writing was becoming more complex because his boat was taking him far out where you don't see the shoreline, observed Paul Hendrickson, author of *Hemingway's Boat*.[64]

As Hendrickson said, if an artist doesn't grow, he is dead.

Hemingway was growing as a writer but dying as a husband. Just as he had gone to their nearby church in Paris when he had a spell of impotency early in the marriage, he should have reached out to God, through the intercession of Our Lady, to cure his spiritual impotency. But it was not to be.

He wrote *Green Hills of Africa* in Suite #511 at the Hotel Ambos Mundo, his principal Cuban residence for most of the 1930s, sailing aboard the *Pilar* to Havana for the first time on July 18, not returning to Key West till October 26, and seeing Pauline only five times while in Cuba. He would take a break to fish, as he always did to recharge his creative batteries. Only this time, he was not only fishing for piscatorial gold. He had begun an affair with Jane Mason. Theirs was a torrid romance, which cooled Hemingway spiritually.

When Donald Ogden Stewart introduced Ernest to Jane aboard *Île de France*, Pauline's pregnancy was coming to term and, while she rested, the men in the party squired Jane around. (Hemingway also met Marlene Dietrich on the same ocean voyage, but their relationship was never sexual.) That Pauline had even become pregnant so soon after giving birth to Patrick went against her doctor's orders. But the Church forbade birth control, the eschewing of artificial contraception the social norm until only recently as Sanger's campaign reached critical mass. Only a year prior, the Lambeth Conference, which governs Episcopal doctrine, had approved birth control. Now Pauline had a real challenge. The Catholic Church remained steadfast in its opposition, as it does to this day, since natural law is immutable. Albeit, she thought coitus interruptus might be a way to avoid future pregnancies.[65] But that is not acceptable, neither for the Church nor for a macho male like Hemingway. Thus, was the stage set for Hemingway's affair in his Ambos Mundos suite—an affair that was not only spiritually toxic but humanly risky given that, like Zelda, Jane was erratic and unpredictable. But all of Hemingway's writing was the product of living. And with Jane he lived. She could not conceive children so she had an unbridled sexual life—"about the most uninhibited person I ever met," Hemingway said.[66]

After Hemingway came back home from a summer of, er, fishing, the family traveled to Piggot for Christmas 1934, and, after spending the holidays in Arkansas, in early 1935, they came home to a changed Key West, courtesy of Depression-era government programs. Their home now occupied a spot on the tourist map at "number 18 between Johnson's Tropical Grove (number 17) and Lighthouse and Aviaries (number 19)," which, Hemingway wrote, in his *Esquire* column for April 1935, "was all very flattering to the easily bloated ego of your correspondent but very hard on production."[67] He was soon making plans to escape for two months to Bimini, forty-five miles due east of Miami, to fish and finalize his book. But as they were heading out, he "shot himself in the calves of both legs" while trying to harpoon a shark, he wrote in his June *Esquire* column, offering advice on how to kill the large animal, not yourself, namely by shooting it in the brain, if close, the heart, if far, or the spine, for immediate killing![68] Once in Bimini with friends, including Strater, who stayed the summer, and the Murphys, he caught his biggest marlin

Hemingway with Pauline, Gregory, John and Patrick Hemingway and four marlins on a dock in Bimini, 20 July 1935. *Source:* In the public domain. Scribner Archives.

ever—545 pounds!—on his thirty-sixth birthday, while Pauline shuttled back and forth. As Michael Reynolds summed it up: "It was, Hemingway wrote MacLeish, the best summer he could remember: clear water in the harbor, huge tuna in the stream, and good whisky afterwards."[69]

Meanwhile, God was reeling him in. He was Havana-bound post Bimini, after a quick visit in Key West, but the Pilar needed work, and the work was delayed. Then the Labor Day hurricane wiped out Matecumbe and with it over 1,000 souls, many wandering, Depression-starved vets and Bonus Army transplants, sent to Key West to work on the connector highway, afforded little respect, which few commanded. Hemingway was one of 200 volunteers helping clean up from the grisly scene about which he wrote in *New Masses*. Though not the ideal venue, he could not stay silent, asking "who sent them there to die?"[70]

With no time for a final relaxing escape in Havana, a month before the *Green Hills of Africa* hit bookstores, the Hemingways went to New York. The real magnet was not Max Perkins but Max Baer fighting Joe Louis on

September 24, 1935, at Yankee Stadium. It was "the most disgusting spectacle" he had ever seen, he wrote that December in *Esquire*. The fear emanating
from Baer, as Louis knocked him out, was palpable and bought to mind his
own fears traversing the slippery ledges in Wyoming crawling for mountain
rams, or his "dread of eternity" after suffering mortar and bullet wounds,
sapping him of all courage for a month, he wrote.[71] Fear could be a great
catharsis and corrective force. Yet the "dread of eternity" seemed remote as
Hemingway continued to drift in his marriage and thereby his spiritual life.
It did not help that his parents' marriage had been a shell of a marriage. Basically, Hemingway was the child of divorce. As Grace had written her son,
surprisingly, upon learning of his split from Hadley, "I'm sorry to hear your
marriage has gone on the rocks. But most marriages ought to. I hold very
modern and heretical views on marriage—but keep them under my hat."[72]

As the year was winding down, with another set of overall bad book
reviews, Hemingway removed his name off the masthead of *Esquire* as a
contributing editor, as Pauline had urged. He had given his warning about
America being swept up in another world war in the September 1935 *Esquire*. It was time to refocus on his real writing that emanated from the world
of his imagination, mirroring his personal life and experience.

Jane Mason would inspire the nastiest femme fatale Hemingway ever
conceived, that of Margot Macomber in the short story, "The Short Happy
Life of Francis Macomber," which ran in the September 1936 issue of *Cosmopolitan*. As Hemingway wrote in the fictional account he began writing
in November 1934, "She was an extremely handsome and well-kept woman
of the beauty and social position which had, five years before, commanded
five-thousand dollars as the price of endorsing, with photographs, a beauty
product which she had never used. She had been married to Francis Macomber for eleven years."[73] Macomber would end up dead at the end of the
story, when Frances's gun accidentally shoots him. In real life, Jane was an
excellent shot, often outpacing Hemingway, which eventually wore thin, and
they finally broke up in the summer of 1936, after which he used their affair
to draw his portrait of an even nastier femme fatale.

Then, too, "The Snows of Kilimanjaro" (1936), published in *Esquire* in
August 1936, was a window into Hemingway's soul and marriage. It featured
a writer on safari on the Serengeti Plain as he lay dying, his leg becoming
gangrene-infected, and, as he waits for the plane he knows will not arrive in
time, he drinks over his squandered time and talent as he lived in luxury with
a rich and manipulative yet faithful wife he does not love, whom he insults in
his waning hours, though regretting his slights. He reminisces about his early
days in Paris, living in that cheap hotel where Verlaine died, where he rented

the top floor to write, as Hemingway himself had done. The implicit contrast between that "very poor and very happy"[74] time and now could not be starker.

Coincident with Hemingway writing this story, six months earlier, Scott was writing his "Crack-Up" series published in *Esquire* starting in February 1936, taking jabs at Ernest, who believed hard work would cure Scott. That, or religion. As he wrote Max, a fallen-away Episcopalian, "Feel awfully about Scott . . . Maybe the Church would help him."[75]

Truth be told, Hemingway needed help too—that doctor for his soul.

Christmas 1935, Pauline and the family stayed in Key West, rather than their usual celebration in Piggott. Hemingway wrote his mother-in-law, Mary, on January 26, thanking her for the generous check from Paul Pfeiffer, and letting her know that he had suffered "a spell when I was pretty gloomy . . . and didn't sleep for about three weeks," thus the delay in writing. He was getting up in the wee hours when his "brain was racing" to write it all down, lest by dawn "it is gone and you are pooped . . . Had never had the real melancholia," he wrote and this episode "makes me more tolerant of what happened to my father."[76]

Two months later, he returned with great fanfare to Havana aboard the Pilar with "Mrs. George Grant Mason." It was April 1936, the first time in eighteen months he would set foot in Havana.[77] Pauline loved Hemingway deeply and looked the other way when the young lovelies gravitated to her husband. She knew how much he valued her, not only personally but professionally. She carefully tended to his career, for instance, making that correct call urging him to pull back from *Esquire*; reviewing every book from Scribners that crossed the transom, telling him which one to read, which to disregard; and masterfully copyediting all of his manuscripts. But after Gregory was born, all of that was less important, as a continuing conjugal life became impossible, so they spent more time apart, as a kind of birth control, and *naturally* Hemingway sought greener pastures.

Yet while his body—that strong, virile Hemingway body—was thrilled, his soul was churning. Because of his sexual wandering, he lost the *supernatural* sources of grace that would have helped him weather his marital difficulties. But Hemingway's healthy sexual appetites and less developed Catholic faith—"a dumb Catholic," as he had written Fr. Donovan—made it difficult. And so, he was starting to exhibit the same anxieties as when he was torn between Hadley and Pauline, now trying to salve his conscience by recalling the early days in Paris and how he had ditched all of that for Pauline.

If only he had availed himself of the grace to stay married—the grace to see contradictions through a redemptive prism.

Spain, too, was churning, with Civil War breaking out on July 16.

It was all such a perfect storm.

Meanwhile, Our Lady, Star of the Sea, understanding Hemingway's weakness, continued to protect him. On May 27, 1936, in her month of May, as he set sail from Havana for Key West, at 11 p.m., five days after Pauline had sailed home, the *Pilar* was buffeted by a huge wave, forcing him to veer off course up the Florida Straits, as progressively higher waves battered the *Pilar*, causing, unbeknown to him, the engine block to crack, taxing all of his strength and wits during the fourteen-hour ordeal that brought him perilously close to death. As he wrote to MacLeish on May 31, "When the Capt. of the Cuba heard we'd left to cross that night he told Sully they'd have to give us up."[78]

But he survived—all of his recent nods to suicide, notwithstanding, as the anxiety of his divided heart mounted—and he spent the month of June in Bimini where he began writing *To Have or Have Not*, another story of survival, the noble "have nots" (rootless vets)—epitomized by salt-of-the earth Harry Morgan forced into smuggling to support his family— stoically holding on in a world of cold "haves" (the ultra-rich and vacuous writers) including the sexually alienated Bradleys, Tom and Helène (i.e., the Grants), and the Gordons, the shape-shifting, regularly drunk novelist, Richard (i.e., Dos Passos), sleeping with Helène—and his slutty, neurotic wife, Helen, who possessing a sheen of elegance, is no better than the prostitute Morgan's wife had started out as.

He feels badly he has once again borrowed from his friends' lives with such abandon. But, as before, the material was just too rich to ignore.

This time, though, there are no cathedrals, no Hail Mary's, in the 175-page novelette, which he finished late November in Wyoming, and has but one Catholic reference, when Helen says her father "went to mass because my mother wanted him to and he did his Easter duty for her and for Our Lord, but mostly for her."[79]

Hemingway was drifting spiritually.

As Frederic Henri said in *A Farewell to Arms*, mirroring Hemingway's predicament, "I don't love much."

Amazing what lust can do to douse the embers of love, and quell the "dread of eternity."

But, of course, there was more at work than lust, as Hemingway struggled for sanctity—trying to reach for more actual grace, but finding unbridled impulses getting in the way.

Then, too, it was Scott's theory that Hemingway needed a new wife for each new novel.[80]

❧❧❧

7

❧❧❧

A Faith Grown Tepid

"For Whom the Bell Tolls"

One day, shortly before Christmas 1936, as Hemingway was enjoying another round of drinks at Sloppy Joe's before heading home for dinner, a young, twenty-eight-year-old blonde, aspiring to literary greatness, came sauntering in. Her name was Martha Gellhorn. Like Hadley and Pauline, she was from St. Louis. Her father, Dr. George Gellhorn, a prominent gynecologist, had died on January 25, and she was on a vacation with her mother, Edna Fischel Gellhorn, co-founder of the League of Women Voters, and her brother, Alfred. Disliking Miami, they had bussed down to Key West on a whim. Her mother had a telegram to send at the nearby Western Union, so the story goes. "Marty," no naïve innocent, had made a pattern of snagging married men,[1] and, knowing the habits and history of her prey, no doubt had this prize game, the iconic writer, relaxing after a hard day's writing, in her sights. She lionized him and had used a Hemingway quote as the epigraph in her first novel, *What Mad Pursuit*, published two years earlier.

They immediately clicked and soon Hemingway was skipping dinner telling Charles Thompson, who had come to fetch him, that Pauline should meet him at Pena's Garden of Roses later on. Charles reported back the reason for the delay: "A beautiful blonde in a black dress."[2] Game on! After Edna and Alfred returned home, like Pauline before, Martha simply moved in and made herself at home in the Hemingways' comfortable estate across from the Key West Lighthouse, as if it was the most normal thing in the world. Normal, if you are planning to make off with the lady of the house's husband.

135

"DUMB CATHOLIC" DETOUR

When she finally motored back to Miami for the trip home on January 10, Hemingway followed her like a lion in heat, Pauline noting wryly for Gingrich responding to a rumor when her husband arrived in Miami, that no, he was not sick, he was the picture of health.

Hemingway was New York–bound to discuss the timeline for *To Have and Have Not* with Max. But he was also laser-focused on the strife in Spain and while in Manhattan signed with the North American News Alliance (NANA) to write dispatches from Madrid, and met with a young novelist about his documentary, *Spain in Flames*. It was a brutal, bloody civil war that was unfolding in the land he loved so, pitting communist Republican Loyalists against monarchist fascist Nationalists, led by Gen. Francisco Franco Bahamonde, who was determined to overthrow the Second Spanish Republic (1931–1939). Hemingway knew full well it was a proxy war—communist Russia fighting against fascist Germany and Italy—using Spain as a testing ground. He felt he needed to be there. He despised fascists. Martha, too, became an adherent to the cause, readily pivoting from the book she was writing on Nazi Germany. Though she evidently had a sympathetic philosophical bent, J. Edgar Hoover's FBI labeling her "a dangerous Communist" for inciting protests in the fall of 1936 over the treatment of the unemployed at the height of the Great Depression.[3]

Hemingway made a second trip to New York in February, this time to meet with the Dutch Communist filmmaker Juris Ivens to discuss supporting his film *The Spanish Earth*, joining a business consortium composed of Dos Passos, MacLeish, and Lillian Hellman.[4] He finally boarded the oceanliner *Paris*, accompanied by Sidney Franklin and Evan Shipman, telling a young reporter, Ira Wolfert, on February 28, 1937, in an interview that his mission was to make Americans aware of the new kind of war—"a total war"—being waged by Franco and his foreign allies, ensnaring the entire civilized population.[5] Wolfert found Hemingway himself of keener interest. "His chest bulged through his coat like a parapet," he wrote of the young and vigorous thirty-seven-year-old legend.[6]

Once in Madrid, he settled at the Florida Hotel. Martha was not far behind, showing up as a correspondent for *Colliers*. Ironically, Patrick Hemingway said,[7] it was the firsthand accounts by Hemingway's documentary filmmaker friends about the Spanish Civil War that inspired her to become a "war correspondent." Before that she hadn't written word one about war.

Hemingway made four trips to Spain, two each in 1937 and 1938. He was a sharp, disciplined observer of the war, writing detailed dispatches about the horror, and, during his first trip, lasting over forty-five days, he was also gathering material for *The Spanish Earth*.

As the war raged, so did their affair.

For Hemingway, the calculus was simple. Besides birth control, the Church's perceived coddling of the fascists was a mortal sin in his book. Of course, it was more complicated than that. The Church portrayed the Spanish Republicans as godless communists, as they were, the obvious corollary being to support the Nationalists, led by Gen. Franco whom foreign powers considered a fascist dictator, albeit 50 percent of his countrymen supported him. Hemingway was now double-alienated. The channels of sacramental grace no longer flowing, he lacked the necessary spiritual fortification and his marriage continued to atrophy, leaving a hole in his soul in need of filling.

Mary Pfeiffer, trying to appeal to her son-in-law's Catholic conscience, had implored him to stay home, and take care of his sons—to no avail. Hemingway arrived back in Paris on May 9, then sailed for America, docking in New York Harbor on the eighteenth, but his heart was in Spain. Once again, Mary wrote asking him to consider his duty to family. But he would not be dissuaded. After spending June in Bimini fishing and writing, followed by a July screening of *The Spanish Earth* at the White House for Martha's friends, President Franklin Delano Roosevelt and First Lady Eleanor Roosevelt, followed by a screening in Los Angeles, this time accompanied by Pauline; he headed back to Spain. Never mind that there was not much action to cover. He had made a promise to return and help the anti-fascist cause. If not, he wrote back to Mary, what kind of example would he be setting for his sons.

More to the point, he had psychologically distanced himself from the Church as he listened to the communist siren song, which caused him to drift further from his faith and family. There was a class aspect to it, as well. The turmoil in Spain was, in many ways, rooted in the class divide, something that St. Josemaria Escrivá had deconstructed: It was not money or position that made you great, but the love of God you put into your work. Pauline and her family were on the rich side of the cultural divide. To preserve her privileged place, she was somewhat aloof from the Key West riffraff. That rubbed Hemingway, who befriended all classes at Sloppy Joe's, on the *Pilar* and elsewhere, the wrong way. But while expressing solidarity with the poor, he was undercutting his own dignity. Alcoholic spirits and surreptitious sex filled the void, but not without consequence.

In Paris that August, en route back to Spain, he complained of liver troubles and insomnia for which Dr. Wallich prescribed Drainochol twice daily, along with halving his alcohol consumption and eliminating fatty eggs and creamy sauces, plus a bedtime dose of Belladenal Sandoz to induce sleep.[8]

Far better to have sought out supernatural spirits—the "ghostly comforts," he found so consoling.[9] As he wrote to Mrs. Pfeiffer in August 1938,[10] he had not been very nice—"intolerant and righteous, and many times, ruthless and cruel"—and admitted he needed to accept "the discipline of the Church" unquestioningly to channel his strong emotions and behave properly. But the church was on the wrong side, "attacking us, I think mistakenly," he wrote. In this letter, warming up to the topic, he meanders—first talking about Mother Pfeiffer's new typewriter and how it has improved her "epistolary style" and what a great word "vicissitudes" is. Then after all this distraction, he hits it, saying what's really on his mind. Implied in his rejection of church discipline is his embrace of his comrade-in-arms, who also happened to be young, svelte, and blonde. That he refers to Paul Pfeiffer as "Pauline's father" early in the letter underscores their less than warm relationship.

Then, too, Hem was helpless to ask for spiritual help because, he wrote Mother Pfeiffer, it seemed "crooked" to petition Heaven for yourself when others were in much more desperate shape, even as he expressed his own neediness. To do so, he wrote over fifteen years later, seemed "egotistical and wicked" when so many were dying by shellfire.[11]

Yes, he was "a dumb Catholic."

Somehow Hemingway escaped unscathed while reporting on the war often in the midst of fusillade that could have easily doomed him, to say nothing of the bombing at the Hotel Florida: His room was on the sixth floor; the seventh and eighth floors were destroyed by bombs. So he did not have the humbling experience of being wounded and scared, he wrote his mother-in-law. (Though he did eat humble pie when the play he wrote during the war's ample down-time, *The Fifth Column*, had but a brief theatrical release.) Clearly Jesus' mother, Mary, was protecting him, Mary Pfeiffer no doubt imploring her to do so now that Hem had stopped praying for himself. But she could not protect him from himself and, not only did his health, spiritual and physical, suffer, so did his reputation, often unfairly.

Critics, said Patrick, were complaining about Hemingway "wasting his time fishing for marlin in Bimini." There was even a picture of him on the cover of *Time Magazine*, the October 18, 1937, issue, in a striped sailor's shirt with a rod. "The image was of someone goofing off when the rest of the nation was preoccupied with their problems." Hemingway had discovered the futility of bobbing and weaving with the ups and downs of world events, and had a "distaste"[12] for both American political parties. "I think you can deal with humanity just so long and then you realize what a waste of time it is," said Patrick. But he made an attempt to engage. "He was pursuing marlin, but he was also explaining to the public in *Esquire* exactly what was going on in Europe and that there was going to be a war and we absolutely ought to stay out of it."

HEMINGWAY'S STRENGTHS AND WEAKNESSES

In that September 1935 *Esquire* column, "Notes on the Next War," he had predicted that Mussolini's imperial ambitions—aimed at reestablishing the Roman Empire, playing out in Africa at the time, along with Hitler's hegemonic reign of terror, designed to subjugate France and England as payback for World War I—made the next European war inevitable. "No European country is our friend nor has been since the last war and no country but one's own is worth fighting for," Hemingway wrote. "Never again should this country be put into a European war through mistaken idealism." The scars Hemingway bore from World War I, the elastic brace on his right knee, a forever reminder, had informed his thinking. "We were fools to be sucked in once on a European war and we should never be sucked in again," he wrote.[13]

Very astutely he observed, "The first panacea for a mismanaged nation is inflation of the currency; the second is war. Both bring a temporary prosperity; both bring a permanent ruin," and are the "refuge of political and economic opportunists." All of which makes his headlong involvement in the Spanish Civil War some eighteen months later confounding, though his purpose was to try and prevent World War II, whereas it only became more inevitable.

Orson Welles met Hemingway when he was finalizing *The Spanish Earth*.

> We hadn't seen each other. This is a dark projection room and I was reading the text. And, I said, "Is it really necessary to say this. Do you think, wouldn't it be better—just see the picture" . . . Then I heard this growl from the darkness. "Some damn faggot who runs an art theatre trying to tell *me* how to write narration" and so on. So, I began to camp it up . . . (and) . . . said, "Oh, Mr. Hemingway, you think because you're so big and strong and have hair on your chest that you can bully me." So, this great figure stood up and swung at me. So, I swung at him. Now you have the picture of the Spanish Civil War being projected on a screen and these two heavy figures swinging away at each other and missing most the time. The lights came up and we looked at each other and burst into laughter and became great friends.[14]

That was Hemingway! "He's a great, great, great artist," said Welles. But more than that was his humanity. "(T)he thing you never get from his books was his humor," said Welles. "He's so tense and solemn and dedicated to what is 'true and good' and all that. But when he relaxed, he was riotously funny. That was the level that I loved about him . . . And I enjoyed being with him."

Clearly, Hemingway's strength was his weakness. As his son, Patrick, said, "He was faulty as a husband. He was faulty as a father. He was faulty as a citizen." But dwelling on his weakness misses the point of Hemingway's strength—the wisdom he imparts, his great humanity, and the sheer beauty of his writing.

Which earned him gobs of actual grace. But he also needed sacramental grace, given his many and undeniable weaknesses that many biographers tut-tut about, careful to miss *not one speck of dirt*.

As he drifted, Pauline, understanding his strengths and his weaknesses, worked to lure him back. After *To Have and Have Not* was published on October 15, 1937, publicized with the aforementioned *Time Magazine* cover story, he disappeared from Pauline's life, spending Christmas in Catalan with Martha. Pauline had already contracted to have the pool built and was now making plans to travel to Madrid to find out why the war in Spain was so important to her man. Hem said he would come to Paris instead. But he was late. Pauline, imagining the worst, when it was weather that detained him, lit into him when he crossed the transom of her room at the Hôtel Elysée and they had a great row and she threatened to jump out the window if he left her.[15] Ernest was having "an intense liver complaint" and consulted Dr. Wallich again, who, this time, prescribed Drainochol *and* Chophytol to cleanse his kidneys and liver of toxins, and, this time, he forbade drinking.[16] Hemingway was in a very foul mood not only from his physical ailments but also over the "remorse" he felt just as he did when he was about to dump Hadley for Pauline. As he wrote in *Death in the Afternoon*, "I would sooner have the pox than to fall in love with another woman loving the one I have."[17]

When they sailed back to America, January 12–29, aboard the MS Gripsholm, four years after their triumphant return from Africa, the dismal weather was an analogy for their marital travails. Ernest's liver ailment darkened his outlook and, once again, the Hemingway DNA of ill-temper, depression, and paranoia swamped him the first few months of the year, the littlest thing sparking a fight as he wallowed in self-pity. When he upbraided Perkins with his time-honored complaint that his novel was not advertised sufficiently—not even a tea party like the one they hosted for Max Eastman—complete with a vituperative one-page screed, Max gently reminded Hem of Thomas Wolfe's manic-depressive episodes, prompting Ernest to note "he was an enormous baby and it must be very difficult to be a genius."[18] Touché!

By the end of March 1938, Hemingway was back in Spain and his first order of business was to plan for evacuations of Americans in the increasingly likely event of the sudden collapse of the Republican government. He attended a screening of *The Spanish Earth* in Barcelona while the Nationalists bombed overhead after which he made the great skedaddle back home.

Waiting for him on May 31, was a big pool, 24 x 60 feet, filled with over eighty thousand gallons of water pumped in from the ocean. The cisterns provided fresh water for home use but it was not enough for the pool so that had to drill down to the salt table and pump in salt water, said Patrick Hemingway.[19] It was the first pool built in Key West and the $20,000 cost was two and a half times the purchase price of the estate. Hemingway was so irritated that Pauline had spent so lavishly (though it was *her money*) that he took a penny from his pocket and dropped it on the ground, saying, "You might as well spend my last cent." Pauline, seeking to inject some levity, had the penny embedded in the concrete and soon Hemingway grew to love the pool and had a fence built around the estate so he could swim in privacy. Ironically, the pool with its salt water, laced with lithium, was "just what the doctor ordered," so to speak, for the hereditary depression that dogged him, especially when exacerbated by all the alcohol, consumed over many years. Prior to the salt pool, as noted, Hemingway would soak with friends in the salt baths in bogs which surely helped balance him mentally and helped catalyze his ample literary output while living in Key West, including *Death in the Afternoon* (1932); *Winner Take Nothing* (1933); *The Green Hills of Africa* (1935); "The Snows of Kilimanjaro" (1936); "The Short Happy Life of Francis Macomber" (1936); *To Have and Have Not* (1937); *The Fifth Column and the First Forty-Nine Short Stories* (1938); in addition to his *Esquire* and *Cosmopolitan* pieces. He also wrote portions of *For Whom the Bell Tolls* (1940) there, and, later on, his book *Islands in the Stream* was found on the property and published posthumously.

Yet, now, his erratic mood swings and outbursts punctuated life in Key West as he continued to give his faith and family short shrift. Once he had finished arranging his next volume—his only play and some five dozen short stories—he headed to Cuba on a fishing trip with Josie Russell. He wanted to avoid the hoopla surrounding the opening of the Overseas Highway, while Pauline, maintaining a façade of normalcy, planned a costume party at the Havana-Madrid club. Hem, arriving back early in a foul mood, refused to attend the party and, angry over not being able to find the key to unlock his writing room, shot off the lock with a gun to the shock and horror of Lorraine Thompson. Doubling down at the club later, Hem got into a row with a drunken guest.

Yes, it was tough being a genius.

After a couple of weeks in August at the L Bar T, he was back in Paris by September, soon arriving at the Spanish and Italian borders to cover the war for *Colliers* and begin work on his next novel with single-minded focus, so Pauline was led to believe, as she continued to hope against hope that their marriage might be mended. In truth he was with Martha much of the time, while Scribners issued his next book, *The Fifth Column and First Forty-Nine Stories*, featuring the play that had left the critics cold, and eliciting Hem's displeasure, once again, for perceived advertising deficiencies, which he trained squarely on Max.

His moodiness was all part of the agonizing and drawn-out process of separating from Pauline, and ending his marriage. Essentially, he was repeating the pattern of his parents, and following the cues of the Protestant utilitarian philosophy that shaped him in his formative years, where good and pleasure are indistinguishable.

MARITAL WOES, "HAPPIEST" WRITING

Finally leaving Key West for Cuba on February 13, 1939, he settled into his suite at the Hotel Sevilla-Biltmore in Havana, while still receiving mail at the Ambos Mundos as a decoy to hide the shambles of his personal life. He was always happiest writing and now he had found both a place to write undisturbed and an epic story to write. As he wrote Max, "Have figured out that in my personal problems I am no good to anyone if I do not work."[20] He had planned to write three short stories including "one about the old commercial fisherman who fought the swordfish all alone in his skiff for 4 days and four nights and the sharks finally eating it after he had it alongside and could not get it into the boat."[21] Instead, he began writing a novel based on a short story about the war that Pauline thought was the best, titled "Under the Ridge," and when he had written 15,000 words, he knew he must continue. He also asked Max to send Scott his "great affection," noting how "excellent" much of *Tender Is the Night* was, and explaining parenthetically, "I always had a very stupid feeling of superiority about Scott—like a tough little boy sneering at a delicate but talented little boy."

Clearly writing was healing for Hem.

He returned to Key West in mid-March to spend time with his eldest son Jack, now fifteen and home for Easter vacation, rejoining Martha in Havana the day after Easter, her first time there, to continue his life of writing, fishing and drinking. (Though Michael Reynolds says he returned to Cuba on Spy Wednesday which, if so, would seem to underscore his weak faith, since it's unlikely he attended Holy Mass on Easter Sunday in Havana.) Initially they stayed at the hotel, but Martha could not abide the mess, so they looked for and found a new home, the "Finca Vigia," twenty minutes outside of Havana, just east of Iglesia de Santa Maria del Rosario. They rented and renovated the ramshackle home, settling in by May as they began their new life in Cuba, albeit still receiving mail at Ambos Mundos.

On September 1, 1939, the first day of World War II, Hemingway, now forty, arrived at the L Bar T, soon to be joined by 44-year-old Pauline, just arriving back from Europe. They had spent so many happy times at the ranch not so many years ago but now Pauline had a bad flu/cold and she only got sicker and, as the week progressed, they decided, then and there, to end their union. While the marriage was not over in the eyes of the Church, recognizing reality, Pauline granted Ernest a divorce. In so doing, she told her husband that the relationship with Martha would not last. She was right, but he would not listen.

Hemingway rejoined Martha in Sun Valley, Idaho, in the fall, his first time there, chosen because it reminded him of Spain. Martha, itching to cover the war, soon departed for Europe, leaving Hemingway alone to his novel. He would find that, with Martha, he would spend much time alone; nor did he have a trust fund to pay for his travel now, though the Hollywood contract to produce the film version of *To Have and Have Not* (1944), starring Humphrey Bogart and Lauren Bacall, replaced those monies. It was only made because Howard Hawks was trying to lure Hem to Hollywood "to write for pictures."[22] No dice, said Hem. "I'm good at what I'm doing and I don't want to go to Hollywood." Hawks said, "You don't have to go to Hollywood. I'll come and meet you and we'll fish and hunt and we'll work on a story." But Ernest hemmed and hawed. And he said, "Ernest, I can make a picture out of your worst book." "What's my worst book?" "*To Have and Have Not* is a bunch of junk," said Hawks. Well, that junk was now gold.

Life was changing in so many ways. By December 1939, longing for his old haunt, he drove back to Key West, once again, with Toby Bruce. But the island was no longer big enough for both Pauline and Ernest and, that same month, he finally made the move to Cuba into his new home, the Finca Vigia, where he finished his masterpiece. In July, he was staying at the Intercontinental New York Barclay Hotel, a few blocks from Scribners, when he put the finishing touches on the novel he christened *For Whom the Bell Tolls*.

The spiritual thirst and memory in the novel that opened and closed on the pine-needle covered floor, though scant, is evident. To wit: One of the main characters, named "Pilar," in another nod to Our Lady of Pilar, keeps

Hemingway posing for a dust jacket photo for the first edition of "For Whom the Bell Tolls" at the Sun Valley Lodge, Idaho, late 1939. *Source:* In the public domain.

the main guerilla band together when her husband "goes bad." Spared a bout of sickness, she says, "There probably still is God after all, although we have banished him."[23] "I do not believe in ogres, nor soothsayers, nor in supernatural things," says Robert Jordan, the protagonist,[24] a humanist who only believes in "the cause." His love interest, Maria, though, makes sure he did not aim at the Sacred Heart medal an enemy combatant wore, the medal that everyone in Navarre wears, she says. He assures her, "No. Below it."[25] And, as the fighter planes near, Joaquim, a member of "Sordo's" band, named after the father of the Blessed Virgin Mary, prays the entire Hail Mary then makes an Act of Contrition, as he faces possible death.[26] (In the 1943 film version, Joachim is only shown moving his lips, praying.) And cathedrals are no longer "places of dignity" but battle posts.

A friend of this author, who prefers remaining anonymous, born in Madrid in 1940, who grew up in Cuba, recounted how, after the Spanish Republicans lost the war, they all sought refuge in Cuba. Her Uncle Jose (not his real name), a prominent Cuban journalist from Catalan, and friend of Hemingway, would bring her to the "Finca Vigia." "They drank like fish" and "they were all communists," she said. Her father did not approve of Jose bringing her to these social gatherings, saying "You take her where the devil won't go." Jose, said my friend, "hated the church." But as for the contention that Hemingway was a "communist," she admits that she was looking at it through the prism of a young child seeing him cavorting with Fidel Castro and Ernesto "Che" Guevara, which, admittedly seems dispositive. But as Hemingway wrote to Charles Scribner, "I can take oath at any time that I am not nor never have been a member of the C.P. (Communist Party.)"[27] My friend said her uncle swore the same. As Jordan said, when asked if he was a communist, "No I am an anti-fascist."[28] John said his father's philosophy was that it was not right to interfere with your host country's management of their affairs.[29]

Then, too, the distaste Hemingway felt for the Church, sewn into him by the antifascist doctrine, was all of a piece. Not to put too fine a point on it, but it sent his personal life careening.

Pauline, for her part, was now experiencing the "Via Dolorosa" ("mournful way") Christ trod on the way to Golgotha. The cross she carried was immense. Truth be told, like Hemingway, she could have helped save the marriage and avoid the heavy cross that dissolution of her marriage inflicted on her. Whereas Hem's blind spot was sex, hers was money. "There was a great deal of bitterness between my father and Pauline," said John. "A lot of it was financial. Papa resented the fact that Pauline was extremely wealthy and still insisted that he pay."[30] (Albeit Martha did as well!) When Hadley and her new husband, Paul Mower, visited her in Key West after the divorce, the first time Hadley had seen her since 1930, their enmity long since dissolved, she observed her "bitterness" over the divorce.[31] A few years later, in April 1945, when they ran into each other at the Algonquin in New York, Hadley recalled how, over lunch, Pauline kept saying how she begged Ernest not to go to Spain with Martha, punctuating it by saying, "Well, I hate him."[32] As a Catholic, she believed in the indissolubility of marriage and was not free to remarry since Ernest's first marriage was annulled, paving the way to a valid marriage.

Now, Pauline had to row her own boat.

As did Ernest.

MEETING "COOP," SAYING GOODBYE TO SCOTT

In the fall of 1940, while once again vacationing at celebrity-rich Sun Valley—the celebrities lured by the beautiful ski resort built in 1936—Hem met and befriended Gary Cooper, one of Hollywood's biggest stars who single-handedly lifted Paramount's sagging Depression-era fortunes with *Mr. Deeds Goes to Town* (1936). He had, of course, famously played Frederic Henry in the film version of *A Farewell to Arms* (1932) and was now working on *Sergeant York* (1941).

Theirs was a warm, enduring friendship, characterized by hours conversing and drinking by the fire at the lodge in Sun Valley, and they became "extraordinarily close," said Coop's daughter, Maria Cooper Janis.[33]

Not long afterward, on the first day of winter, Hemingway's other close friend, F. Scott Fitzgerald, dropped dead of a heart attack in Hollywood.

"His talent was as natural as the pattern that was made by the dust on a butterfly's wings," Hemingway would later write of Scott, showing his lasting regard for his friend. "At one time he understood it no more than the butterfly did . . . Later he became conscious of his damaged wings . . . and could not fly anymore because the love of flight was gone and he could only remember when it had been effortless."[34]

The feeling was mutual.

In his last letter to Ernest, Scott wrote and thanked him for the inscribed copy of *For Whom the Bell Tolls*. "It's a fine novel, better than anyone else writing could do," he wrote. "I envy you like hell . . . and I envy you the time it will give you to do what you want." He closed: "With Old Affection."[35]

Now, from his perch in Heaven, Scott could see he had nothing to envy, and how Hemingway's new friend would provide that stable male friendship he so needed at this critical juncture, bringing him along spiritual paths, both men always carrying a little crucifix. Hemingway was just entering a time in his life when his crosses would become heavier.

8

~~~~

World War II and "Black Ass"

"Across the River and Into the Trees"

It was like clockwork. *For Whom the Bell Tolls* was published on October 21, 1940. On November 5, Hemingway wed Martha, having learned of the final divorce over the AP wire the day before. Then, he bought the Finca Vigia as a Christmas present. After that he stopped writing. Novels, that is.

His celebrity certainly played a role in distracting him from his life's work. When he showed up at the Floridita in Havana in the evenings with his glamorous wife on his arm, the electricity in the air was palpable. The music started playing more loudly, heads turned, conversation quickened. And, while he lived for his writing, he also lived for the thrill of it all, so corrosive to a writer, as he would famously say in the sunset of his life upon receiving the ultimate recognition of literary excellence.

ADRIFT

As he lost his way, his celebrity at its peak, he began to drink a quart of whiskey a day. "He was what in England was known as a 'one bottle man,' tremendously resistant to alcohol. He could drink like a fish," said his son Patrick.[1] At his fortieth birthday party the previous July, still married to Pauline, he got plastered.[2] And while he surely had the habit of working hard and playing hard—drinking, like smoking, being commonplace then—for him, alcohol was more than social convention. It was also a crutch, helping dull the effects of traumatic brain injuries (TBI), two by that time, and shell shock (now called "Post Traumatic Stress Disorder," i.e., PTSD) and helped him medicate the depression he felt after a period of mania, a cycle that dogged him his whole life—an illness that was now only intensifying, given the effects of long-term alcohol consumption, overlaid with the PTSD and TBI, which exacerbated his hypertension, high blood sugar, and genetic hemochromatosis.

Whereas in the thirties, Hemingway's disciplined and prolific writing served as a continuing source of emotional healing, his Catholic faith a healing spiritual salve, all the while his body soaked up healthful salt water; by 1940, in Havana, having cut ties with his faith and family, he was alcoholically self-medicating, in spite of Dr. Wallich's order three years earlier to *stop* drinking. And he was swimming in toxic chlorinated water to boot. Then, too, Martha's career was overshadowing their relationship—taking precedence over hearth and home, which was not to Hemingway's liking and did not help his mood. In the revisionist telling, it's the story of his massive male ego resenting Gellhorn's talent, self-confidence, and independent streak. After all, *he* had mentored her and helped her find her voice. Now he's chafing at the bit, engaging in dissolute living—his writing sort of an afterthought.

Nothing could be further from the truth.

Meanwhile, with no novel in the works, which would have anchored him—using all the pain for his next masterpiece—he took a major detour in his life, doing intelligence work including several OSS missions.

Yes, gone was the anchor.

"We're all communists," Hemingway, so virulently anti-fascist, had said while covering the Spanish Civil War, which Denis Brian deemed akin to a "non-Irishman" saying on St. Patrick's Day, "We're all Irish."[3] One day, Hemingway took it a step further, in Nicholas Reynolds' telling.[4] Estranged former KGB officer Alexander Vassiliev found "verbatim excerpts from Hemingway's official Soviet file that he smuggled out of Russia." Evidently, in December 1940, NKVD agents recruited Hemingway for "[NKVD] work on ideological grounds." This, in spite of Hemingway's forthright assessment of the Spanish Republic's bad behavior in *For Whom the Bell Tolls*, causing the Left to skewer him, notably the *Daily Worker*, for his alleged "class egotism" and his failure to understand neither democracy nor communism. Furthermore, he allegedly cut and ran from the war, "leaving a trail of alibis, whines and slanders."[5] All those strikes against him notwithstanding, Jacob Golos, a top NKVD agent in New York, the smuggled file asserts, "met with Hemingway, giving him the code name 'Argo,'" said Reynolds, the deal evidently sealed on the Lower East Side. Though, what occurred at the meeting and where they even met is all speculative—Golos and Hemingway "would have" said and done this, Reynolds wrote in his book.[6] The fact is, Hemingway never gave them anything of value—not even a signed copy of *For Whom the Bell Tolls*! Still, the anchor was sorely missed.

Hemingway and Martha traveled to China on February 22, 1941, where they spent 100 days reporting for *Colliers*, and honeymooning. Once back in Havana, they entertained lavishly, as always, at their stunning seaside estate in the hills above Havana, and it was at one of these parties that Hemingway chatted up the larger-than-life U.S. Ambassador to Cuba, Spruille Braden, who suggested he might do some counterintelligence work, helping ferret out Nazi spies. Hemingway, though, was more interested in eying Spanish falangists in league with Germany and, in 1942, assembled an anti-fascist spy network composed of Loyalist refugees he knew from Spain, twenty-six informants in all, dubbed "The Crook Factory." Washington sent Gustavo Durán, a lieutenant colonel in the Spanish Republican Army who commanded troops at Boadilla, Brunete, and Valencia, now serving as a U.S. diplomat, and Communist spy and later an aide to Nelson Rockefeller, to help with Hemingway's efforts, according to Professor Jeffrey Meyers.[7] A former pianist and composer, Durán is said to have inspired *For Whom the Bell Tolls*, and it was Hemingway's friendship with him that got Hoover's antennae up and led to the opening of an FBI file, wrote Meyers. Braden had wanted Hemingway to go to Mexico City in early September to snag some "Commies" and "their traveling peace circus." Hemingway did not go. He had already been there in March 1942, according to a confidential FBI informant, albeit "under an assumed name," while meeting with a dispirited communist.[8] While he and his network kept an eye out for the falangists, providing little useful intel, the FBI successfully discredited his efforts and they were disbanded eight months later in April 1943; yet the FBI's surveillance of Hemingway would continue until shortly before his death.

For the rest of 1943, Hemingway patrolled the waters off Cuba, fortified by a stockpile of U.S. government weapons including machine guns, stove-pipes (rocket-propelled anti-tank), and grenades, while keeping eyes peeled for German U-boats that had sunk 263 Allied ships during the Battle of the Caribbean (February 16–November 30, 1942)—hoping to lure them close to the *Pilar*, to disable and sink them. Hemingway was also fighting off feelings of worthlessness fueled by all that talk of his being a loose cannon in official Washington and among intimates, including Martha, seemingly poised for ever-greater glory. As if to underscore these inferior feelings, when he registered for the draft on November 20, 1943, he called himself "an unemployed writer."

RE-ANCHORED, D-DAY AND WWII

Early on the morning of May 25, 1944, eight days after arriving in London to serve as a war correspondent for *Collier's*, Hemingway was in a car accident[9] and suffered yet another traumatic brain injury. Bill Walton, a *Time* reporter, whom Hemingway met in London on May 24, hours before the accident, at one of photographer Robert Capa's patented parties, pegged him a "classic manic-depressive," and he knew it, he said. "I think he was perfectly aware of his own strain of madness."[10] It surely did not help his condition that, after he had made the trip to Europe, embarking on this dangerous mission, in part, to be with Gellhorn, she laughed when she saw him all bandaged up in his hospital room as she continued preparing to cover the Allied invasion of Normandy. Supreme Allied Commander General Dwight D. Eisenhower finally gave the order to commence this, the largest amphibious military operation in history, known as Operation Overlord, on June 6, 1944. Her reaction to Hemingway as she's prepping and he's sidelined, was cruel, given that "she thought he was slightly mad long before his breakdown in the 1940s," said Brian. "The violent rages and wild drunkenness are all symptoms," said Walton. "But they don't exist all the time; they're periodic."

Hemingway was soon right back where he wanted to be—in the thick of it. While Gellhorn landed on Omaha Beach, it was Hemingway who wrote the day's events most compellingly from his vantage point on the landing craft, said Patrick Hemingway: "At the 50th anniversary of D-Day in France, the Navy asked for his piece describing that landing craft and the people going ashore to be read in the ceremony" near Omaha Beach. "It did not ask to read anything by Martha Gellhorn."[11] Touché!

Hemingway had scoped out the war from the day he arrived in London, writing dispatches from his base at the Dorchester Hotel and, after D-Day, was enthralled by the Royal Air Force and their Typhoon squad working to blunt the German buzzbomb campaign over London. He enjoyed hanging with them, drinking a beer at the pub, stopping by, along the way, "at Salisbury Cathedral to pray for the souls of his English Ancestors."[12]

But this consummate risk-taker was not satisfied *just* being the dutiful dispatcher, the Geneva Convention Rules to observe, not join, the fighting be damned. And, before long, he had hooked up with the 4th Armored Division and, by July 28, West-Pointer Col. Charles "Buck" Lanham's forward command post, the 22nd Infantry Regiment. For nine days he accompanied "the Double Deucers" as they advanced south and east toward Saint-Pois, twenty-five miles from Le Mesnil-Herman, writing that it was "a tough fine time with the infantry"[13] as they fought over the farmland topography now scattered with "deads" from both sides. When fighting let up, Hemingway and Lanham managed to bond, in spite of their diverging interests—Lanham focused on literature and his own writing aspirations while Hemingway wanted to talk about, as Lanham dubbed it, that "grace under pressure crap."[14]

Lanham thought that Hemingway "veered back and forth between believing in nothing and being a half-assed Catholic." But, in time, he witnessed how Hemingway's faith was real. "At bullfights some years later he'd go to a Catholic chapel every day and by God he'd pray."[15]

Hemingway evidently did valuable reconnaissance work as the Allies steamed toward Paris to liberate the city in the summer of 1944, especially in Rambouillet about 27.5 miles southwest of Paris and during the Battle of Hürtgen Forest (September 19 to December 16, 1944). "His main job—as he saw it—was to provide information on the disposition of enemy forces far enough in advance to help save the lives of his compatriots," wrote Baker. Naturally, his fellow correspondents resented his heroics and even tried to bring him up on Geneva Convention violations but Col. Lanham stood by him, calling him "probably the bravest man I have ever known."[16]

Walton described the scene in Hürtgen Forest in his *Life Magazine* dispatch published on January 1, 1945: "Other battles in this war have been more dramatically decisive—Normandy, St. Lo, the Falaise pocket—but none was tougher or bloodier than the battle for this Hürtgen Forest" stuffed with "firs towering 75 to 100 feet" rendering it "a gloomy, mysterious world where the brightness of noon is muted to an eerie twilight filtering through dark trees onto spongy brown needles and rotting logs." At 8 a.m., fighter bombers began their mission on the eastern edge. "In the thunder heaped on Grosshau, it seemed impossible for any living thing to survive."

But as bad as the battle was, it was the uncertainty of the silence between the gunfire that seemed worse, alternating between fear and boredom. During these black-jack and conversation-filled intervals Hemingway and Walton bonded.

When they met at the Capa bash, Hemingway was fascinated that Walton, also failing to get credentials, was planning to parachute into Normandy on D-Day with the 82nd Airborne, and was in "Jump School" to learn how. After the accident (in which he was a passenger in a car steered by an intoxicated driver), as he recovered from yet another TBI, Hemingway made his way to liberated France to visit Walton in Cherbourg, pretending to deliver him his mail. Later they enjoyed a week of downtime in August, along with Capa and other correspondents, in liberated Mont-Saint-Michel, drinking and eating to their hearts' content, soon famously celebrating the liberation of Paris together at the Ritz bar.

Now, in the fall of 1944, they huddled in a two-room woodcutter's hut in the forest, with no plumbing nor electricity, but thankfully equipped with a small iron stove, on which Hemingway's driver, Sergeant Archie "Red" Pelkey, who idolized him, cooked for the trio, whipping up a stew by scrounging fresh vegetables to add to the army-issued beef. Firewood he gathered warmed the hut and dried their drenched uniforms. Gin, too, helped keep them warm. At night, the two correspondents could only count on an unreliable army lantern or candles by which to write their cables or read, for about an hour.[17]

In the daytime, the two correspondents went to the front lines, where the soldiers immediately noticed Hemingway's impressive frame. They were immensely fond of him—a frequently photographed celebrity, known for his safaris, often compared to Clark Gable—handsome, tan, with that pearly white smile; a successful novelist, his latest *For Whom the Bell Tolls* recently made into a film starring his friend Cooper and Ingrid Bergman; and now war correspondent. One day, both were clad in warm and bulky sheepskin coats purloined from a German warehouse, on the fronts of which Hemingway had playfully sketched military medals. But they did not don the hoods lest they be mistaken for Germans, instead wearing steel helmets on which was etched their correspondent's "C," so they would be correctly identified.

Hemingway and Walton would often stop by the trailer where Colonel Lanham made his headquarters, always sharing "the true gen"—a phrase first used by the Royal Air Force in World War II to signify the lowdown, the truth. They spent September and October with the regiment, ending with Hürtgen Forest, where thick underground walls protected the remaining Germans. They were following Colonel Lanham's regiment, which had sustained heavy casualties amid heavy shelling.

Theirs was an enduring friendship—both Midwesterners, both possessing a great sense of humor and storytelling prowess, both magnanimously generous. (Just that summer, Hemingway had arranged a $1,500 painting commission for the writer Wyndham Lewis, impoverished at the time, even though Lewis had been harshly critical of Hemingway's writing.) As A. E. Hotchner, known as "Hotch," said, Walton "measured up"—not an easy hurdle to surmount. The key was genuineness. A whiff of phoniness and you were gone. This exclusive club also included Dietrich, Cooper, Ordóñez, Peirce, Beach, Percival, and *New York Post* columnist Leonard Lyons, among others. Loyalty was important but most important was being true to oneself.[18]

The last day of the Hürtgen battle sealed the deal. Pelkey was driving the pair when Hemingway, hearing the familiar sound of enemy aircraft just like in the Spanish Civil War, yelled for Pelkey to stop, then listening, ordered them to jump out into the soggy ditch as the attacking enemy plane flew overhead. Their lives were saved, which Ernest celebrated by passing around his gin-filled canteen, smiling fulsomely.[19]

Walton, who frequently saw Hemingway making the sign of the cross and knocking on wood three times, a sign of his belief in the Trinity, no doubt saw him make that gesture in that moment of saving grace.[20]

No, Hemingway was not just tagging along or carousing, as Gellhorn bravely covered wars.

"Every year," said Patrick, his father "got a Christmas card from General Omar Bradly," who commanded all U.S. ground forces invading Germany. "After the war, I had to listen to endless discussions with members of the 4th Infantry Division and my father. He was revered by these people."[21]

No matter, the revisionists say Hemingway was "jealous" of Gellhorn's writing success during World War II and was all hat, no cattle. So, she finally put him *in his place*, divorcing him in 1945 after which her illustrious career covering wars continued while Hemingway descended into madness. That might make a good feminist storyline. But it's not the real story.

"I don't think his breakup with her had any real bad effect on him as a writer. He went on to triumph. It was breaking up with her that got him writing again!" said Patrick, who observed the transition close-up.

The problem, in fact, was the difference in talent, he said. "It's very difficult when you have two ambitious writers of unequal talent married," said Patrick. His father was, as *Vanity Fair*'s James Wolcott describes him, "America's first and only literary king." Gellhorn was a fine journalist, said Patrick. "But the truth is, Hemingway was better than her *even in that*."

Regarding this, his third marriage, said Patrick, "It was amazing that they stuck together as long as they did. But I think that both were quite happy when it was over. They were both free to fulfill their individual careers."

Furthermore, Hemingway went on to rediscover his faith, starting with building a better foundation on which his humanity could flourish.

On April 2, 1945, as his marriage to Gellhorn was crumbling, he wrote in a letter to Col. Buck Lanham, that he was suffering from "Black Ass," defining it in parentheses as "Depression."[22] Hemingway had married Gellhorn hoping for a baby girl. Yet Martha was so contemptuous of him that she aborted a child she had conceived with him, without even telling him she was pregnant, and carried on an affair with Walton with Hemingway's full knowledge. As Meyers reported, she told an English friend, "'There's no need to have a child when you can buy one' . . . referring to the Italian boy she had adopted after the war. 'That's what I did.'"[23]

At the same time, Hemingway's eyes were reopening to spiritual realities. As he wrote to Thomas Welsh in that famous letter of June 19, 1945, when he was "really scared" in World War I after being wounded, he had prayed for "preservation through prayers for intercession of Our Lady and various saints that prayed to with almost tribal faith."[24]

Hemingway divorced Martha on December 31, 1945, and married Welsh's daughter Mary, a *Time-Life* reporter and colleague of Walton, on March 14, 1946.

While Mary was not Hemingway's cultural equal, she did one thing right. She put Hemingway first, and so it was that Hemingway started writing novels again and getting right with God.

STRUGGLING, SPIRITUALLY AND PHYSICALLY

Sanctity is not about being perfect but about struggling. Hemingway struggled and would talk with Cooper about those struggles and about his Catholic faith, which he had badly fallen away from for a second time. As he warmed up to his faith, Cooper, too, was discovering Catholicism.

But the soul dances in a healthy body, and Hemingway's health was now making that dance a little more difficult. In August 1947, he began suffering from high blood pressure. "Inside his head," writes Baker, "Ernest began hearing a strange buzzing and humming, like the sound made by telephone wires along country roadsides."[25] Besides dietary changes to shed the pounds, his physician, Dr. José Luis Herrera Sotolongo, prescribed medications.

Hemingway had met Dr. Herrera while both were attached to the 12th International Brigade near Madrid in 1937. After the war, Dr. Herrera was incarcerated by Franco, then exiled to Cuba where he became a close associate of Fidel Castro and Che Guevara, which helps explain Hemingway's friendship with the two prominent communists.[26] Now, Dr. Herrera was helping defeat the enemy within Hemingway's mind and body. But how to shed the mounting stress?

That spring, Patrick had a mental breakdown after suffering a concussion in a car crash en route to visit his mother in Los Angeles. Greg recovered quickly. For Patrick it was a different story. On the morning of April 14, shortly after arriving at the Finca Vigia, he awoke with a fever and delirium, and began to go into a psychotic episode. He was nearly disabled for life, during which Hemingway doggedly nursed him back to health at home, which, along with electroshock treatments, enabled his full recovery. Meanwhile, Mary had decamped to Chicago to be at the bedside of her ailing father, suffering with prostate cancer. Shortly after Mary arrived back in Havana on May 18, utterly exhausted, just needing to sleep, Pauline arrived and, to Ernest's surprise and delight, the two women bonded over their shared experience at "Hemingway University."[27]

Mary and Pauline soon realized Hemingway was suffering nervous exhaustion, demonstrated no more clearly than when he exploded in anger over Faulkner calling him a coward. So he thought. Faulkner, now teaching creative writing at the University of Mississippi, had nominated his "five most important contemporaries"—Wolfe, Dos Passos, Hemingway, Willa Cather, and John Steinbeck—stating that American literature had begun with Sherwood Anderson "who has 'no inhibitions,' and who 'writes simply as if he had never read anything.'" He put himself second, only behind Wolfe.[28] By comparison, the six novelists, who arrived on the scene in Anderson's wake, were victims of "splendid Failure," Faulkner told some his Ole Miss students. Hemingway surely did not appreciate the middling rank, nor the comparison to Anderson, nor the "Failure" designation. Believing Faulkner was referring to his physical courage, he sprang into action, asking Col. Lanham to detail for Faulkner his acts of bravery during World War II.

Shortly thereafter, on June 13, Hemingway was awarded the Bronze Star at the American Embassy in Havana for "meritorious service as a war correspondent from 20 July to 1 September, and from 6 November to 6 December, 1944, in France and Germany"—in which he demonstrated military prowess and that special Hemingway "talent of expression."

Faulkner apologized.

No sooner had Hemingway arrived back from the embassy on June 17, than he received the shocking news that Max Perkins had, that very day, died of pneumonia, breathing his last at his historic home in Stamford, Connecticut. Needless to say, Perkins' sudden death was a massive shock to Hemingway's system. That was just the start of the gut-wrenching loss. Three months later, on September 12, Katy Smith Dos Passos was decapitated in a car accident while driving with her husband, who had been blinded by the sun at that horrific moment of impact and, while Dos lived, he lost sight in one eye. Next, two generals in Spain Hemingway had worked with, suddenly died. Then, Mark Hellinger, who had produced the film *The Killers* (1946) based on Hemingway's short story, dropped dead of a heart attack on December 21, seven years to the day after Scott's heart gave out, both chain-smoking, hard-drinking workaholics. Even Hemingway's cook, Ramon, was felled by cardiac arrest.

Hemingway could see his own life winding down, as well.

The biographers and feature writers were not far behind.

During the Christmas season of 1947, the *New Yorker*'s Lillian Ross, a twenty-nine-year-old reporter, phoned regarding a profile she was writing about Hemingway's friend, Sidney Franklin—a kid from Brooklyn, parents from Czarist Russia, father a cab driver, who had become the first successful

American matador in Spain. Hemingway had befriended Franklin while writing his bullfighting magnum opus—one day simply approaching him in a café. The two struck up a conversation and became fast friends. When Ross called, the Hemingways were headed to Ketchum, Idaho, for Christmas. So, she met them there. Her first glimpse of the iconic author completely won her over, and she would soon start writing a profile of *him*.

At a New Year's party on January 1, 1948, Hemingway predicted a terrible year ahead. In fact, that spring, once they got back to Cuba, things got off to a pretty good start as he enjoyed a visit with his old friend Malcolm Cowley who was writing his own profile of Ernest—this one in *Life Magazine*.

Then along came young Aaron Hotchner. He was doing a profile of Hemingway for *Cosmopolitan*. After Hem's hazing of "Hotch" at the Floridita where he downed several Papa Dobles and prevailed upon the young reporter to do the same, they bonded. Hem clued him in that day to the simple fact that his writing was simple because he had a few simple ideas to impart.

Thus, had the chapter of his life begun where the chroniclers were swarming in, intruding on his private life to try and capture it for posterity. If only he could capture his life for himself. If only he could live in peace. The profiles that came out were less than helpful in that regard.

Ross' profile, for one, published two and a half years later, in the May 13, 1950, issue of the *New Yorker* was not exactly a love letter, what with its tight directorial closeups in which she often repeated back every syllable Hemingway uttered and reported every gesture in a mocking way.

Nor was he thrilled about others who started poking around in his life including, from Hemingway's perspective, that pesky biographer Carlos Baker, who would write the authorized biography for Scribners, and this kid named Philip Young who had written a doctoral dissertation on Hemingway, which Rinehart wanted to publish a non-academic version of.

But rising above it all, he soldiered on with his latest novel, *The Garden of Eden*, ironically observing, "Happiness in intelligent people is the rarest thing I know"[29]—all the while accompanied by his new English Springer Spaniel, named Blackie or Black Dog—Hem's most fiercely loyal companion. He had sent Hadley a copy of the 1,000-page draft of the novel in 1946, which included the story of the wife burning up her husband's writings.

In June, after declining the invitation from the Academy of Arts and Letters to be a member, he sent a series of letters to Charles Scribner including one with the humorous observation that when he was working hard, he had to cut back on lovemaking because the two were powered by the same engine.

Then came his forty-ninth birthday, a big cruise bash, celebrated with close family and friends. As the dust settled, it was now time to begin staring down his fiftieth and how to celebrate *that milestone*. And, so it is that he began making plans to travel to Italy. He wanted to gain a new lease on life and leave behind all the problems in America not least of which the new novelists who threatened to overtake him in popularity, if not style.

The month before sailing, news that his entertainment lawyer, Maurice Speiser, who had been gravely ill, had died on August 5, 1948, plunged Hemingway into a deep depression. He had met Speiser in Hendaye 20 years earlier, and the two had formed an unbreakable bond. While Hem had not had good experiences with adaptations of his works for theatre or film—his play, *The Fifth Column*, a case in point—he could, at least, console himself that Maurice would clean up the ensuing mess. No more. Hem's spirits began to lift once he docked in Genoa in late September aboard the Polish ship, *Jagiello*. As they unloaded his glistening royal blue Buick, fastened to the foredeck, and the dozens of pieces of luggage, massive Hemingway, with dainty Mary by his side, made his way down the gangplank to a hero's welcome. Persona non grata during the fascist era, he was now a huge celebrity coming to war-torn Italy, basking in American strength and power that he projected.[30]

He would soon relive his "crowded hour" on that Italian battlefield in the Veneto region thirty years earlier—the moment he was wounded and later anointed. But it was a radically different landscape, now crawling with an entourage of reporters and shutterbug paparazzi, not selfless medical staff and selfless men of the cloth.

The Hemingways hoped to tour Provence, as well, wrapping up in Paris. Instead, they remained in Italy through Christmas as Hemingway soaked in the spirituality of its cathedrals, his faith once again stirring.

Something else was stirring, as well.

They made Venice their home and its splendid Gritti Palace Hotel where they regularly dined at Harry's Bar. Worshipped by the local aristocrats, Hemingway loved shooting ducks, while work on his trilogy, "The Land," "The Sea," and "The Air," languished.

In November, a duck hunt at a private reserve brought him face to face with beautiful, intelligent, aristocratic, *and* artistic Adriana Ivancich, thirty-one years his junior, and a devout Catholic, with whom he fell madly in love.

The relationship was evidently platonic, but in Hemingway's mind it was so much more. Their exchange of letters and time spent together in public was scandalous to Venetians. Adriana, who herself suffered from depression and would end her life thirty-four years later, should have known better than to encourage such an imprudent relationship. She must have intuited that she brought more to the table than his wife Mary, who lacked the intellectual sophistication Hemingway craved. Mary was, Walton observed, inadequate in many ways for Hemingway, resulting in an estrangement in the early fifties. But Adriana was starstruck as was Hemingway who swooned over her. Such are the emotions of artists. Meanwhile Mary suffered through this latest emotional entanglement. Or perhaps she encouraged it, as she evidently encouraged an affair with "an attractive young woman" a few years later.[31]

Adriana was invited to ski with the Hemingways in Cortina D'Ampezzo after which she visited the Finca Vigia for several months with her mother—a May to December romance Hemingway turned into *Across the River and Into the Trees*. He started writing this, his fourth novel, during the Italian ski vacation in early 1949, just as Cowley's "Portrait of Mr. Papa" came out in *Life Magazine* (Jan. 10 issue). "Papa" was the name he had acquired when first visiting Pamplona, in the summer of 1923, when Hadley was pregnant with John. Now it fit him like a glove.

Upon his return to Cuba, he continued writing about the aging fifty-year-old American colonel, a divorcé, who, upon visiting Venice to relive his military glory days, falls in love with a young Italian countess named Renata, Latin for "born again." The colonel's ex-wife was a journalist, now essentially "dead," who "had more ambition than Napoleon and about talent of the average High School Valedictorian," the valedictorian part exactly how Hemingway described Gellhorn, unfairly in his estimation, said Patrick.[32] Renata was a breath of fresh air.[33] As Hemingway writes of the colonel's first impression upon meeting her at Harry's bar, "She turned her head and raised her chin, without vanity, nor coquetry, and the Colonel felt his heart turn over inside him, as though some sleeping animal had rolled over in its burrow and frightened, deliciously, the other animal sleeping close beside."

He asks the nineteen-year-old, "Would you ever like to run for Queen of Heaven?" "That would be sacrilegious,"[34] Renata replies. Adrianna, and her fictional embodiment, was in love with love and the power her older consort infused her with, creative and sensual, affirming her artistry and femininity. But Hemingway could not checkmate the Queen of Heaven, who, after all, was protecting him—in this instance shielding him from another adulterous affair as he kept up his flirtation with the virginal, devoutly Catholic Adrianna. Like the unconsummatable relationship, the novel never quite hung together, though it did have references to God and cathedrals largely abandoned in *For Whom the Bell Tolls*.

He finished the draft manuscript in Paris and completed revisions a year later in Venice, early in the winter of 1950, after which it was serialized in *Cosmopolitan*, February to June 1950.

Ernest Hemingway standing on the Bridge of Sighs in Venice, Italy, 1950. The Bridge of Sighs is so named because, as Lord Byron wrote in his 1812 book, *Childe Harold's Pilgrimage*, it connects "a palace and a prison." *Source:* A. E. Hotchner/ Library of Congress via AP.

In May 1950, with impeccable timing, the Lillian Ross *New Yorker* profile hit. It was based on two days of interviews in New York, November 15–18, 1949, when the Hemingways were staying at the Sherry Netherlands. While Ross' magnifying glass was too harsh at times, Hemingway's endearing side came through. Like when he ran into Winston Guest ("Wolfie") while shopping at Abercrombie and Fitch.

"How's the book now, Papa?" Guest asked.

Hemingway let out his trademark "fist-to-face laugh," wrote Ross, declaring he was defending his title again. "Wolfie, all of a sudden I found I could write wonderful again, instead of just biting on the nail." He spoke slowly and deliberately as he got to the heart of the matter and the need for rebuilding his head "inside," in the wake of so many injuries:

> You should not, ideally, break a writer's head open or give him seven concussions in two years or break six ribs on him when he is forty-seven or push a rear-view-mirror support through the front of his skull opposite the pituitary gland or, really, shoot at him too much.[35]

Then, there was the wonderful visit from Charles Scribner, who had brought along the contract for *Across the River and Into the Trees*. The friendship between the two was palpable and Ross didn't miss a beat, including

Scribner's "Uh-huh" responses and Hemingway's ribbing, telling him when asked whether or not he had read his recent letters, that yes, he kept them tucked away right next to Browning's poems.

Hemingway spoke of "the terrible responsibility of writing." Just because he was letting loose now, he wanted her to know the real Hemingway was a serious writer. As if *that* wasn't *obvious*. Yet Ross's portrait did reveal a bit of hole in his soul that he satiated with food and drink—drink being the constant subtext; he even imbibed from his silver flask while shopping. And, he was constantly focused on what *he* wanted to do or did not want to do. *He* did not want to hang with people he did not like. But *he* loved "the Kraut," as he called Marlene Dietrich.

Showing how far he had drifted spiritually, she quotes him as saying, "Only suckers worry about saving their souls. Who the hell should care about saving his soul when it is a man's duty to lose it intelligently, the way you would sell a position you were defending, if you could not hold it, as expensively as possible, trying to make it the most expensive position that was ever sold. It isn't hard to die."

Clearly, Papa, as the subtitle, "The Moods of Ernest Hemingway," implies and all the drinking underscores, was going in and out of depression— the cycle of mania and depression, said Walton, that plagued him his whole life, intensifying as he aged.

When he was in calmer waters emotionally, "saving his soul," and the souls of loved ones, was important—something Hemingway had scrupulously tended to from his earliest days.

Yes, "The soul dances in a healthy body." And Hemingway's soul was not dancing.

Having just finished *Across the River and Into the Trees*, he was experiencing a bit of a depressive dry spell. And while it is not uncommon for an author to suffer something akin to postpartum depression after finishing a major literary work, for Hemingway it was, of course, so much worse.

Bouncing back from "black ass," as he called it, was no mean feat. But the Heavenly doctor was on the case.

9

꧁꧂

Faith, Tragedy and Triumph
"The Old Man and the Sea"

According to Stoneback, Hemingway's Catholic faith became resurgent after his marriage to Mary Welsh, starting in 1947—the same year his health began to fail, forcing him to confront his mortality and dig deeper for the meaning of it all.

By 1950, Hemingway knew his spiritual "house" was *not* "in order" and, on January 6, while in Venice finishing *Across the River and Into the Trees*, feeling the "need," he wrote Charles Scribner, to "re-inforce" the book, concluded by writing: "Big move in local circles to get me to Rome since it seems sinners of the worst type are being pardoned like flies. I would miss purgatory completely, it seems, though would probably have to take a quick look at hell. Not going to Rome however. Anyway have my personal priest [Andres Untzain] coming here on the twelfth."[1] Don Untzain had served as a machine gunner for the Loyalists. And, now he had just discovered the "wonders of the 23/1 shot" at the racetrack, which took discipline to forego, but then, wrote Hemingway, "a priest must make some sacrifices besides the vow of chastity."[2]

Hemingway worked to discipline himself, too, when it came to popping pills and sipping whiskey, which crowded out his creative juices, and brought on a case of "black ass."

His mood finally calmed, Hemingway started writing again in December 1950, when he began one of his greatest works ever, once again, crediting Adriana, his muse, with priming the pump. Not the first writer who had a muse while staying married to his wife, wrote Baker. His "huge working streak" was unbroken for the first three weeks of December, and on Christmas Eve he declared one of his "sea books," of three he envisioned, finished.[3]

Soon thereafter, Gary Cooper visited Hemingway at the Finca Vigía over Christmas joined by his lovely and voluptuous *Fountainhead* (1949) co-star, Patricia Neal, twenty-five years his junior. Coop, as madly in love with Neal, as Hem was with Adriana, planned to leave "Rocky," and marry Neal, he said. Hem, no doubt, saw himself in his friend—finding younger women rejuvenating as the years ticked by—and gave Coop a big thumb's down. Hemingway knew an adulterous affair with a younger woman spelled trouble. Plus, Mary liked Rocky.

Hemingway could see how silly these dalliances were, even if his own thirst for a muse always needed quenching. So he thought. Yet, he also knew both of them were living out their final years. Leaving Rocky would not be good for Coop's soul. Meanwhile, as the page turned to the new year, reminders of his own soul's reckoning were all around.

REMINDER OF FINAL THINGS, LIFE'S PILGRIMAGE

On June 29, 1951, his ailing mother, Grace, suffering from severe dementia, died. She was seventy-nine. Hemingway had highlighted his mother's advanced age for Scribner two years earlier, noting her "spotty" memory and addiction to "fantastic statements," saying he would cut her off completely if she gave any more interviews like the recent one in *McCall's* for its feature digging into Hemingway's private life. He had stayed away from Grace, upset, as he told Bill Walton in that woodcutter's hut, that, after giving her so much of his largesse, all she could do was criticize his writing. Recently, though, he was the "devoted son," hoping to please his ailing mother, he wrote in his August 1949 letter. Albeit he did not sugarcoat the strained relations. They hated each other's guts. "She forced my father to suicide," he wrote, and then, in the wake of his father's untimely death, when he ordered her to divest herself of "worthless" tax-draining properties, she responded swiftly. "Never threaten me with what to do. Your father tried that once when we were first married and he lived to regret it."[4] Ernest did not attend her funeral.

Then, Pauline, suffering unexplained headaches and a recent blood pressure spike,[5] died on October 1, 1951, when an adrenal gland tumor suddenly hemorrhaged.

Late the night before, she and Ernest had argued bitterly after police found Greg smoking pot in a women's restroom at an LA theater, dressed as a woman, and arrested him. The inevitable recriminations were hurled in that late-night phone call about their maladjusted son, and who was to blame, some critics pointing to *Garden of Eden*, which, ironically, he was writing at the time, to suggest Hem was a gender bender. Not so, said Charles Scribner III. "Hemingway's literary exploration of 'gender exchange' (something that goes back to Ancient Greece and Shakespeare) is far from the trans-vestism and trans-sexuality of poor Gregory, which so upset his father."[6] And, "after Gregory late in life had his gender-reassigning surgery, he regretted it and went back to his original gender assigned at birth" though the press failed to honor his wishes, *Time* naming him as a woman, Gloria, in his obituary. As Greg tried to come to terms with his psychological problems, he told Paul Hendrickson, he had ninety-eight electroshock treatments and had popped every pill under the sun. Talking to his father after the 1951 arrest, Gregory dismissed it as a "nothing." To which Hemingway shot back, "Nothing? It killed your mother!"[7] Three years later, there was a thaw in the relationship.

At the time of Pauline's death, she was living in her San Francisco apartment and had come rushing down to Los Angeles to try and keep Greg out of jail and the story out of the papers. She was going to stay at the Hollywood Hills home her sister Jinny shared with her lesbian lover. When Jinny picked her up at the airport, she complained of "a sharp pain in her stomach."[8] Sometime after midnight, Pauline woke "screaming," and they rushed her to St. Vincent's Hospital in downtown LA, snaking around the winding curves and hairpin turns of the Hollywood Hills to get there. The doctors did all they could to try and stop the bleeding, but, around 4 a.m., she "died of shock on the operating table." While she was suffering so intensely, the Daughters of Charity consoled her spiritually including, no doubt, reciting the "Chaplet of Divine Mercy" and the "Commendation of the Dying," among other spiritual ministrations. That she lived out her final hours at a Catholic Hospital with all its reminders of Heaven was providential. Albeit, she was buried in Hollywood Memorial Cemetery, in an unmarked grave, her divorce preventing a Catholic burial.

Then, came the third blow. Charles Scribner Jr., who had long suffered from "an enlarged heart and aneurysm of the aorta,"[9] was felled by a fatal heart attack on February 11, 1952, the Feast of Our Lady of Lourdes, which hit Hemingway particularly hard, the pain of which he expressed in condolence letters to his widow and namesake son. As he wrote to Vera, her husband was the one person he could "trust or confide in or to make rough jokes with."[10] Now that he was gone, he wrote, "I feel so terribly about [it] that I can't write anymore." Likewise, while admitting to Scribner's son that no words could make it "any easier," he added, "Since he had to die at least he has gotten it over with." And he implored him to convey any "practical" needs as he sought to lighten his burden of worry, including "finances," knowing his triple responsibilities of "Navy, Estate and the House of Scribner" was burden enough. Scribner was then serving, for a second time, now during the Korean

War, as a naval lieutenant deciphering enemy codes. "My father," wrote Charles Scribner III, "later commented in his book of essays, *In the Web of Ideas: The Education of a Publisher*, on Hemingway's extraordinarily "delicate assurance of loyalty. And in the lovely phrase of Dickens, he was better than his word . . . as easy to work with as any author I have ever known."[11]

In the wake of Scribner's death, Hemingway began cultivating his friendship with American art historian Bernard Berenson, a Catholic convert, known for *The Drawings of Florentine Painters*. "I prayed for you sincerely and straight in Chartres, Burgos, Segovia and two minor places," Hemingway wrote the ailing Berenson. He regretted not making it to the "home office of Santiago de Compostela"[12]—as he called this final stop on the "Way of St. James," a pilgrimage he cherished.

As Stoneback wrote, "Pilgrimage . . . is at the center of Hemingway's religious vision and his work . . . Most notable . . . is Hemingway's long-standing devotion to the specifically Catholic Pilgrimage of Santiago de Campostela."[13] He had visited Santiago de Compostela on numerous occasions, including, as noted, following his wedding to Pauline, and in 1929 after he finished *A Farewell to Arms*, capping off "three summers trying to learn when I was working on my education," he wrote Berenson in 1955.[14]

OUR LADY'S ENDURING ROLE IN HEMINGWAY'S LIFE

"The home office" mirrors Hemingway's longing for and bond with Mary—Santiago de Compostela, being, as noted, the burial place of St. James, who had such a close relationship with "Our Lady of Pillar." Hemingway's love of Mary, the mother of Jesus, who saved his life, over and over, was strong, as was his love of pilgrimage, both of which came shining through in that "sea novel" he had started writing Christmas 1950. It is "no accident," Hemingway wrote in a letter four years later to a "Mr. Robert Morgan Brown," that he chose "the name" Santiago (i.e., James) for the protagonist in what would come to be known as *The Old Man and the Sea*.[15]

In this story of chasing a marlin only to have it devoured by sharks, Santiago, though "not religious," says, "I will say ten Our Fathers and ten Hail Mary's that I should catch this fish, and I promise to make a pilgrimage to the Virgin of Cobre if I catch him. That is a promise."[16] He then proceeds to say one Hail Mary after another, adding, "Blessed Virgin, pray for the death of this fish. Wonderful though he is." Later, feeling "faint and dizzy," he asks to endure, promising to pray "a hundred Our Fathers and a hundred Hail Marys,"[17] just as Hemingway had done in the summer of 1933, while fishing for marlin.

Santiago later opined that lack of "hope" is "a sin," though catching himself not to dwell on sin.[18] Hemingway had nurtured hope, starting on that Italian battlefield along the Piave River. Though, he had stopped praying for himself in Madrid in 1937. Quite a change from the young man who prayed for "preservation through prayers of intercession to Our Lady and various saints . . . with almost tribal faith."

Now Our Lady continued to steer him to safe harbors—in spite of himself.

As Mary Welsh Hemingway told Charles Scribner late in the summer of 1951, while caring for her dying father—she needed to ensure Ernest's temperament remained calm "because, as he says, a good half of his work is done in the subconscious . . . It has to be there before it can go on paper."[19] So, if he was suffering troubled waters, his writing would suffer as well. And since his writing was a healing salve, his inability to write only reinforced his "black ass" mood.

He vaulted over his anxiety and depression and finished *Old Man and the Sea* by year's end. It was published in *Life Magazine* on September 1, 1952, selling five million copies. Soon thereafter, it was published in book form by Charles Scribner's Sons. "In my father's personal copy (now at Princeton)," wrote Charles Scribner III, "the author inscribed his famous motto: '*D'abord il faut durer*' [First of all, one must endure]." He had gotten up off the mat after the bad reviews just two years earlier to make "the biggest splash of his career."[20]

In 1953, Hemingway won the Pulitzer Prize for his novelette—the milestone feat announced at Columbia University on May 3—as the month of May, dedicated to Mary, was just beginning.[21] The prize, first awarded in 1917, "for distinguished fiction published in book form during the year by an American author, preferably dealing with American life," came with a reward of "Five hundred dollars ($500)."

His latest literary achievement improved his outlook greatly but spiritually he had yet to set his "house in order" as he had done over twenty-five years earlier. His checkered marital history, he incorrectly believed, precluded him from full communion with the Church. But when Pauline died in the fall of 1951 the way was opened to straighten out his marriage to Mary Welsh. But he chose not to. Understandably, he had great remorse over leaving Hadley and his young son and, in later years, romanticized his relationship with Hadley as being his one true love.

Yet his truest love, again and again, was Mary, the Mother of Jesus, who continued to watch over him. Now, she would save his life and that of his wife. This latest rescue occurred on January 24, 1954, the Feast of Our Lady of Peace (in the United States).

Our Lady of Peace, shown holding a dove and an olive branch, dates back to early 1500s France when her statue was given by Jean Joyeuse to his bride. Known as Virgin of Joyeuse, this cherished family heirloom was later bequeathed to the Capuchins, who housed it in their chapel for 200 years in the wake of Jean's grandson becoming a friar. After that, it took a circuitous journey—finally crowned by the Archbishop of Paris in the name of Pope Pius X on July 9, 1906. Pope Benedict XV added "Our Lady of Peace" to the Litany of Loreto during World War I, and authorized its canonical coronation on November 21, 1921, the Feast of the Presentation of the Virgin Mary, exactly a month before Hemingway and his first wife arrived in Paris.

By the end of 1952, after focusing on the sea, Hemingway had grown anxious to get back to big-game hunting in Africa, telegraphing this desire in the book's last line: "The old man was dreaming about the lions." But more death, including that of Sunny's husband by cardiac arrest in early 1953, kept delaying the trip.

Finally, that summer, after celebrating the Fiesta of San Fermín in Pamplona, Papa and Mary were off to Mombasa, the Kenyan colony's southeastern coastal city along the Indian Ocean. It was a glorious trip, replete with great hunting and warm camaraderie capped off by a celebration of Christmas with grand African traditions and New Year's Eve with tea and minced pies brought by the Percivals. Mary captured all of this in her diary: Ernest said he was "not a phony" but "a terrible braggart." "No. Just full of joy," she thought. "We were smart kittens to come to Africa," said Ernest, who had been deputized an "Honorary Game Warden," and was enjoying himself capitally.[22]

On January 22, 1954, they took off in a chartered plane from West Nairobi for a splendid sight-seeing tour the country, a 600-mile flight over the Serengeti Plain including Lake Victoria and Lake Albert en route to Uganda. On the third day, they detoured to the Victoria Nile so Mary could photograph the 400-foot Murchison Falls, the plane circling and winging over to maximize her picture-taking. But the third time, a group of ibis disrupted the flight path and the plane dived to avoid them, striking an old telegraph wire strung across the gorge, and making a crunch landing into the trees. The Hemingways jumped out, free and clear, touching down on Uganda soil for the first time. Mary was in shock with an aching chest, and Ernest had a sprained right shoulder.

They were finally rescued, but neither the new plane, a twelve-seater de Havilland Dragon Rapide, nor the poorly plowed airfield inspired confidence. "The Aircraft was properly warmed up, took off and was not airborne until near the end of what may be called a runway!" Hemingway wrote in a

Photograph of Ernest Hemingway sitting at a table writing while at his campsite in Kenya, c. 1953. *Source:* Look Magazine, Photographer (NARA record: 1106476). In the public domain.

statement after they were nearly killed.[23] Given how bumpy the runway was, "at no time was the Aircraft given . . . a decent chance to take off" and after being "airborne" for mere "seconds," "it went into the ground hitting with the tail" and burst into flames on the starboard side. Mary, sitting on the first port seat, was able to escape to safety through a front "passage," with few injuries. But Hemingway, sitting in the second port seat, evidently had to use his head as a battering ram to escape through the door passengers usually enter, which was tightly closed shut. As the *New York Times* reported, after the accident, "His head was swathed in bandages and his arm was injured, but the novelist, who is 55 years old, quipped: 'My luck, she is running very good.' . . . He waved a swollen arm, wrapped in a torn shirt, and appeared to be in high spirits as he shrugged off the crashes."[24] In fact, his injuries were much worse than he was letting on. As Baker reported, "Apart from a full-scale concussion, his injuries included a ruptured liver, spleen and kidney, temporary loss of vision in the left eye, loss of hearing in the left ear, a crushed vertebra, a sprained right arm and shoulder, a sprained left leg, paralysis of the sphincter, and first degree burns on his face, arms and head from the plane fire."[25]

As he recovered, he visited Venice in March, falling right into bed when he arrived at his Gritti Hotel room, later receiving the usual parade of visitors, who were aghast after taking one look at him. He was healing the burns, he told them, with lion fat. But he was also collecting urine samples and visiting the Clinica. "His right kidney was badly ruptured and two of his lumbar vertebrae were crushed," wrote Baker.[26] He visited other cities in Italy while making Venice his base and professing his love for Adriana, now twenty-four, expressing the illusory hope that she would one day marry him.

In May he decamped to Spain with A. E. Hotchner, stopping by the Cathedral of Saint Mary at Burgos, about 150 miles north of Madrid. Dedicated to the Virgin Mary, this French Gothic cathedral, is one of the stops along the "Way of St. James." Five-hundred years in the making, it was constructed in the shape of a Latin Cross, starting in 1221.

Hemingway was in seventh heaven, but it was a cross ascending the steps of the cross-shaped cathedral. "With my help," wrote Hotchner, "Ernest pulled himself tortuously from the car and went slowly up the cathedral steps, bringing forth both feet together on each step." After entering the cathedral and dipping his finger into the Holy Water and blessing himself, he walked to a side chapel, "his moccasins barely audible on the stone floor," and just stood and gazed at the magnificent scene—perhaps the Chapel of the Presentation with its marvelous star ceiling, oil painting, and reredos.

"Then, holding tightly, he lowered his knees onto a prayer bench and bent his forehead onto his overlapped hands. He stayed that way for several minutes."

Afterward, as he slowly descended St. Mary's steps, he said, "Sometimes I wish I were a better Catholic."[27] Jake Barnes in *The Sun Also Rises* said much the same thing, ruing the fact that he was "such a rotten Catholic." It was Hemingway's lifelong struggle. And if he could not make it himself, Mary was there for him every, now halting, step of the way.

Arriving back in Havana that summer, he was heartened to receive a letter from Adriana and immediately replied to her after which he rested, unable to write word one. Dr. Herrera advised rest, exercising in the pool and placing a board under his mattress to ease the pressure on his back. By late summer, early fall, he was finally starting to write some short stories about the Africa safari, wanting to capture it while it was still fresh in his mind, and also to maintain his sanity given the intense back pain he was suffering from those injuries in the second plane crash. Before long, he had written 10,000 words. In his letter to Berenson on September 24, he wrote, that presently he worked at about 50 percent of his capacity but that "everything is better all the time."[28] That same day he wrote to the aforementioned Robert Morgan Brown noting, regarding the Africa novel, that he thought it would be "better to wait until I'm dead to publish it. But it is an awfully good story, and I was born to write stories not to please the authorities. The story is so rough and I am trying to write it so delicately that it is quite difficult."

Brown was working on a thesis evidently focused on Hemingway, the man, as reflected in *The Old Man and the Sea*.[29] That day, the old man was not feeling too well. He was still "pretty beat up," he wrote, though his two kidneys were now "functioning" and his "head is OK" but he still needs to "take it easy" and his "12th vertebra" was coming along. Given that his ailments were holding up Brown's thesis, Hemingway wrote: "I think the simplest way to get a Ph.D., under the circumstances, would be to write that I am a no good, worthless son of a bitch. I would be glad to sign a statement to this effect."[30]

Then, he doubled down. Regarding "the immortality of the human soul," he wrote "I know nothing of it." But he added, "I respect and admire those who believe in it without fear." Fear was the emotion his father had sown into him, which he had dealt with all his life, while the God of love that his grandfather had schooled him in was a faraway and distant memory.

As to "details of what I believe," he wrote, "you might as well ask someone who is dead." He goes on to write about imperfect "human beings," noting that "I have certainly lived more of my life in a state of sin than in a state of grace. I am living, in the present time, in a state of sin, according to the church, but I have no feeling of sin." Yet he was quite certain he would end up in hell, or at least, he would go there so that he could see how his friends were doing! Basically, throughout this correspondence with Brown, he shows that rich sense of humor that, Welles said, defined him. Brown wants to receive some good reviews about *The Old Man and the Sea*, and Hemingway goes through a leather-bound book Scribners had sent him with all the reviews, highlighting one in particular—the one Will Lissner had written for the *Catholic Messenger* on September 4, 1952, which he thought was quite good but for it being marred by Lissner's reference to the "great fish" as a "giant tuna." Then, he veers off into a discussion of the nitwits who are writing about him and the African novel, among other topics, winding up the letter by expressing the hope that Lissner's review might be just what he needs for his thesis, before once again bemoaning the "giant tuna" reference.

WRITING, HIS SAVING GRACE

In spite of his defects, his writing was his saving grace: "Work could cure almost anything, I believed then, and I believe it now," he wrote in his Paris memoir.[31]

Possessing the soul of a writer, he rose early each morning, he wrote Brown, "living in a world he is trying to come alive and true in his writing, not even speaking to his wife until his work is done," which he wrote, "is most important to him."

Ah, the healing creativity! And why, he asked, should he interrupt all that to answer questions about his private life and affairs and his beliefs, or lack thereof?

No, his work was most important and, more than healing, it was sanctifying. It brought that actual grace he had enthused about to Withington Church so many years earlier that he could win in the arena of life.

Yet he did not consider himself holy.

"Please do not try to make me out a good man," he wrote. "I have tried to be but have failed. But I try to be a very good writer. And it is difficult enough under the circumstances."

Yes, work was the stuff of sanctity for someone like Hemingway, defects and all, St. Josemaria would have told him.

His ailments, too, were reaching a critical mass as the Holy Spirit sanctified the Pulitzer Prize–winning writer through his work—his sanctity, which means trying to be good, in every aspect of life, and letting God be the judge.

The critics were judging his writing and thought it quite good. Rumors were swirling that Hemingway would be awarded the Nobel Prize in Literature. In late October, as he was writing about Africa, he finally got the call. After he hung up, he phoned Col. Lanham about "the thing." "What thing?" asked Lanham. "The Swedish thing. You know."[32]

On October 28, when the formal press release was issued, he was inundated with requests for interviews, including from his friend Harvey Breit of the *New York Times*, whom Ernest granted an interview. After getting into a comfortable chair, tape recorder rolling, Hemingway said he regretted that "Mark Twain, nor Henry James," his own "countrymen," never received it because the prize was only created in 1901.

Not to be outdone, NBC showed up with a film crew and he kindly spoke to them, though, his halting speech showed just how impaired he still was.

He was awarded the Nobel "for his mastery of the art of narrative, most recently demonstrated in *The Old Man and the Sea*, and for the influence that he has exerted on contemporary style." Dr. Herrera advised him not to attend the ceremony since he was still recovering. Oh, but what a gala affair it was in the Stockholm Concert Hall held on December 10, 1954, with elegantly dressed guests greeting the arrival of the Swedish Royal family including King Gustaf VI Adolf, Queen Louise, Princesses Sibylla and Margaretha, and Princes Wilhelm and Bertil. After dinner, Birger Ekeberg, chairman of the Nobel Foundation, gave opening remarks, after which each Nobel Laureate was introduced and Nobel Prizes awarded—John C. Cabot, United States Ambassador to Sweden, accepting it on Hemingway's behalf, reading this statement Hemingway wrote and would later deliver in an audio recording at the Finca, which read in part:

> Writing, at its best, is a lonely life. Organizations for writers palliate the writer's loneliness but I doubt if they improve his writing. He grows in public stature as he sheds his loneliness and often his work deteriorates. For he does his work alone and if he is a good enough writer he must face eternity, or the lack of it, each day.

In his earlier draft, he described the loneliness of the writer as no more so than that of "the suicide."[33] As St. Augustine famously wrote in *Confessions*, "the heart is restless until it rests in God." Now that Hemingway had won the Nobel, as in high school when he achieved those two prizes, he surely realized that it could not fill him up.

He needed God.

And so it was that Hemingway donated his 1954 Nobel solid gold medal to the Virgin of Cobre—Our Lady of Charity—Cuba's national saint. Several sources, including Stoneback and Hemingway's wife, confirmed that he, in fact, gave his Nobel to Our Lady, not the Cuban Church or the people of Cuba, as others wrongly assert. This act on Hemingway's part mirrors what the "Old Man" in his novel—Santiago—promises: To make that pilgrimage to her shrine if he catches the fish.

Hemingway had caught the biggest fish of all, while, at the same time, as in *The Old Man and the Sea*, the sharks constantly threatened him.

He was suffering immensely. In late December, he wrote in a letter to his friend from World War I, "Chink," now Eric Dorman O'Gowan, who changed his name after being forcibly retired from the British Army in 1944: "This has been sort of a rough year . . . We call this 'black-ass' and one should never have it. But I get tired of pain sometimes, even if that is an ignoble feeling."[34]

As 1955 opened, his health continued to lag—feeling "not so hot," he wrote Charles Scribner—his back still constantly hurting a year after the plane crash. Mary's absence when her father died in mid-February only added to his misery.[35]

Still he had been writing the Africa novel from the beginning of the year, in spite of the constant barrage of uninvited visitors to the Finca Vigía wanting to bask in the glory of his celebrity especially now that he had won the Nobel.

During Holy Week, some Princeton students showed up and no sooner had he exchanged pleasantries with them than another student showed up wanting Hemingway to critique his short stories, which he did with great graciousness and kindness.

Then, on Good Friday—April 8, 1955—a professor from Buffalo named Drew Frasier came by invitation and would later write poignantly about his visit with "EH."

"He shakes hands and welcomes me and seems shy at first, as if I, not he, were the important man."[36]

After a tour of the first floor, it was on to the swimming pool by which time Hemingway was relaxed and more talkative—"a very easy person to be with, slow-moving and slow speaking, and with a gentle manner," wrote Frasier.

When he visited, Papa was a suffering soul. His painful back made it difficult to exercise and so he had fattened up, but he would slim down soon enough with a trip on the *Pilar* with Mary, as more and more his boat became his refuge. Later in the summer, his go-to trainer, George W. Brown, based in New York City, who had famously gotten Babe Ruth back into shape in the twenties, came down and gave him some rubdowns with the gracious solicitousness for which he was famous.

Just what the doctor ordered.

But he was also out of shape spiritually, as Frasier revealed:

He asked me if I went to church and I told him that I am a Roman Catholic, though originally a Congregationalist. This interested EH. He said, I like to think that I'm Catholic, as far as I can be. I can still go to Mass, although many things have happened—the divorces, the marriages. He spoke with admiration of Catholicism and then of his friend, the Basque priest [Don Andres] whom he had known in Spain and now lived in [Cuba]. He comes here a great deal, said EH. He prays for me every day, as I do for him. I can't pray for myself any more. Perhaps it is because in some way I have become hardened.

SUFFERING PHYSICALLY, GROWING SPIRITUALLY

He was still reeling from the December 13, 1954, *Time Magazine* cover story, which, wrote Frasier, "had commented that he had been born a Congregationalist, had become a Roman Catholic, and now no longer went to church." *Time* betrayed further ignorance when they wrote, "In a sense, Hemingway perhaps never fully faced up to the concept of soul in his writing. Religion is a subject he refuses to discuss at all"—telegraphing their lack of depth and understanding. His wife Mary, a Christian Scientist, revealed in many lengthy conversations with Stoneback, that, in fact, he was quite devout. In their first exchange of letters, Mary wrote that "whenever we explored cathedrals in France, Spain and Italy, he used to light candles for friends."[37] Regarding his Protestant upbringing, it was her sense that "he disapproved of the falsity between their protestations of faith and their behavior." Stoneback dug deep to understand Hemingway's spiritual life and devotion and found that his faith was rekindled and strengthened during his marriage to Mary. As he wrote:

> Mary had made a real effort to see that the texture of her daily life with Hemingway was Catholic: eating fish on Fridays, observing Lent, singing Christmas carols and fixing the crèche under the tree, celebrating Ernest's saint's day, having prayers and masses said for friends and family, observing Catholic feasts and holy days, driving miles out of the way on journeys to visit and revisit churches and cathedrals, and attending religious processions.[38]

The "joy" that he gave others was, to Mary, Hemingway's essence. But he himself was suffering greatly, abandoning the Africa novel in June only to pick it up again in October 1955. "Am trying to write now like a good sorcer's [*sic*] apprentice," he wrote Berenson, noting he had written 650 pages and "always start to write as an apprentice. By the end of a book you are a master but if you commence as a master, in writing anyway, you end as a bloody bore."[39]

By Thanksgiving, though, he was bedridden with two kidney ailments, nephritis, and hepatitis, and was still ailing at the start of 1956. His red corpuscle count was much too low, causing weakness, fast heart rate, and shortness of breath, likely due to an iron deficiency. Genetic hemochromatosis, which causes an abnormal build-up of iron in the bloodstream, likely accounted for that—his brother Leicester confirming that, like their father, his brother Ernest, in fact, had hemochromatosis.[40] (Mary, too, had anemia, though there is no indication she had the gene for hemochromatosis. At any rate, women rarely exhibit this condition.)

By January 1956, he acknowledged, in a letter written on the second anniversary of the African plane crashes, to Alfred Rice that he could not recall the trip very clearly given the trauma endured, and he had simply abandoned the project for the time being.[41]

At his fifty-seventh birthday that July, Papa was drinking copiously, to Mary's chagrin, but he had pain to dull—pain that spirits of a supernatural sort could have helped him with, if only to give meaning to his suffering. Writing, too, was a continuing struggle. As he told Charles Scribner on August 14, "I find it impossible to resume work on the Africa book without some disciplinary writing."[42] (The book, *True at First Light*, would finally be published posthumously by his son Patrick and grandson Sean. And, while Hemingway's writing shines through, the necessary reworking caused some critics to value it not an authentic Hemingway.)

As he suffered physically, he was spiritually adrift, as well. As Mary had told Stoneback, when pressed, he "probably did 'take communion'" and viewed Don Andres as his "personal priest and confessor."[43] But Don Andres had died on June 24, 1955, the Nativity of St. John the Baptist, so Papa was without a regular confessor going on two years.

And he had yet to establish the validity of his marriage, which would have opened up the channels of sacramental grace. It was a straightforward proposition: Under church doctrine, marriage is indissoluble—a solemn "till death do we part" vow—"forsaking all others." In the eyes of the church, he was married to Pauline until her death on October 1, 1951, making his marriage to Martha Gellhorn, his third marriage, invalid. Mary Hemingway's prior marriages could have been invalidated under the ironically named, "Pauline Privilege," if she had become Catholic, but it was not to be. Certainly, during his affair with and marriage to fellow war correspondent Martha Gellhorn (1936–1945), he could not participate in the sacraments, but once that marriage ended and he married Mary, he started becoming more spiritual and needed the grace of the sacraments to continue growing spiritually.

All the fame, too, had had a certain corrosive effect, as he had pointed out in his Nobel Prize acceptance speech. His writing was his healing. Then, too, was his faith.

❧❧❧

10

~~~

The Final Years

"A Moveable Feast"

"As became more obvious in later life," wrote Michael Reynolds, "Hemingway was deeply drawn to all things medieval, which is to say all things ancient and Catholic."[1]

His regular visits to famous European cathedrals—Burgos, after those near-fatal plane crashes; and Galicia, the "home office;" among other great cathedrals through the years—were suffused with piety and reverence. He attended Mass (although, later, he did not receive communion) and confessed to Don Andres until 1955. His sacramental deficits notwithstanding, his observance of rituals surrounding Christmas and Easter and other special feast days was constant. And he loved and revered the Pope, as evidenced by the scene in early October 1958, when, while driving with Mary to Ketchum, Idaho, for the winter, he made the sign of the cross as news of the dying Pope Pius XII came across the radio.

Yes, Hemingway was a complex man with a simple faith. Those hidden crucifixes, untrumpeted visits to cathedrals, and private celebrations of feast days were as much a part of the legendary writer as all his labors winning "actual grace"—now, more and more, won through his daily struggle just to ascend the steps of a cathedral, and to string a few words, if not sentences, together on a page.

AN UNEXPECTED GIFT INSIDE A PARIS TRUNK

"His decline and death took place at an earlier age than most people expect nowadays," Patrick Hemingway said. "We all go into decline and death.

With Hemingway it happened in rather spectacular form in that he evidently did lose his mind at the end. But what is also interesting is that he was producing *A Moveable Feast* within that time frame. He didn't find *A Moveable Feast* in the suitcase. It was written a year before his death."[2]

While staying at the Hôtel Ritz Paris in November 1956, hotel management notified him of two small vintage twenties' steamer trunks containing papers he had put in storage before leaving for Key West years earlier. Upon retrieving it, Hemingway was transfixed by what he found—notebooks and writing from his Paris years, giving him a veritable window into the days when life was so much simpler. He was deeply moved and once he arrived back in Cuba in early 1957, he took the first steps toward shaping the material into a literary gem. Then, as he pivoted back to David and Catherine Bourne and Martita, and their ménage à trois in *The Garden of Eden*, life in steaming hot Cuba became one big series of distractions—Jack, now a Havana stockbroker, becoming ill; Evan Shipman dying; his lawyer, Alfred Rice, mismanaging his affairs, including the Key West property; Ezra Pound going nuts; Mary not saving enough money—all the while he cut alcohol out of his life, relying on pharmaceuticals to stay calm; and though his cholesterol, weight, and BP went down, his boring and dullness factor went up—no Floridita!—and he was anything but calm. Rather like his father, he was a depressed bundle of nerves.[3]

Still, in spite of the administrative and other headaches, he managed some impressive literary output. But his heart was in those papers he found in the Ritz trunk and, by year's end, he had returned to the Paris memoir. New Year's Eve, Mary learned of her mother's death and hit the road New Year's day, taking the first plane out, while Hem, once again, hit the bottle, and his memories of Paris, where he enjoyed the good Martinique rum in that delightful café, sharpened.

In the spring of 1958, as Hemingway worked on the manuscript, Bunny and Bill Horne visited the Finca. Horney noted "Ernie's" beard and the wonderful dinner at the Floridita which Hem had put on the map, he said. "We were much impressed with Mary—she seemed a fine wife for Ernie."[4]

By fall 1958, seeing the handwriting on the wall concerning the brutality of the Cuban Revolution where at night he could become a dispensable bourgeoisie, the Hemingways made arrangements to move to Ketchum, Idaho, a mile south of Sun Valley, where he pivoted to the serious work of meticulously crafting his Paris memoir—as usual, rising each day at sunset to write, standing over his writing board. He was coming full circle—back to those innocent days of 1920s Paris, before he became famous. Scheduled for publication in 1960, it would, in time, be called *A Moveable Feast,* at Hotchner's suggestion—"feast" imaging religious holidays that move throughout the church calendar, as well as changing venues of conviviality, both so abundant in Paris.

After shaking off Old Man Winter, in May 1959, Hemingway returned to Cuba where he planned to write for another month or so to finish the memoir, though, in a sit-down interview with the *Honolulu Advertiser*, he "could not say definitely" how long it would take him to have a final manuscript to his publisher. He would spend his sixtieth in Madrid and Pamplona, then "Africa, maybe." Then, he caught himself and said, "No, I am going to let it sit until I return from my trip. Then I will return to it again."[5]

Asked why he was going to Spain, he said, "I like Spain. And, there are the bullfights. Hunting in Africa. And, I still have uncompleted writing on Spain and Africa that I must finish." When asked how his writing was going, he refused to say. "I don't talk about my work at all when I am still at it. You lose a lot that way."

But he was willing to talk about the art of writing. "You do not put symbolism in your work. But if you are good enough the symbolism is there truer than if you had put it in by some preconceived plan."

"Hemingway had a quiet head-to-chest laugh, accompanied by a hunched rocking of the shoulders, raising of the eyelids, and a wide grin that, despite the white beard, [gave] his face a startlingly boyish appearance," the *Advertiser* reported. Yet despite what he said about his plans, after he returned from Spain, skipping Africa, *A Moveable Feast* just sat and collected dust. Meanwhile, the three other books he had worked on from 1957–1959—*True at First Light*, about his 1953–1954 African safari; *The Garden of Eden* to which he had added a few chapters; and *Islands in the Stream* (his "sea books" set in Bimini, Havana, and at sea, written in 1950–1951, telling the story of artist Thomas Hudson's different stages of life)—sat securely in a safe deposit box in Havana.

The real story, as Patrick noted, was this: That May in Havana, on the eve of his sixtieth, Hemingway spiraled downward mentally—events, habits, and heredity all conspiring with unrelenting rapidity to engulf him. Events in Cuba were surely destabilizing. On January 1, 1959, Castro's revolution had succeeded in expelling Fulgencio Batista from power. When asked about the Revolution, he was noncommittal. "It is hard to say, truly," he said." I would like to wait until I get back. I hope for the very best."[6]

Hemingway was also bound for Spain because he had contracted with *Life Magazine* to write a 40,000-word article "about Spain's reigning matadors, the brothers-in-law Antonio Ordóñez and Luis Miguel Dominguín," wrote A. E. Hotchner. "He cabled me, urging me to join him for the tour. It was a glorious summer, and we celebrated Ernest's 60th birthday with a party that lasted two days."[7]

"DANGEROUS SUMMER" AND DECLINE

Joining in the two-day festivities was Colonel Lanham, jetting in on the eighteenth for a late-night dinner, where he poignantly read from a volume on the history of the 22nd Infantry Regiment, bringing Hemingway to tears. Two nights later, though, it was a different story. At the end of a lavish dinner at the Grand Hotel Miramar, Lanham affectionately placed his hand on Hemingway's shoulder as he was leaving, twenty minutes shy of the twenty-first. Then he brushed the back of Hemingway's head, prompting Papa to wince and loudly proclaim that *no one* was allowed to touch his head. The party also included Ambassador and Mrs. David Bruce, Annie and Nathan (Bill) Davis, who were hosting the Hemingways at their seaside estate, Valerie Danby-Smith, Hotch and Mary, and, as they all exchanged uncomfortable glances, Hemingway caught up with Lanham, all contrite, explaining the obvious: He was bald and had a comb-over to hide his thinning hair and if Lanham would just forgive him, he would go to the barber the next day to have all his hair shaved off. Lanham showed no mercy and said he would leave Malaga right away but for the fact there was no flight out. Hemingway's poor treatment of Mary, limping with a broken toe, as he complained about her lavish spending and unsuccessfully prevailed upon the doctor to change his diagnosis, is what really stuck in Lanham's craw.[8] Of course, he lacked depth and, though he was right to balk at Hem's ill-treatment of Mary, Hemingway was also a suffering soul, who, truth be told, needed to rush to God, asking for help to shave off his excesses.

But then, he evidently wasn't praying for himself, though he kept struggling and, upon his return to Cuba, after six months in Malaga, running with the bulls joined by a bevy of celebrities, including Ava Gardner and Lauren Bacall, and his usual disciplined writing in the mornings, he worked to come to grips with both his deteriorating health and the deteriorating political situation. Finally, as the year came to a close, he began preparing to write his *Life Magazine* article.

Then, too, he was intent on completing his memoirs. To get into the right frame of mind, he read Harold Loeb's autobiography *The Way It Was.*[9] The pathos of Loeb's "search for how he wished things to have been" touched him deeply, calling to mind the winter of 1925–1926 in Schruns,

Ernest Hemingway and Gary Cooper, with Bobbi Powell, Silver Creek, Idaho, January 1, 1959. *Source:* Photograph in the Ernest Hemingway Photograph Collection, John F. Kennedy Presidential Library and Museum, Boston.

when Pauline, Gerald, and Sara Murphy and John Dos Passos invaded what he now viewed as a paradise-like existence in which he described Dos as the "pilot fish," the other three, by inference, the sharks—a mutually beneficial relationships in which sharks, free of parasites the pilot fish eats, gain protection from predators. Dos and Hem had clearly had a falling out. As for Loeb, upon hearing that he had angina pectoris, the very ailment that afflicted his father, Hemingway prayed that he would have "the grace of a happy death."[10]

It was Hemingway, though, who was facing his own mortality in the nearer term, given habits that would have felled a lesser person far sooner. He would need to start praying for himself, if only he could find it in himself to do so.

"Hemingway's later physical and mental decline," said Charles Scribner III, "was due primarily to long-term consumption of excessive quantities of alcohol, and, more immediately, to brain injuries sustained in two plane crashes."[11] What's more, after those dual plane crashes, he drank more to dull the pain. His doctor had told him he could hold his liquor ten times better than the average person, but it finally reached a tipping point, overlaid as it was with toxic prescription drug interventions to deal with the ill effects of bad health habits; heredity factors, notably undiagnosed and untreated hemochromatosis;

and the need, suddenly, in July 1960, to pull up stakes from his beloved Finca Vigia as Castro's Revolution showed up on his doorstep.

Emotionally, he was a wreck.

He powered through the *Life Magazine* article even as he had nightmares, calling Hotch for help with the manuscript that had ballooned to over 90,000 words. By May 28, weighing in at 120,000, he declared, what he would call "The Dangerous Summer," finished. Three days later came the first sign he was untethered from reality when he wrote in a letter to his friend Carlos Quintana in Spanish that all that forced labor ("trabajando forzado") had confused his brain.[12] Helpless to excise the excess, beyond a paltry 530 words, an "exhausted" Hem sent another SOS to Hotch who came to Cuba to help with the edits, but Hem protested. "What I've written is Proustian in its cumulative effect, and if we eliminate detail we destroy that effect."[13] By some alchemy, Hotch managed to coax 55,000 words of cuts, leaving *Life* to finish the surgery so they could publish "The Dangerous Summer" in three tidy parts. "I got on the plane back to New York knowing my friend was 'bone-tired and very beat-up,' but thinking he simply needed rest and would soon be his old dominating self again."

Think again.

By fall, Hem became convinced that the FBI was tailing him. When Hotch visited for their annual pheasant shooting, Hem adopted all kinds of paranoid duck and hide maneuvers, for instance not wanting to have a drink with Hotch at the bar across from the train depot in Shoshoni before the ride to Ketchum, lest the Feds overhear their conversation. Hotchner deemed all of this a dangerous sign that Hem's "brain" was, indeed, "confused." The thing is, the FBI, by now, did have a thick file on Hem. But the existence of his FBI file was, of course, unknown and so Hemingway was considered crazy, as opposed to being hypervigilant about something that was, in fact, grounded in reality. Even so, it became an obsession with him as he eyed after-hours cleaning ladies at the bank, as Hotch wrote, viewing them as examiners pouring through his financial records late at night—a prominent New York psychiatrist confidentially diagnosing his condition as "depressive persecutory." Then, too, he worried about little things, for instance whether Valerie, his assistant from Ireland, who, like all the other young lovelies, he wanted to marry, would be deported.

By year's end, everything spiraled out of control and he was admitted to the Mayo Clinic in Rochester, Minnesota.

It was late November 1960. JFK had just been elected president. In the initial evaluation, both Dr. Hugh Butt, an internist, and Dr. Howard Rome, chief of psychiatry, believed Serpasil, one of Hemingway's blood-pressure medications prescribed in the late forties, may have caused what Rome described as "depression, agitation and tension." So, they took him off both Serpasil, as well as Ritalin, prescribed to counteract the side effect of Serpasil.[14]

Hemingway thought all the drugs being poured into his system were toxic and the source of his depression and anxiety. He was right. The changes were obvious—something Sunny had observed in her husband, Ernie Miller, as hypertensive drugs dampened his mood. Over Hemingway's last decade or so of life, he took Oreton M (a synthetic testosterone), along with Serpasil (an anti-hypertensive), Doriden (a sedative), Ritalin (a stimulant), Eucanel (an anti-anxiety drug), Seconal (a barbituate hypnotic sleeping pill discontinued in January 2022); and massive doses of vitamins A and B.[15] (He was taking blood-pressure meds and Seconal as early as November 1949, likely sooner, telling the *New Yorker*'s Ross that he did not even allow his cat Boise, who ate everything humans ate, to ingest these meds.) All of this, on top of the alcohol—the first drug Hemingway poured into his system that gradually stripped away his vitamin B, and was so dehydrating—was too much for his body. Initially, he took vitamin B, he wrote Breit in early 1952, noting alcohol depleted it, implying that's all he took, along with the testosterone and vitamin A. If true, he was soon enough prescribed blood pressure meds, then barbiturates to try and alleviate depression, which blood pressure meds—alleviating the effects of alcohol, rich foods, and the stress of life—had caused. It was a vicious cycle of taking one drug to mask the effects of the last.

If only he had substituted Vichy water for all the alcohol, as he did in 1929, he could have obviated the need for all these medications the transformed medical system prioritizing pharmaceutical interventions, starting in 1910—pushed at the behest of John D. Rockefeller, rebranded "philanthropist," as he began funding medical schools in exchange for their fealty to the wonders of these lucrative drugs that he was heavily invested in.[16] Of course, some of these drugs are necessary evils, and even transformative, apropos of which, mental illness was, after all, part of the Hemingway DNA. So even if he was perfect when it came to alcohol, hydration, food, exercise and sleep, he would have suffered and likely would have needed some kind of intervention. John Sanford, recounting the Hemingway curse for this author, noted that he, too, had taken pills for depression.[17] John's own mother, Marcelline, Ernest's elder sister, was a suspected suicide.

That last year, Hemingway was "entirely in control of himself," said Welles, but the old zest for life was gone. "And, I saw him then," said Welles. "But we never discussed bullfighting because, except on the subject of Ordóñez, we disagreed profoundly on too many points. And, he thought

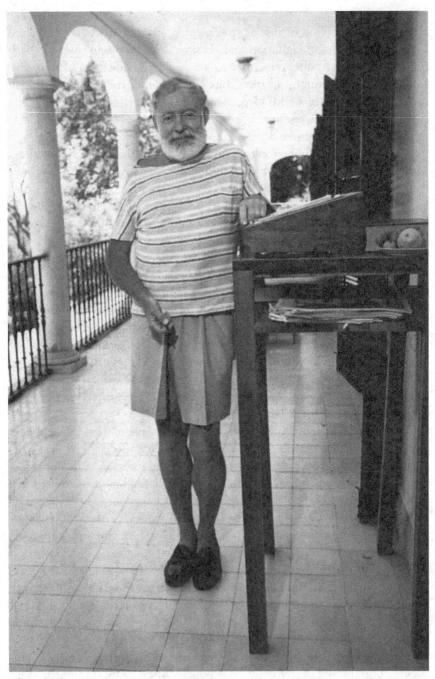

Photo of Hemingway near Malaga, Spain, 1960. At his writing desk on the balcony of Bill Davis's home where he wrote "The Dangerous Summer" in 1959. *Source:* Loomis Dean. Time-Life.

he invented it. You know . . . Maybe he did." He did write that "superb" book about bullfighting, *Death in the Afternoon,* said Welles, who observed that "There are very few important writers, with the exception of Nabokov, who have not been influenced to some degree by him."[18] But by the time he got around to the subject of bullfighting again in the spring of 1960, in the ironically titled "The Dangerous Summer," published posthumously as a book in 1985, he was becoming unhinged, and that summer he would stay inside for his birthday.

In Hemingway's initial evaluation at Mayo, his symptoms most definitely pointed to hemochromatosis, a leading cause of suicide, induced by toxic levels of iron in the blood because of the body's inability to absorb it, causing severe depression, which heavy alcohol consumption only exacerbates. His enlarged liver certainly pointed to that diagnosis. Yet, confoundingly, a liver biopsy required to determine definitively his condition was not done, Dr. Butt deeming him too ill to undergo the procedure. At any rate, he evidently believed excessive alcohol consumption was the main cause of Hemingway's enlarged liver. Dr. Rome, the psychiatrist, should have known better. The symptoms he exhibited, including diabetes, memory impairment, and depression, strongly suggests Hemingway did, indeed, have hemochromatosis. Then, too, a quick look at his family history would have affirmed the diagnosis—a condition, as noted, his brother Leicester said he had. The simple treatment of drawing blood, though not very lucrative, would have helped Hemingway heal. Meanwhile, this undiagnosed and untreated disorder caused Hemingway indolent pain and joint stiffness, exacerbating his mental anguish. Rome seems to be the driving force in attributing Hemingway's enlarged liver to excessive alcohol, rather than to hemochromatosis, because in place of Serpasil and Ritalin he substituted Librium, a sedative, which had recently been approved, to reduce anxiety and alcohol withdrawal symptoms, including tremor.

Besides changing his drugs, Rome also proposed electroshock treatment in spite of the fact that Hemingway had made clear, his son John said, that he never wanted electroshock treatment. Nonetheless, Rome administered electroshock treatment—25 in all, 15 in the first admission; 10 in the second.[19] How terrible to think in his final days, on each occasion, the nurse would transport this ailing and vulnerable soul, one of America's most gifted writers, into an antiseptic room, put him to sleep with an injection, insert a rubber gag in his mouth, before fitting the electrodes onto his head, a greased patch easing the shock as the switch went on, with all the deleterious effects.

As Hemingway told Hotchner in January shortly before being discharged, "What is the sense of ruining my head and erasing my memory, which is my capital, and putting me out of business? It was a brilliant cure but we lost the patient. It's a bum turn, Hotch, terrible."[20] In today's dollars, one treatment alone cost over $1,000. It was then a twenty-year-old treatment, which, quite clearly, Hem did not approve of. By law, it required "informed consent." Mary, with the power of attorney, obviously approved, but had evidently not analyzed the situation, deferring to the doctor's judgment. As a result of these ill-advised treatments, his psyche gravely deteriorated because he had lost his memory—his main writing tool. And, as Dr. Andrew Farah notes in *Hemingway's Brain*, the treatments would have exacerbated his TBI-induced dementia.

Yes, it was a "bum turn."

But God allowed him to suffer—ironically at the same time Gary Cooper was dying from prostate and colon cancer. Coop had received his diagnosis around Christmas, he told Hotch over lunch in January. He was in New York City filming *The Real West*, his last on-screen work, which reflected his "real love of the West," his daughter Maria Cooper Janis said.[21] Coop told Hotch, "I'm not gonna hang around too long." Hotch kept Hemingway's real diagnosis from Coop, though, of course, Coop knew his issues—in spades, his daughter said. Hotch, not wanting Coop to suffer more, said he was at Mayo for hypertension. Coop, for his part, insisted Hotch level with Hem about his fatal cancer, lest he find out in the news. When Hotch told him in mid-January that Coop was dying, he wrote, "He didn't say anything. Just looked at me as if I had betrayed him." Then, he just put on his coat and slowly made his way "out of his prison."[22]

For Hemingway, 1960–1961 was a "Period of despair," wrote Stoneback, "which he had earlier noted was the sin against the Holy Ghost, a sin he had not committed—it is not known that electroshock causes despair; it is known it does not cure it."[23]

During his first stay at Mayo Clinic, Hemingway lamented to Hotchner that he was a "failed Catholic" and that the "shock doctors" knew nothing about writers and what "remorse and contrition" does to them, revealing his craving for spiritual healing.

In the late fall of 1960, shortly after Hotch's fall visit, Hemingway should have been admitted to Menninger Clinic in Houston, the top psychiatric clinic in the country for anxiety and depression. But given Hemingway's fame, they wanted to keep his mental illness under wraps. After the story leaked, it was reported that he was in for hypertension. He was admitted under the name "George M. Savier," the name of his doctor in Ketchum. He was so paranoid that he thought the FBI would investigate him for registering under an assumed name, Dr. Butt told Denis Brian.[24] When the source of the leak was revealed, Hemingway threw his metal dinner tray at the fellow, who beat a quick retreat.

By Christmas Eve, Mary knew the treatment was not working. "After 24 days and nine electric shock treatments, he seemed to me today to be almost as disturbed, disjointed mentally as he was when we came here," though, "He no longer insists that an FBI agent is hidden behind the door of the bathroom with a tape recorder." Nonetheless, on January 22, with the blessing of Drs. Butt and Rome, Hemingway was discharged from St. Mary's Hospital at Mayo Clinic after fifty-three days of treatment. In the instructions, Rome wrote that he could drink wine but no more than a liter daily. "It is my judgment," wrote Rome, "that you have fully recovered from this experience and I see no reason to anticipate any further difficulty on this score."[25]

It is a mystery how Dr. Rome could believe Hemingway was "fully recovered." The fact is he was still a very sick man and, back in Ketchum, he could not write, taking a week to compose a simple note of congratulations to newly inaugurated President John F. Kennedy Jr. He was writing in between tears, frustrated that the words were so slow in coming. The man who had cheated death so many times was now deathly afraid the FBI was tailing him. The thing is, they were—FBI agents now sent in to snoop around even though he was so ill.

While suffering bouts of depression and the suicidal impulses that hemochromatosis causes, the frail, ailing Hemingway wrote one final chapter of *A Moveable Feast* the first three days of April—doing, as he wrote, what "I was born to do,"[26] while repeating the "Nada, Pues Nada" of "A Clean Well-Lighted Place." He had written this earlier work after his accident in Billings, Montana, that had plunged him into a deep, depressing place he only escaped by imagining this well-ordered, clean, lit place, while splicing his nothingness, his "nada," into his prayers.

Now the lights went out. "(M)y heart," he wrote in this final, initially unpublished chapter, "does not exist"—"my memory . . . tampered with."

Oh, but he had a heart—a big heart, evidenced by the letter he would write to his doctor's ailing son. As for his memory, it had surely been "tampered with." He was readmitted to Mayo Clinic on April 25 when his "memory" would once again be "tampered with." As they refueled in Rapid City, South Dakota, on the return trip, he attempted suicide twice, the second time walking toward the plane's rapidly spinning propeller, evidently concluding it would be a quick way to finish himself off. But the pilot cut the engine just in the nick of time.[27] After they sedated him, Hemingway was able to make the rest of the trip without incident.

Once back at St. Mary's, he was given amazing freedom to walk around town and enjoy the beautiful scenery, but along with that freedom came more electroshock therapy. Mary visited in May and was greeted by a distraught husband, feeling imprisoned. "You think as long as you can keep me getting electric shocks, I'd be happy," he said.[28] Mary wanted to take him out of the Mayo Clinic because she thought he was not getting better and asked Rome to transfer him to the Institute of Living in Hartford, but Rome insisted he was getting better and so he stayed. By 1965, Rome became head of the American Psychiatry Association.

A DYING COOPER GIVES HIS AILING FRIEND A SPIRITUAL BOOST

That May, as Cooper lay dying, writhing in pain, he wanted to give his tortured friend, now suffering so greatly at St. Mary's, a morale and faith boost. As Hotchner, who had visited Coop, wrote, "When the pain had passed, Cooper reached his hand over to the bed table and picked up a crucifix, which he put on the pillow beside his head . . . 'Please give Papa [Hemingway] a message. It's important and you mustn't forget because I'll not be talking to him again. Tell him . . . that time I wondered if I made the right decision'—he moved the crucifix a little closer so that it touched his cheek—'tell him,'" he said, referring to his conversion to Catholicism, "'it was the best thing I ever did.'"[29]

Cooper died on May 13, 1961, the Feast of Our Lady of Fatima.

In early June, Hotch visited "Papa," taking a walk with him in the woods. As they sat on a stone wall, Hem told him, in response to a question, that he wanted to kill himself because of "that thing in my head," which, he said, prevented him from writing. "Hotch, if I can't exist on my own terms, then existence is impossible."

Yet he continued to share his "joy," evident in his last letter, dated June 15, 1961, from Rochester, to young nine-year-old Fritz Saviers, hospitalized for viral heart disease:

I was terribly sorry to hear . . . from your father that you were laid up in Denver . . . I've had a chance to see some of the wonderful country along the Mississippi where they used to drive logs in the old lumbering days and the trails where the pioneers came north. Saw some good bass jump in the river. I never knew anything about the upper Mississippi before and it is really a very beautiful country and there are plenty of pheasants and ducks in the fall . . . But not as many as in Idaho and I hope we'll both be back there shortly and can joke about our hospital experiences together . . . Best always to you, old timer from your good friend who misses you very much. (Mister) Papa[30]

Like his mother, Grace, who could still play the piano as life was waning, by feeling the tempo, Hemingway could still feel the beats of his writing in this beautiful letter while he struggled immensely.

Beats inspired by the Holy Spirit.

In late June, Rome called Mary into his office, and she was surprised to see her husband dressed in regular clothes, "grinning like a Cheshire cat."[31] The doctor said he was discharging him because he would best recover at home. Mary could not disagree more but there was no arguing the point with this expert, who had read Dostoyevsky to try and understand a patient's mental condition when all he need do was read Hem's medical chart and family medical history, and read his suffering face.

Hotch had begged Mary not to let him come home and to wait until they could transfer him to a more suitable place of healing, but she followed Rome's orders.

In truth, Mary was quite ill herself. Clara Spiegel, ex-wife of Hem's Italian ambulance corps buddy Frederick, who had left Chicago in the forties to settle in Ketchum, Idaho, becoming a close friend of the Hemingways, had observed Mary's alcoholism. One day as their lives were unraveling, she told Mary she must cut back on her drinking. Mary thanked her then went to the refrigerator and took out a bottle of Tanqueray and downed the whole thing right in front of Clara.[32]

On June 26, they began the long journey home to Ketchum, with George Brown at the wheel driving the 1,786-mile trip over five days—longer than usual because Hemingway wanted to stop early each day lest they not find a motel room. Such was his growing paranoia.

On Saturday, July 1, Hemingway and Mary had their last meal together at a local Chinese restaurant, Christiana—Christy's as Hem called it—joined by Brown. Sitting in his favorite booth, he enjoyed a New York strip steak, and delicious French wine. But during dinner, he thought two men at a table farther back were the feds coming to get him. At home later, Brown went to sleep in the guest room while Mary sang Ernest an Italian folk song, as he said, "Good night, my kitten."—his final words to her.

On Sunday morning, Hemingway rose early and went downstairs to the gun case. Mary had left it open the night before, reasoning that he was so beautifully calm that it would be fine to do so, lest he feel constrained and become agitated. In the intervening hours, his mood had darkened and in his frenzied state of mind, he grabbed his cherished Boss gun and blew his brains out. Mary found him at the bottom of the stairs, slumped over, a bloody mess, and called a friend, Chuck Atkinson, to put out a statement, which read: "Mr. Hemingway accidentally killed himself while cleaning a gun this morning at 7:30 a.m."[33] After a week of seclusion, Mary told the *New York Times* what good spirits Hemingway had been in the day before and that she thought his death had to have been an accident.[34]

Sunny wrote that when they arrived at the Ketchum home the day after Hemingway died, there was no sign of the dramatic events of one day earlier. Most unusual, she thought. She also wondered if her brother had slept-walked, as he did as a child, and killed himself unknowingly—not being in his right mind and that, in a trance-like state, as if on autopilot, he grabbed the gun and did the deed, now the hunted one, because of various things preying on his mind.

No one was there to rescue him that day at his home in Ketchum.

Or maybe there was.

"He was sick. He was sick," said Welles. "But he did talk about suicide . . . And, he talked to me about it several times in a sort of obsessive way. He was a sick man. He was not well mentally. He's not to be judged as himself. The Hemingway we are talking about did not choose his death. He might have. But he wasn't that man."[35]

OUR LADY OF THE SNOWS, THE END AND THE BEGINNING

Hemingway was given a Catholic burial from Our Lady of the Snows in Ketchum, Idaho, his gravesite blanketed with red roses. Rev. Robert J. Waldman, who officiated at Hemingway's gravesite Catholic memorial service, said, "We pass no judgment on [his suicide]."

"I think Hemingway truly was a Catholic down deep, however much he might have ignored it for convenience and posturing," said Charles Scribner III. "Think Graham Greene's characters. Or even Greene himself, who was more conspicuously and intellectually engaged with aspects of the Faith. The fact that Mary chose a Catholic service of burial for him speaks volumes."[36]

As his friend George Herter, who knew him in Paris, Key West, and Havana and visited him in Idaho in those last years, wrote in a letter to Stoneback after his death, "(H)e was a very strong Catholic. He had complete faith in God, Jesus, the Virgin, the Holy Ghost, guardian angels. Much more than nearly all Catholics I have known. I have often wondered what he would have done and how he would have reacted to the church today. He was a traditional Catholic as we all were at the time."[37]

When told of his father's belief in Mary's apparitions, citing particularly the "Miracle of the Sun" at Fatima on October 13, 1917, Patrick, absorbing the magnitude of this event, said, "Maybe he did believe in miracles."[38]

His sister "Sunny" (Madelaine) Mainland—who said, to understand Hemingway's writing, you need to understand his spirituality—wrote in her book *Ernie* how deeply concerned she was about his soul after he took his own life. But when she visited the local Episcopal church the day he was buried—miraculously, a smiling Hemingway, albeit with "sad eyes" appeared on the aisle carpet. Hemingway, she was assured, was now experiencing that "best thing" of which Cooper spoke in his last message to his dear friend.

His "sad eyes" intimated his dismay with his biographers—"pleading for more light, more charity, more accuracy from his biographers," wrote Stoneback.[39] Hopefully, this book has provided a portrait of Hemingway that shows, along with the shadows, the light of faith that shone so brightly in the "writing" he was "born to do," reflecting a rich interior life.

The stuff of sanctity!

Bibliography

A&E Biography, *Ernest Hemingway: Wrestling with Life,* 1996.

A&E Biography, *The Lost Generation,* 2001.

Adams, Lucia. *Wahoga: Bror Blixen in Africa.* Kindle Direct Publishing, May 2019.

AP. "Novelist Ernest Hemingway Dies of Gun Wounds." *Los Angeles Times,* July 3, 1961.

Baker, Carlos. *Ernest Hemingway: A Life Story.* New York: Charles Scribner's Sons, 1969.

Baker, Carlos. "Ernest Hemingway: Living, Loving, Dying." *The Atlantic Monthly,* January 1969.

Baker, Carlos ed. *Ernest Hemingway: Selected Letters,* 1917–1961. New York: Charles Scribner's Sons, 1981.

Barnett, Andrea. "The Moderns: 'SISTER BROTHER Gertrude and Leo Stein.'" *New York Times Book Review,* June 2, 1996.

BBC One. *The Great Gatsby, Midnight in Manhattan,* 2000.

Benton, Charlotte, Benton, Tim, and Wood, Ghislaine. *Art Deco: 1910–1939.* New York: Bulfinch Press, 2003.

Blume, Lesley M. M. *Everybody Behaves Badly: The True Story Behind Hemingway's Masterpiece* The Sun Also Rises. New York: Eamon Dolan/ Houghton Mifflin Harcourt, 2016.

Bowen, Stella. *Drawn from Life.* London: Virago Press Limited, 1941.

Bracker, Milton. "1953 Pulitzer Prizes Won by Hemingway and 'Picnic.'" *New York Times,* May 4, 1953.

Brasch, James D. "Hemingway's Doctor: José Luis Herrera Sotolongo Remembers Ernest Hemingway." *Journal of Modern Literature.* Indiana University Press, Vol. 13, No. 2, July 1986.

Brian, Denis. *The True Gen: An Intimate Portrait of Hemingway By Those Who Knew Him.* New York: Grove Press, 1988.

Brooklyn Daily Eagle. "Novelist Hurt in Paris," March 7, 1928.

Bruccoli, Matthew J., ed. *Conversations with Ernest Hemingway.* Jackson: University Press of Mississippi, 1986.

Bruccoli, Matthew. *F. Scott Fitzgerald: A Life in Letters.* New York: Charles Scribner's Sons, 1994.

Bryer, Jackson Robert, Margolies, Alan, and Prigozy, Ruth. *F. Scott Fitzgerald: New Perspectives.* Athens: University of Georgia Press, 2000.

Burdine, Hank. "Papa and Piggott: How a Small Arkansas Delta Town Helped Change the Course of American Literature." *Delta Magazine,* March 13, 2022.

Burgess, Anthony. *Ernest Hemingway.* London: Thames & Hudson, 1978.

Buske, Morris. "Hemingway Faces God." *The Hemingway Review,* Vol. 22, 2002.

Callaghan, Morley. *That Summer in Paris.* Ontario: Exile Editions, 2022.

Capshaw, Ron. "Hemingway the Communist." *The Liberty Conservative,* January 24, 2017.

The Catholic Transcript. "G. K. Chesterton Gives the Reasons for His Conversion: Hilaire Belloc Helped Famous Convert to See the Light." Volume XXIX, Number 12, 2 September 1926.

Chesler, Ellen. *Woman of Valor: Margaret Sanger and the Birth Control Movement in America.* New York: Simon and Schuster, 1992.

CBS This Morning-Saturday-Anthony Mason. "Was Ernest Hemingway a Player in International Espionage?" March 11, 2017.

Chicago Tribune. "Ernest Hemingway Pens Short Stories of Unusual Merit," December 24, 1927.

Chicago Daily Tribune. "Dr. Hemingway, Writer's Father, Ends Own Life." December 7, 1928.

Church, Ralph W. *A Study in the Philosophy of Malebranche.* London: Routledge, 1931.

Cray, Robert E., Jr. "Hemingway Goes Sub Chasing; Author Ernest Hemingway Tracked German U-boats Aboard His Yacht in the Caribbean." www.warfarehistorynetwork.com, June 2010.

Davis, Tom. "American Woman." *Hatch Magazine,* January 16, 2019.

Dearborn, Mary V. *Ernest Hemingway: A Biography.* New York: Alfred A. Knopf, 2017.

Dicastery for Communication, Vatican Publishing House. Address of His Holiness John Paul II to the Students of Catholic University. Washington, DC, October 7, 1979.

Diliberto, Gina. *Paris Without End.* New York: Harper Perennial, 1992.

DiRobilant, Andrea. "Retracing Hemingway's Road Trip Through Northern Italy." *Departures*, December 15, 2016.

Donaldson, Scott. "The Jilting of Ernest Hemingway." *VQR, A National Journal of Literature and Discussion*, Autumn 1989.

Donaldson, Scott. *Archibald MacLeish: An American Life*. New York: Houghton, Mifflin Company, 1992.

Donaldson, Scott. *Hemingway vs. Fitzgerald: The Rise and Fall of a Literary Friendship*. New York: The Overlook Press, 1999.

Donaldson, Scott. *The Paris Husband: How It Really Was Between Ernest and Hadley Hemingway*. Scott Donaldson, 2018.

Dos Passos, John. *The Best Times: An Informal Memoir*. New York: Open Road Distribution, 1966.

Douglas, William A. "The Sun Also Sets." *BOGA: Basque Studies Consortium Journal*, October 2015, Vol. 3, Issue 1.

Driver, Julia. "The History of Utilitarianism." University of Texas at Austin, March 27, 2009; revised September 22, 2014. *Stanford Encyclopedia of Philosophy*.

Eastman, Max. *Einstein, Trotsky, Hemingway, Freud and Other Great Companions*. New York: Collier Books, 1962.

Escrivá de Balaguer, St. Josemaria. *The Way*, "Our Lady." Chicago: Scepter, 1954.

Fadiman, Clifton. "Ernest Hemingway Crosses the Bridge: The Transformations of 'For Whom the Bell Tolls.'" *The New Yorker*, October 18, 1940.

Farah, Andrew. *Hemingway's Brain*. Columbia, SC: University of South Carolina Press, 2017.

Fenton, Charles A. "Ernest Hemingway: The Young Years." *The Atlantic Monthly*, April 1954.

Fenton, Charles A. "Ernest Hemingway: The Paris Years." *The Atlantic Monthly*, May 1954.

Fenton, Charles A. *The Apprenticeship of Ernest Hemingway*. New York: Compass Books Edition, 1958.

Fortini, Amandi. "The Importance of Not Being Ernest." *New York Times*, October 24, 2013.

Fountain, Gary and Brazeau, Peter. *Remembering Elizabeth Bishop: An Oral Biography*. Amherst: University of Massachusetts Press, 1994.

Freedman, Richard. "Hemingway's Spanish Civil War Dispatches." *Texas Studies in Literature and Language*, University of Texas Press, Vol. 1, No. 2, Summer 1959.

Fulbright.org, "Remembering Earl 'Bud' Rovit," May 9, 2018.

Gopnik, Adam. "Hemingway, the Sensualist: The Macho Icon Has Been Recast as a Gender-Bending Progressive. But What Really Made His Pulse Race?" *The New Yorker*, June 26, 2017.

Granta. *The 1930s: Martha Gellhorn.* https://granta.com/the-thirties/.

Griffin, Peter. *Along with Youth: Hemingway, The Early Years.* New York: Oxford University Press, 1985.

Hackett, Mary, and Kendall, Mary Claire, ed. *William 'Bill' Walton: A Charmed Life.* Wellesley, MA: Branden Books, 2013.

Hammond, Percy. "The Theaters." *Chicago Tribune*, October 17, 1920.

Heise, Kenan. "Madelaine Miller; Hemingway's Sister." *Chicago Tribune*, January 27, 1995.

Hemingway, Ernest. "Confessions." Oak Park Public Library Special Collections, 1917.

Hemingway, Ernest. *in our time.* Paris: Three Mountains Press, 1924.

Hemingway, Ernest. *In Our Time.* New York: Charles Scribner's Sons, 1925.

Hemingway, Ernest. *The Sun Also Rises.* New York: Charles Scribner's Sons, 1926.

Hemingway, Ernest. *Men Without Women.* New York: Charles Scribner's Sons, 1927.

Hemingway, Ernest. *A Farewell to Arms.* New York: Charles Scribner's Sons, 1929.

Hemingway, Ernest. *Death in the Afternoon.* New York: Charles Scribner's Sons, 1932.

Hemingway, Ernest. *Winner Take Nothing.* New York: Charles Scribner's Sons, 1933.

Hemingway, Ernest. *Green Hills of Africa.* New York: Charles Scribner's Sons, 1935.

Hemingway, Ernest. "The Short Happy Life of Francis Macomber." *Cosmopolitan*, September 1936.

Hemingway, Ernest. *A Moveable Feast.* New York: Charles Scribner's Sons, 1964.

Hemingway, Ernest. *A Moveable Feast, The Restored Edition.* New York: Scribner, 2009.

Hemingway, Ernest. "The Sights of Whitehead Street; A Key West Letter." *Esquire*, April 1935.

Hemingway, Ernest. "A Gulf Stream Letter, On Being Shot Again." *Esquire*, June 1935.

Hemingway, Ernest. "A New York Letter: Million Dollar Fight." *Esquire: The Magazine for Men*, December 1935.

Hemingway, Ernest. *To Have and Have Not.* New York: Charles Scribner's Sons, 1937.

Hemingway, Ernest. *For Whom the Bell Tolls*. New York: Charles Scribner's Sons, 1940.

Hemingway, Ernest. *The Garden of Eden*. New York: Charles Scribner's Sons, 1986.

Hemingway, Ernest. *Across the River and Into the Trees*. New York: Charles Scribner's Sons, 1950.

Hemingway, Ernest. *The Old Man and the Sea*. New York: Charles Scribner's Sons, 1952.

Hemingway, Ernest. *The Dangerous Summer*. New York: Charles Scribner's Sons, 1985.

Hemingway, Ernest. *True at First Light: A Fictional Memoir*. New York: Scribner, 1999.

Hemingway, Ernest. *The Short Stories*. New York: Scribner, 1999.

Hemingway, Ernest. Statement on the Second Plane Crash, January 1954. Hemingway Collection, JFK Library.

"Hemingway Is Injured," New York Times, May 26, 1944.

Hemingway, Leicester. *My Brother, Ernest Hemingway*. Sarasota, FL: Pineapple Press, 1996.

Hemingway, Mary. *How It Was*. New York: Ballantine Books, 1976.

Hemingway, Patrick, and Hemingway, Sean, ed. *Hemingway on War*. New York: Scribner, 2004.

Hemingway, Valerie. *Running with the Bulls: My Years with the Hemingways*. New York: A Ballantine Book, 2004.

Hendrickson, Paul. *Hemingway's Boat: Everything He Loved in Life and Lost, 1934–1961*. New York: Alfred A. Knopf, 2011.

Henrickson, Paul. "Ernest Hemingway and the Sea." John F. Kennedy Presidential Library, October 12, 2011.

Hendrickson, Paul. "Hemingway and son," *The Financial Times*, January 13, 2012.

Horne, Bill, 1913, as told to Virginia Kleitz Moseley. "First Person: The Hemingway I Remember." *Princeton Alumni Weekly*, November 11, 1979.

Hotchner, A. E. *Papa Hemingway*. New York: Random House, 1966.

IOANNES PAULUS PP. II, From the Vatican, April 19, 2000. CONGREGATION FOR THE DOCTRINE OF THE FAITH, *THE MESSAGE OF FATIMA*. https://www.vatican.va/roman_curia/congregations/cfaith/documents/rc_con_cfaith_doc_20000626_message-fatima_en.html.

Isabelle, Julianne. "Hemingway's Religious Experience," MA Thesis. Northern Michigan University, 1963.

Index of Modernist Magazines. "This Quarter."

Irish Times, "Once a Catholic, always . . ." June 16, 2001. https://www.irishtimes.com/news/once-a-catholic-always-1.313453.

Katakis, Michael, ed. *Ernest Hemingway: Artifacts from A Life*. New York: Scribner, 2018.

Kellogg, Louise Phelps. Charlevoix, Pierre-Francois-Xavier De. *Journal of a Voyage to North America*. London: Dodsley, 1761, XV.

Kendall, Mary Claire. "Hemingway on Hemingway & Hollywood," *Forbes*, July 21, 2012.

Kendall, Mary Claire. "Hemingway's Catholic Heart." *St. Austin Review*, January/February 2019.

Kendall, Mary Claire. "America Loses Pre-Eminent Civil War Historian; Professor Edward C. 'Eddie' Smith Viewed History through a Lens of Truth and Healing." *"Old Hollywood and Beyond,"* *Substack*, April 13, 2023.

Kendig, Jeanne. "The Nobel and the Addict." *The American Dissident*, 2001.

Kert, Bernice. *The Hemingway Women*. New York: W.W. Norton & Company, 1983.

Kipen, David. "Ernest Hemingway's Long-Lost Los Angeles Visit." *Los Angeles Times*, July 13, 2017.

Lynn, Kenneth S. "Hemingway's Private War." *Commentary*, July 1981.

Lynn, Kenneth S. *Hemingway*. New York: Simon and Schuster, 1987.

Lyons, Leonard. "The Lyon's Den." *New York Post*, July 21, 1959.

Maziarka, Cynthia and Vogel Jr., Donald ed. *Hemingway at Oak Park High*. Oak Park: Oak Park and River Forest High School, 1993.

McAlmon, Robert. *Being Geniuses Together 1920–1930*. San Francisco: North Point Press, 1984.

McInerney, Ralph. "F. Scott Fitzgerald: The Authority of Failure," 2005.

Meyers, Jeffrey. "Wanted by the FBI!" *New York Review of Books*, March 31, 1983.

Meyers, Jeffrey. *Hemingway: A Biography*. New York: Harper & Row Publishers, 1986.

Meyers, Jeffrey. "The Hemingways: An American Tragedy." *VQR: A National Journal of Literature and Discussion*, Spring 1999.

Meyerson, Harvey. "They All Like the Ernest Hemingways." *The Honolulu Advertiser*, May 3, 1959.

Miller, Madelaine Hemingway. *Ernie: Hemingway's Sister "Sunny" Remembers*. New York: Crown Publishers, 1975.

Mitgang, Herbert. "Publishing FBI File on Hemingway." *New York Times*, March 11, 1983.

Moraglio, Massimo. "1922: The Motorway from Milan to the Prealpine Lakes." *Driving Modernity*, Vol. 3, 2017.

Morris, Edmund. *Colonel Roosevelt*. New York: Random House, 2010.

Morris, James McGrath. *The Ambulance Drivers: Hemingway, Dos Passos, and a Friendship Made and Lost in War*. Boston: Da Capo Press, 2017.

Mort, Terry. *Hemingway at War: Ernest Hemingway's Adventures as World War II Correspondent*. New York: Pegasus Books, 2016.

New York Times. "Widow Describes Hemingway MSS.; Tells of Unpublished Work—Calls Death Accident," July 9, 1961.

Nickel, Matthew. *Hemingway's Dark Night: Catholic Influences and Intertextualities in the Work of Ernest Hemingway*. Wickford, RI: New Street Communications, LLC, 2013.

Nilsson, Anton. "Ernest Hemingway and the Politics of the Spanish Civil War." *The Hemingway Review*, Volume 36, Number 1, Fall 2016, p. 81–93. Published by The Hemingway Foundation and Society.

Oliver, Charles M. *Ernest Hemingway A to Z: The Essential Reference to the Life and Work*. New York: Checkmark, 1999.

Orson Welles, Interview with Michael Parkinson, BBC, 1974. https://www.youtube.com/watch?v=6dAGcorF1Vo.

Paul, Steve. "'Drive,' He Said: How Ted Brumback Helped Steer Ernest Hemingway into War and Writing." Chestnut Hill College. *Hemingway Review*, Vol. 27, Issue 1, Fall 2007.

Paul, Steve. "Hemingway Left a Legacy, and Much of His Heart, in Cuba." *The Kansas City Star*, July 19, 2013.

Pawley, Daniel. "Ernest Hemingway: Tragedy of an Evangelical Family." *Christianity Today*, November 17, 1984: 20–27.

PBS documentary. *Paradise and Purgatory: Hemingway of the L Bar T and St. V's*. October 31, 2016.

Poore, C. G. "Ernest Hemingway's Story of His African Safari." *New York Times*, October 27, 2022.

Pope Leo XIII. "Iucunda Semper Expectatione." Encyclical of Pope Leo XIII on the Rosary. The Vatican, September 8, 1894.

Price, Reynolds. "For Ernest Hemingway," *Ernest Hemingway*. Harold Bloom, ed., New York: Chelsea House, 1985, p. 137–60. Reprinted from *Things Themselves*, New York: Athaneum, 1972.

Reynolds, Michael. *Hemingway's First War*. New York: Basil Blackwell Inc., 1987.

Reynolds, Michael. *The Young Hemingway*. New York: W.W. Norton & Co., 1998.

Reynolds, Michael. *Hemingway: The Paris Years*. New York: W. W. Norton & Company, 1989.

Reynolds, Michael. *Hemingway: The Homecoming*. New York: W.W. Norton & Co., 1992.

Reynolds, Michael. *Hemingway: The 1930s*. New York: WW Norton & Co., Inc., 1998.

Reynolds, Michael. *Hemingway, The Final Years*. New York: W.W. Norton & Co., 1999.

Reynolds, Nicholas. "A Spy Who Made His Own Way; Ernest Hemingway, Wartime Spy; Novelist Spy?" *Unclassified Studies in Intelligence*, Vol. 56, No. 2 Extracts, June 2012.

Reynolds, Nicholas. *Writer, Sailor Soldier Spy*. New York: Harpers Collins, 2017.

Rosengren, John. "The Old Man and the Clinic." *Minneapolis-St. Paul Magazine*, February 2019.

Rosengren, John. "The Last Days of Hemingway at Mayo Clinic." *Minneapolis St. Paul Magazine*, March 1, 2019.

Ross, Lillian. "How Do You Like It Now Gentlemen?: The Moods of Ernest Hemingway." *The New Yorker*, May 13, 1950.

Sanford, Marcelline Hemingway. *At the Hemingways* (Moscow: University of Idaho Press, 1999), p. 14.

Sarason, Bertram. *Hemingway and the "Sun" Set*. Washington, DC: NCR/ Microcard Editions, 1972.

Schickel, Richard. "You Must Remember This: The Warner Brothers Story," American Masters, PBS, 2008.

Schiller, Bill. "My Afternoon with Hemingway's Sister." THE INSIDER. *Toronto Star*, Summer 1981.

Scribner, Charles III. *Scribners: Five Generations in Publishing*. Essex, CT: Lyons Press (Rowman & Littlefield), 2023.

Sears, David. "When Ernest Hemingway Went from Writer to Fighter." *World War II*, June 25, 2020.

Sokoloff, Alice Hunt. *Hadley: The First Mrs. Hemingway*. New York: Dodd, Mead & Company, 1973.

Spanier, Sandra & Trogdon, Robert W., ed. *The Letters of Ernest Hemingway, 1907–1922*. New York: Cambridge University Press, 2011.

Stewart, Donald Ogden. *By A Stroke of Luck! An Autobiography By Donald Ogden Stewart*. New York: Paddington Press, Ltd., 1975.

Stillwater Gazette. "William Faulkner Picks Five Literary Greats," June 6, 1947.

Stoneback, H. R. "Hemingway's Catholicism and the Biographies," in *Hemingway: Essays of Reassessment*. Scafella, Frank, ed. New York: Oxford University Press, 1991.

Stoneback, H. R. "Pilgrimage Variations: Hemingway's Sacred Landscapes." The University of Notre Dame, Vol. 35, No. 2/3. Summer–Autumn, 2003.

Stoneback, H. R. *Reading Hemingway's* The Sun Also Rises. Kent, OH: Kent State University Press, 2007.

Stoneback, H. R., *Hemingway's Paris: Our Paris?* New Street Communications, 2010.

Time Magazine. "Books: An American Storyteller," December 13, 1954.

UPI. "Hemingway Out of Jungle; Arm Hurt, He Says Luck Holds." *New York Times*, January 25, 1954.

Vaill, Amanda. *Everybody Was So Young: Gerald and Sara Murphy: A Lost Generation Love Story.* New York: Broadway Books, 1998.

Villard, Dr. Henry S. and Nagel, James. *Hemingway in Love and War.* New York: Hyperion, 1989.

Wickes, George. "Little Magazines and Other Publishing Ventures." *The Paris Review*, Issue 47, Summer 1969.

Wikipedia. "Basilica of St. Mary Star of the Sea. (Key West, Florida)."

Wilmington Morning News. "Among Local Folk: M/M Fr. Scott Fitzgerald Sailed at Midnight Last Night," April 21, 1928.

Wilson, Edmund. "Mr. Hemingway's Dry-Points." *The Dial*, October 1924, p. 340.

Woodress, James. *Booth Tarkington, Gentleman from Indiana.* Philadelphia: JB Lippincott Company, 1955.

https://oprfmuseum.org/this-month-in-history/st-edmunds-parish-dedicates-new-oak-park-church

https://www.pleasanthome.org/about#

https://www.graceoakpark.org/

https://cnrse.cnic.navy.mil/Installations/NAS-Key-West/About/History/

Notes

INTRODUCTION

1. As told to the author by Redd Griffin, founding member and past president of the Ernest Hemingway Foundation of Oak Park, and her mentor. His mother gave birth to him in the same hospital in Oak Park as Madelaine "Sunny" Hemingway Mainland (later: Miller) when she gave birth to her son, Ernest Hemingway Mainland. The two mothers and their newborns shared the same room.

2. Anthony Burgess, *Ernest Hemingway* (London: Thames & Hudson, 1978), p. 48, 52, 60.

3. Frank Scafella, ed., *Hemingway: Essays of Reassessment* (New York: Oxford University Press, 1991), "Hemingway's Catholicism and the Biographies" by H. R. Stoneback, p. 138.

4. Letter from Ernest Hemingway to Robert Morgan Brown, July 22, 1954, Ernest Hemingway Collection, Harry Ransom Center, Box 3.8, The University of Texas at Austin.

5. Correspondence with Charles Scribner III via email, dated September 12, 2011.

6. Harold Bloom, ed., *Ernest Hemingway* (New York: Chelsea House), 1985.

7. Harold Bloom, ed., *Ernest Hemingway* (New York: Chelsea House, 1985), p. 137–60: "For Ernest Hemingway" by Reynolds Price, reprinted from *Things Themselves*, (New York: Athaneum, 1972): 176–213.

8. Scafella, ed., and Stoneback, *Hemingway: Essays of Reassessment*, p. 135–36.

9. Mary Claire Kendall, "Hemingway on Hemingway & Hollywood," *Forbes*, July 21, 2012.

10. Scafella, ed., and Stoneback, *Hemingway: Essays of Reassessment*, p. 120.

CHAPTER ONE

1. Carlos Baker, *Ernest Hemingway: A Life Story* (New York: Charles Scribner's Sons, 1969), p. 3.

2. Seventy-four years later First Congregational became First United Church of Oak Park, formed by uniting with the First Presbyterian.

3. Morris Buske, "Hemingway Faces God," *The Hemingway Review*, Vol. 22, 2002.

4. Sandra Spanier and Robert W. Trogdon, ed., *The Letters of Ernest Hemingway*, 1907–1922 (New York: Cambridge University Press, 2011), p. 6 footnote.

5. Buske, "Hemingway Faces God." JFK Library, Hemingway Collection. Scrapbook II, 19.

6. Baker, *Ernest Hemingway*, p. 5.

7. Marcelline Hemingway Sanford, *At the Hemingways* (Moscow: University of Idaho Press, 1999), p. 14.

8. https://www.graceoakpark.org/.

9. Daniel Pawley, "Ernest Hemingway: Tragedy of an Evangelical Family," *Christianity Today*, 17 Nov. 1984: 20–27.

10. Sanford, *At the Hemingways*, p. 15.

11. Julianne Isabelle, "Hemingway's Religious Experience," MA Thesis, Northern Michigan University, 1963.

12. Sanford, *At the Hemingways*, p. 12.

13. Scrapbook II, 31; Scrapbook III, inside front cover, JFK Library, Hemingway Collection.

14. Scrapbook #2, 19, February 12, 1902, JFK Library, Hemingway Collection.

15. Scrapbook #2, 41, JFK Library, Hemingway Collection.

16. Scrapbook II, 69, JFK Library, Hemingway Collection.

17. Scrapbook IV, 4, JFK Library, Hemingway Collection.

18. Mary V. Dearborn, *Ernest Hemingway: A Biography* (New York: Alfred A. Knopf, 2017) p. 12.

19. Miller, *Ernie*, p. 6 and 15.

20. Miller, *Ernie*, p. 50.

21. Miller, *Ernie*, p. 50.

22. Michael Reynolds, *The Young Hemingway* (New York: W.W. Norton & Co., 1998), p. 82–83.

23. Sanford, *At the Hemingways*, p. 31.

24. Buske, "Hemingway Faces God."

25. Miller, *Ernie*, p. 71.

26. Letter from Ernest Hemingway to Robert Morgan Brown, July 1, 1956, Ernest Hemingway Collection, Harry Ransom Center, Box 3.8, The University of Texas at Austin.

27. Baker, *Ernest Hemingway*, p. 670.

28. Denis Brian, *The True Gen: An Intimate Portrait of Hemingway by Those Who Knew Him* (New York: Grove Press, 1988), p. 300.

29. Ernest Hemingway, *Winner Take Nothing*: "Fathers and Sons" (New York: Charles Scribner's Sons, 1933).

30. Letter from Ernest Hemingway to Marcelline Hemingway, June 17, 1909, Hemingway Collection, Box #OC01, JFK Library.

31. Letter from Marcelline Hemingway to Grace Hall Hemingway, August 31, 1919, Humaniies Research Center, University of Texas.

32. BBC One, *The Great Gatsby, Midnight in Manhattan*, 2000.

33. Letter from and to Ernest Hemingway, to and from Dr. Clarence Hemingway, July 1907, Scrapbook III, JFK Library.

34. Letter from Ernest Hemingway to Clarence Hemingway, Hemingway Collection, Scrapbook IV, JFK Library.

35. Address of His Holiness John Paul II to the Students of Catholic University, Washington, DC, Sunday, 7 October 1979, Dicastery for Communication, Vatican Publishing House.

36. Leicester Hemingway, *My Brother, Ernest Hemingway* (Sarasota, FL: Pineapple Press, 1996), p. 62.

37. Buske, "Hemingway Faces God."

38. https://oprfmuseum.org/this-month-in-history/st-edmunds-parish-dedicates-new-oak-park-church.

39. https://www.pleasanthome.org/about#.

40. Ernest Hemingway, "Confessions," 1917, *Oak Park Public Library Special Collections.*

41. Ernest Hemingway, "Confessions."

42. Charles A. Fenton, "Ernest Hemingway: The Young Years," *The Atlantic Monthly*, April 1954.

43. A&E, *Ernest Hemingway: Wrestling with Life.*

44. Ellen Chesler, *Woman of Valor: Margaret Sanger and the Birth Control Movement in America* (New York: Simon and Schuster, 1992), p. 66.

45. Edmund Morris, *Colonel Roosevelt* (New York: Random House, 2010), p. 267–72 and 660–63.

46. Letter from Ernest Hemingway to Grace Hall Hemingway, September 8, 1914, Hemingway Collection, Box #OC01, JFK Library.

47. Brian, *The True Gen*, p. 14.

48. Bill Schiller, THE INSIDER, "My afternoon with Hemingway's sister," *Toronto Star*, Summer 1981.

49. Letter from Ernest Hemingway to Marcelline Hemingway, May 5, 1915, Hemingway Collection, Box #OC01, JFK Library.

50. Brian, *The True Gen*, p. 12.

51. Fenton, *Atlantic Monthly.*

52. Ernest Hemingway, "Confessions."

53. Fenton, *Atlantic Monthly.*

54. Ernest Hemingway, "Confessions."

55. Sanford, *At the Hemingways*, p. 150.

56. Brian, *The True Gen*, p. 13.

57. Brian, *The True Gen*, p. 15.

58. Spanier & Trogdon, ed., *Letters, 1907–1922*, p. 24–25.

59. William E. Barton Letters at Syracuse University, https://library.syracuse.edu/digital/guides/b/barton_we.htm.

60. Redd Griffin, interview with author, over Thanksgiving 2011.

61. Letter from Ernest Hemingway to Grace Hall Hemingway, September 14, 1917, Hemingway Collection, Box #OC01. JFK Library.

62. Fenton, *Atlantic Monthly*.

63. Fenton, *Atlantic Monthly*.

64. Letter from Ernest Hemingway to Anson Hemingway, August 6, 1917, Hemingway Collection, Box #OC01. JFK Library.

65. Letter from Ernest Hemingway to Anson Hemingway, August 3, 1917, Hemingway Collection, Box #OC01. JFK Library.

66. Letter from Ernest Hemingway to Fanny Biggs, Spring 1917, Hemingway Collection, Box #OC01, JFK Library.

67. Steve Paul, "'Drive,' He Said: How Ted Brumback Helped Steer Ernest Hemingway into War and Writing," Chestnut Hill College, *Hemingway Review*, Vol. 27, Issue 1, Fall 2007.

68. Letter from Ernest Hemingway to Grace Hall Hemingway, January 16, 1918, Hemingway Collection, Box#OC01, JFK Library.

69. Scafella, ed., and Stoneback, *Hemingway: Essays of Reassessment*, p. 117.

70. Baker, *Ernest Hemingway*, p. 59.

71. Carlos Baker, ed., *Ernest Hemingway: Selected Letters*, 1917–1961 (New York: Charles Scribner's Sons, 1981), p. 7–8.

72. Brian, *The True Gen*, p. 16–17.

73. Brian, *The True Gen*, p. 17.

74. Bill Horne, 1913, as told to Virginia Kleitz Moseley, "First Person: The Hemingway I Remember," *Princeton Alumi Weekly*, November 11, 1979.

75. Sanford, *At the Hemingways*, p. 154 and 156.

CHAPTER TWO

1. Horne, "The Hemingway I Remember."

2. Dr. Henry S. Villard and James Nagel, *Hemingway in Love and War* (New York: Hyperion, 1989), p. 207.

3. Villard and Nagel, *Hemingway in Love and War*, p. 209.

4. Villard and Nagel, *Hemingway in Love and War*, p. 10.

5. Baker, *Ernest Hemingway*, p. 40–41.

6. Ernest Hemingway, *Death in the Afternoon* (New York: Charles Scribner's Sons, 1932), p. 135–36. He also included the same passage in his next volume: Ernest Hemingway, *Winner Take Nothing* (New York: Charles Scribner's Sons, 1933), p. 98–99.

7. Baker, *Ernest Hemingway*, p. 41.

8. Horne, "The Hemingway I Remember."
9. Villard and Nagel, *Hemingway in Love and War*, p. 10.
10. Baker, *Ernest Hemingway*, p. 43.
11. Baker, *Ernest Hemingway*, p. 44.
12. Baker, *Ernest Hemingway*, p. 43.
13. Brian, *The True Gen*, p. 18
14. Horne, "The Hemingway I Remember."
15. Baker, *Ernest Hemingway*, p. 44.
16. McKey, not Hemingway, as is frequently misstated, was the first American to be wounded in Italy—fatally. Hemingway was the first American to be wounded and survive.
17. Villard and Nagel, *Hemingway in Love and War*, p. 210.
18. Cynthia Maziarka and Donald Vogel Jr., ed., *Hemingway at Oak Park High* (Oak Park: Oak Park and River Forest High School, 1993), p. 118.
19. Baker, *Ernest Hemingway*, p. 44.
20. Brian, *The True Gen*, p. 19.
21. Scafella, ed., and Stoneback, *Hemingway: Essays of Reassessment*, Letter to Thomas Welsh, June 19, 1945, p. 127.
22. Baker, p. 45.
23. Spanier and Trogdon, ed., *Letters, 1907-1922*, p. 115.
24. Spanier and Trogdon, ed., *Letters, 1907-1922*, p.115
25. Baker, ed., *Selected Letters*, p. 15-16.
26. Baker, ed., *Selected Letters*, p. 15-16.
27. Villard and Nagel, *Hemingway in Love and War*, p. 216–17.
28. Charles Scribner III email correspondence with the author, September 12, 2011.
29. Scafella, ed., and Stoneback, *Hemingway: Essays of Reassessment*, "Hemingway's Catholicism and the Biographies," p. 107–8, citing Grace Hall Hemingway's Scrapbook I, 68.
30. Villard and Nagel, *Hemingway in Love and War*, p. 8.
31. Scott Donaldson, *Hemingway vs. Fitzgerald: The Rise and Fall of a Literary Friendship* (New York: The Overlook Press, 1999), p. 39.
32. Donaldson, *Hemingway vs. Fitzgerald*, p. 40.
33. Scott Donaldson, "The Jilting of Ernest Hemingway," *VQR, A National Journal of Literature and Discussion*, Autumn 1989.
34. Donaldson, *Hemingway vs. Fitzgerald*, p. 40–41.
35. Ernest Hemingway, *A Farewell to Arms*, (New York: Charles Scribner's Sons, 1929), p. 71–72.
36. Donaldson, "The Jilting of Ernest Hemingway."
37. Horne, "The Hemingway I Remember."
38. Ernest Hemingway to "Dearest Family," November 11, 1918, in Villard and Nagel, *Hemingway in Love and War*, p. 184.
39. Donaldson, "The Jilting of Ernest Hemingway."

40. Donaldson, "The Jilting of Ernest Hemingway."

41. Donaldson, "The Jilting of Ernest Hemingway."

42. Villard and Nagel, *Hemingway in Love and War*, p. 13.

43. Ernest Hemingway, *In Our Time* (New York: Charles Scribner's Sons, 1925), p. 65.

44. Scafella, ed., and Stoneback, *Hemingway: Essays of Reassessment*, p. 111.

45. Hemingway, *In Our Time*, p. 65–66.

46. Letter from Ernest Hemingway to Bill Horne, March 30, 1919, Hemingway Collection, Box #OC01, JFK Library.

47. IOANNES PAULUS PP. II, From the Vatican, 4-19-2000. CONGREGATION FOR THE DOCTRINE OF THE FAITH, *THE MESSAGE OF FATIMA*. https://www.vatican.va/roman_curia/congregations/cfaith/documents/rc_con_cfaith_doc_20000626_message-fatima_en.html.

48. Scafella, ed., and Stoneback, *Hemingway: Essays of Reassessment*, p. 134.

49. Pope Leo XIII, "Iucunda Semper Expectatione," Encyclical of Pope Leo XIII on the Rosary, The Vatican, September 8, 1894.

CHAPTER THREE

1. Donaldson, "The Jilting of Ernest Hemingway."

2. Ernest Hemingway, *In Our Time* (New York: Charles Scribner's Sons), 1925, p. 66.

3. Horne, "The Hemingway I Remember."

4. Maziarka and Vogel, ed., *Hemingway at Oak Park High*, p. 16.

5. Maziarka and Vogel, ed., *Hemingway at Oak Park High*, p. 117–19.

6. Maziarka and Vogel, ed., *Hemingway at Oak Park High*, "Hemingway Speaks to High School," *The Trapeze*, March 21, 1919, image on p. 116.

7. Sanford, *At the Hemingways*, p. 183–84.

8. Ernest Hemingway, letter to Lawrence T. Barnett, April 30, 1919, Hemingway Collection, Box OC01, JFK Library; Baker, *Selected Letters*, p. 24.

9. Hemingway, *My Brother, Ernest Hemingway*, p. 56.

10. Ernest Hemingway, *Men Without Women* (New York: Charles Scribner's Sons, 1927), p. 145–53.

11. Hemingway, *My Brother, Ernest Hemingway*, p. 59.

12. Sanford, *At the Hemingways*, p. 205.

13. Ernest Hemingway, *In Our Time* (New York: Charles Scribner's Sons), 1925, p. 71–72.

14. Ernest Hemingway, *In Our Time*, p. 75.

15. Ernest Hemingway, *In Our Time*, p. 76–77.

16. Baker, *Ernest Hemingway*, p. 63.

17. Ruth Arnold to Grace Hall Hemingway, August 4, 1919, Humanities Research Center, University of Texas.

18. Baker, *Ernest Hemingway,* p. 66.

19. Michael Reynolds, *Young Hemingway*, p. 103–4. Letter from Grace Hall Hemingway to Ernest Hemingway, February 8, 1920, Hemingway Collection, Box IC11, Kennedy Library.

20. Reynolds, *Young Hemingway*, p. 138.

21. Baker, *Ernest Hemingway,* p. 71–72.

22. Spanier and Trogdon, ed., *Letters, 1907–1922*, p. 238.

23. Baker, *Ernest Hemingway,* p. 73. (Based on a letter Ernest wrote to Grace Quinlan on September 30, 1920, postmark Boyne City, MI, October 1, 1920, Boyne City. Letter in Yale Collection.)

24. Louise Phelps Kellogg, Pierre-Francois-Xavier De Charlevoix, *Journal of a Voyage to North America* (London: Dodsley, 1761), xv.

25. Spanier and Trogdon, ed., *Letters, 1907–1922*, p. 244.

26. Reynolds, *The Young Hemingway*, p. 213.

27. Percy Hammond, "The Theaters" *Chicago Tribune*, October 17, 1920.

28. Alice Hunt Sokoloff, *Hadley: The First Mrs. Hemingway* (New York: Dodd, Mead & Company), 1973, p. 6.

29. Charles M. Oliver, *Ernest Hemingway A to Z: The Essential Reference to the Life and Work* (New York: Checkmark, 1999), p. 139.

30. Gina Diliberto, *Paris Without End* (New York: Harper Perennial, 1992), p. 11.

31. Diliberto, *Paris Without End*, p. 18.

32. Diliberto, *Paris Without End*, p. 24.

33. Brian, *The True Gen*, p. 9.

34. Horne, "The Hemingway I Remember."

35. Letter from Ernest Hemingway to Hadley Richardson, December 23, 1920, Spanier and Trogdon, ed., *Letters, 1907–1922*, p. 258–59.

36. Horne, "The Hemingway I Remember."

37. Peter Griffin, *Along with Youth: Hemingway, The Early Years* (New York: Oxford University Press, 1985), p. 153.

38. Scafella, ed., and Stoneback, *Hemingway: Essays of Reassessment*, p. 113.

39. Scafella, ed., and Stoneback, *Hemingway: Essays of Reassessment*, p. 170.

40. Horne, "The Hemingway I Remember."

41. Sokoloff, *Hadley*, p. 24.

42. Sokoloff, *Hadley*, p. 24.

43. Diliberto, *Paris Without End*, p. 66.

44. Horne, "The Hemingway I Remember."

45. Sokoloff, *Hadley*, p. 24.

46. Spanier and Trogdon, ed., *Letters, 1907–1922*, p. 288.

47. Sokoloff, *Hadley*, p. 32–34.

48. Letter from Hadley Richardson to Ernest Hemingway, April 23, 1921, Hemingway Collection, Box IC25, JFK Library.

49. https://archive.org/details/virginiahotelchi00lawr/page/n1/mode/2up.

50. Diliberto, *Paris Without End*, p. 78.

51. Diliberto, *Paris Without End*, p. 79.

52. Sokoloff, *Hadley*, p. 35.

53. Spanier and Trogdon, ed., *Letters, 1907–1922*, p. 292.

54. Ernest Hemingway, *In Our Time*, "The Three-Day Blow" (New York: Charles Scribner's Son, 1925), p. 46.

55. Diliberto, *Paris Without End*, p. 81.

56. Sokoloff, *Hadley*, p. 36.

57. Madelaine Hemingway Miller, *Ernie: Hemingway's Sister "Sunny" Remembers* (New York: Crown Publishers, 1975), p. 99.

58. Diliberto, *Paris Without End*, p. 87–88.

59. Sokoloff, *Hadley*, p. 40.

60. Sokoloff, *Hadley*, p. 41.

CHAPTER FOUR

1. Sokoloff, *Hadley*, p. 42.

2. Baker, *Ernest Hemingway*, p. 83.

3. Sokoloff, *Hadley*, p. 43.

4. "G.K Chesterton Gives the Reasons for His Conversion: Hilaire Belloc helped famous convert to see the light," *The Catholic Transcript*, Volume XXIX, Number 12, 2 September 1926, p. 10.

5. Hilaire Belloc, *Paris* (London: Methuen & Co. Ltd., 1902), p. 92–94.

6. BBC One, *The Great Gatsby, Midnight in Manhattan*, 2000.

7. Diliberto, *Paris Without End*, p. 96.

8. Michael Reynolds, *Hemingway: The Paris Years* (New York: W. W. Norton & Company, 1989), p. 10.

9. Ernest Hemingway, *A Moveable Feast* (New York: Charles Scribner's Sons, 1964), p. 35.

10. Sokoloff, *Hadley*, p. 48–49.

11. Ernest Hemingway, *A Moveable Feast*, p. 3–8.

12. Sokoloff, *Hadley*, p. 46.

13. Sokoloff, *Hadley*, p. 48.

14. Sokoloff, *Hadley*, p. 51.

15. Ernest Hemingway, *A Moveable Feast*, p. 108.

16. Ernest Hemingway, *A Moveable Feast*, pp. 133 and 138.

17. Andrea Barnett, "The Moderns: 'SISTER BROTHER Gertrude and Leo Stein,'" *New York Times Book Review*, June 2, 1996.

18. A&E Biography, *Ernest Hemingway: Wrestling with Life*, 1996.

19. Burgess, *Ernest Hemingway*, p. 39.

20. "Once a Catholic, Always . . ." *The Irish Times*, June 16, 2001. https://www.irishtimes.com/news/once-a-catholic-always-1.313453.

21. https://www.hemingwaysociety.org/seeking-double-dealer-part-i.

22. Baker, *Ernest Hemingway*, p. 100.

23. Ernest Hemingway, *A Moveable Feast*, p. 55.

24. Letter from Ernest Hemingway to Gertrude Stein and Alice B. Toklas, June 11, 1922, Hemingway Collection, Box OC01, JFK Library.

25. Ernest Hemingway, *A Moveable Feast*, p. 43–44.

26. Sokoloff, *Hadley*, p. 52.

27. Ernest Hemingway, *A Moveable Feast*, p. 51–52.

28. Ernest Hemingway, *A Moveable Feast*, p. 54.

29. Ernest Hemingway, *A Moveable Feast*, p. 55.

30. Ernest Hemingway, *A Moveable Feast*, p. 56.

31. Ernest Hemingway, *A Moveable Feast*, p. 57–58.

32. Baker, *Ernest Hemingway*, p. 91.

33. Scafella, ed. and Stoneback, *Hemingway: Essays of Reassessment*, p. 134.

34. Sokoloff, *Hadley*, p. 56.

35. Sokoloff, *Hadley*, p. 38.

36. Scott Donaldson, *The Paris Husband: How It Really Was Between Ernest and Hadley Hemingway* (Scott Donaldson, 2018), Location 601 in Kindle Edition.

37. Letter from Hadley Richardson Hemingway to Clarence and Grace Hemingway, December 11, 1922, Hemingway Collection, Box IC26, JFK Library.

38. Sokoloff, *Hadley*, p. 61.

39. Brian, *The True Gen*, p. 41.

40. Reynolds, *Hemingway: The Paris Years*, p. 124.

41. Ernest Hemingway, *in our time* (Paris: Three Mountains Press, 1924) p. 12.

42. A&E Biography, *Ernest Hemingway: Wrestling with Life*, 1996.

43. Brian, *The True Gen*, p. 44–45.

44. Morley Callaghan, *That Summer in Paris* (Ontario: Exile Editions, 2022), p. 17–18.

45. Callaghan, *That Summer in Paris*, p. 19–20.

46. Brian, *The True Gen*, p. 44–45.

47. Letter from Ernest Hemingway to Mrs. John Sanford, October 14, 1923, Hemingway Collection, Box OC01, JFK Library.

48. These stories included a robbery and murder in Kansas City Hemingway covered as a cub reporter; the story of the public hanging of the Chicago mobster Sam Cardinelli; and an interview with the King Constantine I of Greece and his wife Sophia of Prussia during the Revolution, titled *"L'Envoi."*

49. Donaldson, *Hemingway vs. Fitzgerald*, p. 62.

50. Ernest Hemingway, *A Moveable Feast*, p. 76–77.

51. Ernest Hemingway, *A Moveable Feast, The Restored Edition* (New York: Scribner, 2009), p. 72.

52. Baker, *Ernest Hemingway*, p. 126.

53. Lillian Ross, "How Do You Like It Now Gentlemen?: The Moods of Ernest Hemingway," *The New Yorker*, May 13, 1950.

54. Letter to Gertrude Stein, August 15, 1924, Hemingway Collection, Box OC01, JFK Library.

55. Ernest Hemingway, *A Moveable Feast*, p. 69.

56. Ernest Hemingway, *Green Hills of Africa* (New York: Charles Scribner's Sons, 1935), p. 50.

57. A&E Biography, *The Lost Generation*, 2001.

58. Callaghan, *That Summer in Paris*, p. 108.

59. Scott Donaldson, *Archibald MacLeish: An American Life* (New York: Houghton, Mifflin Company, 1992), p. 144–45.

60. Brian, *The True Gen*, pp. 37 and 52.

61. Brian, *The True Gen*, p. 54.

62. John Dos Passos, *The Best Times: An Informal Memoir* (New York: Open Road Distribution, 1966), p. 139.

63. Dos Passos, *The Best Times*, p. 140–41.

64. Dos Passos, *The Best Times*, p. 142.

65. Ernest Hemingway, *A Moveable Feast* (New York: Charles Scribner's Sons, 1964), p. 64.

66. Dos Passos, *The Best Times*, p. 140–41.

67. Letter from Ernest Hemingway to Harold Loeb, December 29, 1924, Hemingway Collection, Box OC01, JFK Library.

68. Baker, *Ernest Hemingway*, p. 133.

69. St. Josemaria Escrivá de Balaguer, *The Way*, "Our Lady" (Chicago & London: Scepter, 1954), p. 127.

70. Ernest Hemingway, *The Sun Also Rises* (New York: Charles Scribner's Sons, 1926; Collier Books 1986), p. 78.

71. H. R. Stoneback, *Hemingway's Paris: Our Paris?*, New Street Communications, 2010.

72. Hemingway, *The Sun Also Rises*, p. 97.

73. Hemingway, *A Farewell to Arms*, p. 105.

CHAPTER FIVE

1. Ernest Hemingway, *A Moveable Feast*, p. 81.

2. Index of Modernist Magazines, "This Quarter," https://modernistmagazines.org/european/this-quarter/.

3. Ernest Hemingway, *A Moveable Feast*, p. 79.

4. Letter from Ernest Hemingway to Dr. Clarence Hemingway, March 20, 1925, Ernest Hemingway Collection, JFK Library, Box #OC02.

5. A&E Biography, *The Lost Generation*, 2001.

6. Michael Reynolds, *Hemingway: The Homecoming* (New York: W.W. Norton & Co., 1992), p. 24.

7. Stella Bowen, *Drawn from Life* (London: Virago Press Limited, 1941), p. 119.

8. Michael Parkinson interview of Orson Welles, BBC, 1974. https://www.youtube.com/watch?v=6dAGcorF1Vo.

9. Charlotte Benton, Tim Benton, and Ghislaine Wood, *Art Deco: 1910–1939* (New York: Bulfinch Press, 2003), p. 16.

10. Edmund Wilson, "Mr. Hemingway's Dry-Points," *The Dial*, October 1924, p. 340.

11. Letter from Max Perkins to Ernest Hemingway, February 21, 1925; replacement letter dated Feb. 26, 1925 was sent because the address on the first letter was deemed "insufficiently specific."

12. Letter from Max Perkins to F. Scott Fitzgerald, April 28, 1925, Princeton University Library Special Collections.

13. Hemingway, *A Moveable Feast*, p. 149.

14. Brian, *The True Gen*, p. 43.

15. As told to the author by Peet's grandson, Scott Johnston, on April 22, 2023.

16. James Woodress, *Booth Tarkington, Gentleman from Indiana* (Philadelphia: JB Lippincott Company, 1955), p. 265.

17. Callaghan, *That Summer in Paris*, p. 136.

18. Matthew Bruccoli, *F. Scott Fitzgerald: A Life in Letters* (New York: Charles Scribner's Sons, 1994), p. 115.

19. Baker, *Ernest Hemingway Selected Letters*, p. 162–63; June 9, 1925.

20. James Woodress, *Booth Tarkington*, p. 265.

21. Letter from Ernest Hemingway to F. Scott Fitzgerald, July 1, 1925, Hemingway Collection, Box #OC02, JFK Library.

22. Diliberto, *Paris Without End*, p. 246.

23. Brian, *The True Gen*, p. 55–56.

24. Kenneth S. Lynn, *Hemingway* (New York: Simon and Schuster, 1987), p. 123.

25. Baker, *Selected Letters*, p. 272–74 (Letter to Max Perkins, March 17, 1928, Princeton University Library).

26. Hemingway, *A Moveable Feast*, p. 29.

27. Baker, *Ernest Hemingway*, p. 155–56.

28. The 1930 edition led off with a new addition, "On the Quai at Smyrna."

29. Callaghan, *That Summer in Paris*, p. 158.

30. Julia Driver, "The History of Utilitarianism," University of Texas at Austin, March 27, 2009; revised September 22, 2014, *Stanford Encyclopedia of Philosophy* https://plato.stanford.edu/entries/utilitarianism-history/.

31. Letter to Ernest Walsh from Ernest Hemingway, January 2, 1926, Hemingway Collection, Box #OC02, JFK Library.

32. Ernest Hemingway, *A Moveable Feast, The Restored Edition* (New York: Scribner), 2009, pages 218–19.

33. Scafella, ed., and Stoneback, *Hemingway: Essays of Reassessment*, pages 135–36.

34. Hemingway, *The Sun Also Rises*, p. 31.

35. Hemingway, *The Sun Also Rises*, p. 86–87.

36. Hemingway, *The Sun Also Rises*, p. 90.

37. Hemingway, *The Sun Also Rises*, p. 93.

38. Hemingway, *The Sun Also Rises*, p. 97.

39. Hemingway, *The Sun Also Rises*, p. 108–09.

40. Hemingway, *The Sun Also Rises*, pgs. 121–24.

41. Testimony of Blessed Alvaro del Portillo, March 5, 1976 regarding a conversation he had with Pope Paul VI, which he shared with the Pope's authorization.

42. Hemingway, *The Sun Also Rises*, p. 149.

43. Hemingway, *The Sun Also Rises*, p. 151.

44. Hemingway, *The Sun Also Rises*, p. 155.

45. Hemingway, *The Sun Also Rises*, p. 181–82.

46. Hemingway, *The Sun Also Rises*, p. 208–09.

47. Hemingway, *The Sun Also Rises*, p. 245.

48. Brian, *The True Gen*, p. 57.

49. Scafella, ed., and Stoneback, *Hemingway: Essays of Reassessment*, p. 135–36.

50. Hemingway, *A Moveable Feast*, p. 210.

51. Hemingway, *The Sun Also Rises*, p. 77.

52. Sokoloff, *Hadley*, p. 86.

53. Letter from Ernest Hemingway to Clarence Hemingway, *Selected Letters*, p. 207.

54. Letter from Pauline Pfeiffer to Ernest Hemingway, May 20, 1926, Hemingway Collection, Box IC15, JFK Library. Also, Reynolds, *The Homecoming*, p. 34.

55. Reynolds, *Hemingway: The Homecoming*, p. 38.

56. Miller, *Ernie*, p. 104.

57. Callaghan, *That Summer in Paris*, p. 66.

58. Baker, *Ernest Hemingway*, p. 175.

59. Baker, *Ernest Hemingway*, p. 185.

60. Diliberto, *Paris Without End*, p. 255.

61. Letter from Hadley Hemingway to Ernest Hemingway, August 20, 1926, Hemingway Collection, Box IC26, JFK Library.

62. Letter from Hadley Hemingway to Ernest Hemingway, September 7, 1926, Hemingway Collection, Box IC26, JFK Library.

63. Sokoloff, *Hadley*, p. 90.

64. Letter from Hadley Hemingway to Ernest Hemingway, October 16, 1926, Hemingway Collection, Box IC26, JFK Library.

65. Donaldson, *Archibald MacLeish: An American Life*, p. 161.

66. Reynolds, *Hemingway: The Homecoming*, pp. 68 and 67.

67. A&E Biography, *Ernest Hemingway: Wrestling with Life*, 1996.

68. Letter from Grace Hall Hemingway to Ernest Hemingway, December 4, 1926, Ernest Hemingway Collection, JFK Library.

69. Baker, *Ernest Hemingway*, p. 183.

70. Letter to Fr. Vincent C. Donovan from Ernest Hemingway, December 9, 1927, Hemingway Collection, Box OC02. JFK Library.

71. Diliberto, *Paris Without End*, p. 246.

72. Baker, *Ernest Hemingway*, p. 571.

73. Baker, *Ernest Hemingway*, p. 186.

74. Letter to Dr. and Mrs. C.E. Hemingway from Ernest Hemingway, September 14, 1927, Hemingway Collection, Box #OC02, JFK Library.

75. "Ernest Hemingway Pens Short Stories of Unusual Merit," *Chicago Tribune*, December 24, 1927, p. 8.

76. Miller, *Ernie*, p. 104.

77. Baker, *Selected Letters*, pages 272–74, Princeton University Library.

78. Donaldson, *Hemingway vs. Fitzgerald*, p. 124.

79. Callaghan, *That Summer in Paris*, p. 176.

80. A&E Biography, *The Lost Generation*, Donald Faulkner.

81. F. Scott Fitzgerald, *The Great Gatsby* (New York: Charles Scribner's Sons, 1925) p. 189.

82. Bruccoli, *F. Scott Fitzgerald: A Life in Letters*, p. 115. Letter from F. Scott Fitzgerald to Zelda, summer 1930, Princeton University Special Collection.

83. Lillian Ross, "How Do You Like It Now Gentlemen?: The Moods of Ernest Hemingway," *The New Yorker*, May 13, 1950.

84. Reynolds, *Hemingway: The Homecoming*, p. 167.

CHAPTER SIX

1. "History, Commander, Navy Region Southeast," Official United States Navy Website, https://cnrse.cnic.navy.mil/Installations/NAS-Key-West/About/History/.

2. Wikipedia, "Basilica of St. Mary Star of the Sea" (Key West, Florida).

3. Reynolds, *The Homecoming*, p. 176–77.

4. "Papa and Piggott: How a Small Arkansas Delta Town Helped Change the Course of American Literature," by Hank Burdine, *Delta Magazine*, March 13, 2022.

5. Letter from Ernest Hemingway to Grace and Clarence Hemingway, July 4, 1928, with note added July 15, Hemingway Collection, JFK Library.

6. Horne, "The Hemingway I Remember."

7. Baker, *Ernest Hemingway*, p. 196.

8. Reynolds, *The Homecoming*, p. 189.

9. Ernest Hemingway, *Winner Take Nothing*, p. 116.

10. From author's many conversations with Redd Griffin, founding member of the Hemingway Foundation of Oak Park, especially over Thanksgiving 2011.

11. Kenan Heise, MADELAINE MILLER; HEMINGWAY'S SISTER, *Chicago Tribune*, January 27, 1995.

12. Hemingway, *My Brother, Ernest Hemingway*, p. 109–11.

13. *Chicago Daily Tribune*, "Dr. Hemingway, Writer's Father, Ends Own Life," December 7, 1928.

14. Reynolds, *Hemingway: The Homecoming*, p. 85.

15. Sanford, *At the Hemingways*, p. 234.

16. Letter from Marcelline Hemingway Sanford to Grace Hall Hemingway, April 14, 1939, Humanities Research Center, University of Texas.

17. Author's conversation with John Sanford in Oak Park over dinner at the Carleton, July 19, 2016.

18. Buske, "Hemingway Faces God."

19. Hemingway, *My Brother, Ernest Hemingway*, p. 111.

20. Ernest Hemingway, *In Our Time*, p. 44.

21. Miller, *Ernie*, p. 115.

22. Letter from Ernest Hemingway to Mary Pfeiffer, December 13, 1927, Princeton Special Collection.

23. Baker, *Selected Letters*, p. 296.

24. Michael Reynolds, *Hemingway: The 1930s* (New York: WW Norton & Co., Inc., 1998), p. 1.

25. Bruccoli, *F. Scott Fitzgerald: A Life in Letters,* p. 164–67. (Letter from F. Scott Fitzgerald to Ernest Hemingway, June 1929, Hemingway Collection, JFK Library.)

26. Scafella, ed., and Stoneback, *Hemingway: Essays of Reassessment*, p. 131–32.

27. Callaghan, *That Summer in Paris*, p. 77.

28. Letter from Hadley Richardson to Ernest Hemingway, January 26, 1930, Hemingway Collection, Box IC26, JFK Library.

29. Hemingway, *A Farewell to Arms*, p. 263.

30. From author's many conversations with Redd Griffin, founding member of the Hemingway Foundation of Oak Park, especially over Thanksgiving 2011.

31. Hemingway, *A Farewell to Arms*, p. 147.

32. Hemingway, *A Farewell to Arms*, p. 152–53.

33. Hemingway, *A Farewell to Arms*, p. 248.

34. Hemingway, *A Farewell to Arms*, p. 327.

35. Letter from F. Scott Fitzgerald to Ernest Hemingway, June 1929, Hemingway Collection, JFK Library.

36. Callaghan, *That Summer in Paris*, p. 182.

37. Callaghan, *That Summer in Paris*, p. 202.

38. Donaldson, *Hemingway vs. Fitzgerald*, p. 290 (Article published in *Spur Magazine*, December 1, 1929).

39. Letter from Ernest Hemingway to Max Perkins, August 28, 1929, Baker, *Selected Letters*, p. 302–3.

40. F. Scott Fitzgerald to Ernest Hemingway, August 23, 1929, Hemingway Collection JFK Library.

41. Baker, *Ernest Hemingway*, p. 204.

42. Horne, "The Hemingway I Remember."

43. *Paradise and Purgatory: Hemingway of The L Bar T and St. V's*, PBS documentary, October 31, 2016.

44. Baker, *Selected Letters*, Letter from Ernest Hemingway to Henry Strater, c. September 10, 1930, p. 328–29.

45. Horne, "The Hemingway I Remember."

46. Ernest Hemingway, *Winner Take Nothing*, p. 129–48.

47. *Paradise and Purgatory: Hemingway of the L Bar T and St. V's*, Montana PBS, March 31, 2016. https://www.montanapbs.org/programs/ParadiseAndPurgatory/.

48. As told to author by Todd Asti, who spent time in Key West in the late 1980s and would talk with Russell's daughter.

49. Letter from Ernest Hemingway to Mary Pfeiffer, November 12, 1931, Princeton Special Collection.

50. Reynolds, *Hemingway: The 1930s*, p. 107.

51. Scafella, ed., and Stoneback, *Hemingway: Essays of Reassessment*, p. 127.

52. Reynolds, *Hemingway: The 1930s*, p. 127.

53. A&E Biography, *Ernest Hemingway: Wrestling with Life*, 1996.

54. Correspondence with Charles Scribner III dated October 4, 2022.

55. Scafella, ed., and Stoneback, *Hemingway: Essays of Reassessment*, p. 132–33.

56. Miller, *Ernie*, p. 104.

57. Carlos Baker, *Ernest Hemingway*, p. 228.

58. A&E Biography, *Ernest Hemingway: Wrestling with Life*, 1996.

59. Letter from Ernest Hemingway to Waldo Peirce, June 6, 1932, Hemingway Collection, Box OC03, JFK Library.

60. Key West Log Book, 1933, January 25–May 15 (JFK Library).

61. Reynolds: *Hemingway: The 1930s*, p. 140; EH Fishing Log, JFK, 1933.

62. Lucia Adams, *Wahoga: Bror Blixen in Africa*, Kindle Direct Publishing, May 2019.

63. C. G. Poore, "Ernest Hemingway's Story of His African Safari," *New York Times*, October 27, 2022.

64. Paul Henrickson, "Ernest Hemingway and the Sea," John F. Kennedy Presidential Library, October 12, 2011.

65. Baker, *Ernest Hemingway*, p. 491.

66. Tom Davis, "American Woman," *Hatch Magazine*, Wednesday, January 16, 2019.

67. Ernest Hemingway, "The Sights of Whitehead Street; A Key West Letter," *Esquire*, April 1935, pp. 125 and 156.

68. Ernest Hemingway, "A Gulf Stream Letter, On Being Shot Again," *Esquire*, June 1935, p. 25.

69. Reynolds, *Hemingway: The 1930s*, p. 202.

70. Reynolds, *Hemingway: The 1930s*, p. 211–12.

71. Ernest Hemingway, "A New York Letter: Million Dollar Fight," *Esquire: The Magazine for Men*, December 1935, p. 35.

72. Letter from Grace Hemingway to Ernest Hemingway, February 20, 1927, Hemingway Collection, Box IC11, JFK Library.

73. Ernest Hemingway, "The Short Happy Life of Francis Macomber," *Cosmopolitan*, September 1936.

74. Ernest Hemingway, *A Moveable Feast*, p. 211.

75. Letter from Ernest Hemingway to Max Perkins, February 7, 1936, Princeton Special Collection; also in Baker, *Select Letters*, p. 436–37.

76. Baker, *Selected Letters*, p. 433–37.

77. Reynolds, *Hemingway: The 1930s*, p. 226.

78. Letter from Ernest Hemingway to Archie MacLeish, May 31, 1936, Library of Congress.

79. Ernest Hemingway, *To Have and Have Not* (New York: Charles Scribner's Sons, 1937), p. 127.

80. Callaghan, *That Summer in Paris*, p. 137.

CHAPTER SEVEN

1. Dearborn, *Ernest Hemingway: A Biography*, p. 168–70.
2. Bernice Kert, *The Hemingway Women* (New York: W.W. Norton & Company, 1983), p. 282.
3. Granta, *The 1930s: Martha Gellhorn*, https://granta.com/the-thirties/.
4. Carlos Baker, "Ernest Hemingway: Living, Loving, Dying," *The Atlantic Monthly*, January 1969, p. 49.
5. Richard Freedman, "Hemingway's Spanish Civil War Dispatches," *Texas Studies in Literature and Language*, University of Texas Press, Vol. 1, No. 2 (Summer 1959), p. 171–80.
6. Carlos Baker, "Ernest Hemingway: Living, Loving, Dying," p. 49.
7. Mary Claire Kendall, "Hemingway on Hemingway and Hollywood," *Forbes*, July 21, 2012.
8. Reynolds, *Hemingway: The 1930s*, p. 276.
9. Scafella, ed., and Stoneback, *Hemingway: Essays of Reassessment*, p. 127.
10. Letter from Ernest Hemingway to Mary Pfeiffer, August 18, 1938, Princeton University Special Collection.
11. Letter from Ernest Hemingway to Robert Morgan Brown, September 24, 1954, Ernest Hemingway Collection, Harry Ransom Center, Box 3.8, The University of Texas at Austin.
12. Reynolds, *Hemingway: The 1930s*, p. 100.
13. Ernest Hemingway, "Notes on the Next War: A Serious Topical Letter," *Esquire: The Magazine for Men*, September 1935, pp. 19 and 156.
14. Michael Parkinson interview of Orson Welles, BBC, 1974.
15. Kert, *The Hemingway Women*, p. 312.
16. Carlos Baker, "Ernest Hemingway: Living, Loving, Dying," p. 59.
17. Ernest Hemingway, *Death in the Afternoon*, p. 122.
18. Carlos Baker, "Ernest Hemingway: Living, Loving, Dying," p. 59.
19. Author Interview with Patrick Hemingway, December 11, 2018.
20. Letter from Ernest Hemingway to Maxwell Perkins, March 25, 1939, Princeton University Special Collection; also, Baker, *Selected Letters*, pages 482–483.
21. Letter from Ernest Hemingway to Maxwell Perkins, February 7, 1939, Princeton University Special Collection; also, Baker, *Selected Letters*, p. 479. This is his outline of what would become *The Old Man and the Sea*.
22. Richard Schickel, "You Must Remember This: The Warner Brothers Story," American Masters, PBS, 2008.
23. Ernest Hemingway, *For Whom the Bell Tolls* (New York: Charles Scribner's Sons, 1940), p. 88.
24. Ernest Hemingway, *For Whom the Bell Tolls*, p. 250.
25. Ernest Hemingway, *For Whom the Bell Tolls*, p. 269.

26. Ernest Hemingway, *For Whom the Bell Tolls*, p. 321.

27. Letter from Ernest Hemingway to Charles Scribner Jr., June 29, 1948, Princeton University Special Collection.

28. Ernest Hemingway, *For Whom the Bell Tolls*, p. 66.

29. A&E Biography, *Ernest Hemingway: Wrestling with Life*, 1996.

30. Brian, *True Gen*, p. 135.

31. Sokoloff, *Hadley*, p. 101.

32. Diliberto, *Paris Without End*, p. 265.

33. Author Interview with Maria Cooper Janis, September 20, 2022.

34. Ernest Hemingway, *A Moveable Feast*, p. 147.

35. Bruccoli, *F. Scott Fitzgerald: A Life in Letters*, p. 469–70.

CHAPTER EIGHT

1. Author interview with Patrick Hemingway, July 14, 2023.

2. Jeffrey Meyers, *Hemingway: A Biography* (New York: Harper & Row, Publishers, 1986), p. 332.

3. Capshaw, *The Liberty Conservative*, "Hemingway, The Communist," January 24, 2017.

4. *CBS This Morning-Saturday*-Anthony Mason, "Was Ernest Hemingway a Player in International Espionage," March 11, 2017.

5. Carlos Baker, "Ernest Hemingway: Living, Loving, Dying," *The Atlantic Monthly*, p. 67.

6. Nicholas Reynolds, *Writer, Sailor Soldier Spy* (New York: Harpers Collins, 2017), p. 79.

7. Herbert Mitgang, "Publishing FBI File on Hemingway," *New York Times*, March 11, 1983; Jeffrey Meyers, "Wanted by the FBI!," *New York Review of Books*, March 31, 1983.

8. Nicholas Reynolds, "A Spy Who Made His Own Way: Ernest Hemingway, Wartime Spy," *Studies in Intelligence*, Vol. 56, No. 2, June 2012, p. 3.

9. "Hemingway Is Injured," New York Times, May 26, 1944.

10. Denis Brian, *The True Gen: An Intimate Portrait of Hemingway By Those Who Knew Him* (New York: Grove Press, 1988), p. 302.

11. Mary Claire Kendall, "Hemingway on Hemingway & Hollywood," *Forbes*, July 21, 2012. Hemingway's eyewitness account of D-Day was republished in *Hemingway at War*: Patrick Hemingway and Sean Hemingway, ed., *Hemingway on War* (New York: Scribner, 2004), p. 314–26.

12. Baker, *Ernest Hemingway*, p. 395–96.

13. David Sears, "When Ernest Hemingway Went from Writer to Fighter," *World War II*, June 25, 2020.

14. Sears, "When Ernest Hemingway went from Writer to Fighter."

15. Brian, *The True Gen*, p. 157.

16. David Sears, "When Ernest Hemingway went from Writer to Fighter," *World War II*, June 25, 2020.

17. Mary Hackett, ed. by Mary Claire Kendall, *William 'Bill' Walton: A Charmed Life* (Wellesley, MA: Branden Books, 2013), p. 75–82.

18. A. E. Hotchner, *Papa Hemingway* (New York: Random House, 1966), p. 119.

19. Michael Reynolds, *Hemingway, The Final Years* (New York: W.W. Norton & Co., 1999), p. 123.

20. Jackson Robert Bryer; Alan Margolies, and Ruth Prigozy, *F. Scott Fitzgerald: New Perspectives* (Athens: University of Georgia Press, 2000), p. 239.

21. Mary Claire Kendall, "Hemingway on Hemingway & Hollywood," *Forbes*, July 21, 2012.

22. Baker, *Selected Letters*, p. 578.

23. Jeffrey Meyers, "The Hemingways: An American Tragedy," *VQR: A National Journal of Literature and Discussion*, Spring 1999.

24. Scafella, ed., and Stoneback, *Hemingway: Essays of Reassessment*, Letter to Thomas Welsh, June 19, 1945, p. 127.

25. Baker, *Ernest Hemingway*, p. 462.

26. James D. Brasch, "Hemingway's Doctor: José Luis Herrera Sotolongo Remembers Ernest Hemingway," *Journal of Modern Literature*, Indiana University Press, Vol. 13, No. 2 (July 1986), p. 185–210.

27. Dearborn, *Ernest Hemingway*, p. 499.

28. "William Faulkner Picks Five Literary Greats," *Stillwater Gazette*, June 6, 1947, p. 3.

29. Ernest Hemingway, *The Garden of Eden* (New York: Charles Scribner's Sons, 1986), p. 97.

30. Andrea DiRobilant, "Retracing Hemingway's Road Trip Through Northern Italy," *Departures*, December 15, 2016.

31. Brian, *The True Gen*, p. 302–3.

32. Ernest Hemingway, *Across the River and Into the Trees* (New York: Charles Scribner's Sons, 1950), p. 195–96.

33. Mary Claire Kendall, "Hemingway on Hemingway & Hollywood," *Forbes*, July 21, 2012.

34. Ernest Hemingway, *Across the River and Into the Trees* (New York: Charles Scribner's Sons, 1950), p. 81.

35. Lillian Ross, "The Moods of Ernest Hemingway," *The New Yorker*, May 13, 1950.

CHAPTER NINE

1. Baker, *Selected Letters*, p. 685–86.

2. Baker, *Ernest Hemingway*, p. 372.

3. Baker, *Ernest Hemingway*, p. 488.

4. Baker, *Selected Letters, Hemingway*, p. 670.

5. Mary Hemingway, *How It Was* (New York: Ballantine Books, 1976), p. 365.

6. Correspondence with Charles Scribner III, dated October 4, 2022.

7. Dearborn, *Ernest Hemingway: A Biography*, p. 544.

8. Paul Hendrickson, *"Hemingway and Son," The Financial Times, January 13, 2012. The other two quotes in this paragraph are from the same source.*

9. Charles Scribner III, *Scribners: Five Generations in Publishing* (Essex, CT: Lyons Press, 2023), p. 89.

10. Baker, *Ernest Hemingway*, p. 499.

11. Scribner III, *Scribners*, p. 89-90.

12. Letter from Ernest Hemingway to Bernard Berenson, August 11, 1953, Hemingway Collection, BOX#OC10, JFK Library.

13. H. R. Stoneback, "Pilgrimage Variations: Hemingway's Sacred Landscapes," The University of Notre Dame, Vol. 35, No. 2/3 (Summer–Autumn, 2003), p. 49–65.

14. Letter from Ernest Hemingway to Bernard Berenson, October 25, 1955; Baker, *Selected Letters*, p. 848.

15. Letter from Ernest Hemingway to Robert Morgan Brown, September 14, 1954, Ernest Hemingway Collection, Harry Ransom Center, Box 3.8, The University of Texas at Austin.

16. Ernest Hemingway, *The Old Man and the Sea* (New York: Charles Scribner's Sons, 1952), p. 64–65.

17. Ernest Hemingway, *The Old Man and the Sea*, p. 87.

18. Ernest Hemingway, *The Old Man and the Sea*, p. 104–5.

19. Baker, *Ernest Hemingway*, p. 495.

20. Scribner III, *Scribners*, p. 94.

21. Milton Bracker, "1953 Pulitzer Prizes Won by Hemingway and 'Picnic,'" *New York Times*, May 4, 1953.

22. Baker, *Ernest Hemingway*, p. 518.

23. Ernest Hemingway Statement on the Second Plane Crash, Jan. 1954, Hemingway Collection, JFK Library.

24. UPI, "Hemingway Out of Jungle; Arm Hurt, He Says Luck Holds," *New York Times*, January 25, 1954.

25. Baker, *Ernest Hemingway*, p. 522.

26. Baker, *Ernest Hemingway*, p. 523.

27. Hotchner, *Papa Hemingway*, p. 129–30.

28. Letter from Ernest Hemingway to Bernard Berenson, September 24, 1954, Hemingway Collection, BOX#OC10, JFK Library.

29. Robert Morgan Brown was a lawyer who lived in Massapequa, New York, formerly a Jesuit novitiate, now working on his PhD thesis at Fordham.

30. Letter from Ernest Hemingway to Robert Morgan Brown, September 24, 1954, Ernest Hemingway Collection, Harry Ransom Center, Box 3.8, The University of Texas at Austin.

31. Ernest Hemingway, *A Moveable Feast*, p. 21.

32. Baker, *Ernest Hemingway*, p. 527.

33. A&E Biography, *Ernest Hemingway: Wrestling with Life*, 1996.

34. Baker, *Selected Letters*, p. 843.

35. Baker, *Ernest Hemingway*, p. 530.

36. Matthew J. Bruccoli, ed., *Conversations with Ernest Hemingway* (Jackson: University Press of Mississippi, 1986), p. 96.

37. Scafella, ed., and Stoneback, *Hemingway: Essays of Reassessment*, p. 118.

38. Scafella, ed., and Stoneback, *Hemingway: Essays of Reassessment*, p. 119.

39. Baker, *Selected Letters*, p. 848.

40. Brian, *True Gen*, p. 252.

41. Letter from Ernest Hemingway to Alfred Rice, January 24, 1956, Hemingway Collection, JFK Library, Box#OC10.

42. Baker, *Selected Letters*, p. 868.

43. Scafella, ed., and Stoneback, *Hemingway: Essays of Reassessment*, pp. 119–120.

CHAPTER TEN

1. Reynolds, *Hemingway: The Paris Years*, p. 346.

2. Kendall, "Hemingway on Hemingway & Hollywood," *Forbes*.

3. Reynolds, *Hemingway, The Final Years*, p. 303–6.

4. Horne, "The Hemingway I Remember."

5. Harvey Meyerson, "They All Like the Ernest Hemingways," *The Honolulu Advertiser*, May 3, 1959.

6. Myerson, "They All Like the Ernest Hemingways," , May 3, 1959.

7. A. E. Hotchner, "Hemingway, Hounded by the Feds," *New York Times*, July 1, 2011.

8. Baker, *Ernest Hemingway*, p. 548.

9. Harold Loeb, *The Way It Was* (New York: Criterion Books, 1959).

10. Baker, Ernest Hemingway, p. 552.

11. Correspondence with Charles Scribner III dated October 4, 2022.

12. Baker, Ernest Hemingway, p. 552.

13. A. E. Hotchner, "Hemingway, Hounded by the Feds," *New York Times*, July 1, 2011.

14. John Rosengren, "The Last Days of Hemingway at Mayo Clinic," *Minneapolis St. Paul Magazine*, March 1, 2019.

15. "The Nobel and the Addict," by Jeanne Kendig, *The American Dissident*, March 22, 2001.

16. Robert F. Kennedy Jr., *The Real Anthony Fauci Movie*, 2022.

17. Chat with John Sanford, July 19, 2016, over dinner at the Carleton Hotel during Hemingway conference in Oak Park, Illinois.

18. Michael Parkinson interview of Orson Welles, BBC, 1974. https://www.youtube.com/watch?v=6dAGcorF1Vo.

19. Leicester Hemingway, *My Brother, Ernest Hemingway*, p. 281–82.

20. Hotchner, *Papa Hemingway*, p. 280.

21. Mary Claire Kendall, *Oasis: Conversion Stories of Hollywood Legends*, p. 33.

22. Hotchner, *Papa Hemingway*, p. 279.

23. Scafella, ed., and Stoneback, *Hemingway: Essays of Reassessment*, p. 118.

24. Brian, *The True Gen*, p. 249.

25. John Rosengren, "The Old Man and the Clinic," *Minneapolis-St. Paul Magazine*, February 2019.

26. Ernest Hemingway, *A Moveable Feast, The Restored Edition* (New York: Scribner), 2009, p. 225.

27. Hotchner, *Papa Hemingway*, p. 288–89.

28. Mary Hemingway, *How It Was*, p. 632.

29. Hotchner, *Papa Hemingway*, p. 290.

30. Baker, *Selected Letters*, p. 921, published in *Life Magazine*, August 25, 1961.

31. John Rosengren, "The Old Man and the Clinic," *Minneapolis-St. Paul Magazine*, February 2019.

32. A&E Biography, *Ernest Hemingway: Wrestling with Life*, 1996.

33. AP, "Novelist Ernest Hemingway Dies of Gun Wounds," *Los Angeles Times*, July 3, 1961.

34. "Widow Describes Hemingway MSS.; Tells of Unpublished Work—Calls Death Accident," *New York Times*, July 9, 1961.

35. Michael Parkinson interview of Orson Welles, BBC, 1974. https://www.youtube.com/watch?v=6dAGcorF1Vo.

36. Correspondence with Charles Scribner III dated October 4, 2022.

37. Scafella, ed., and Stoneback, *Hemingway: Essays of Reassessment*, p. 134.

38. Patrick Hemingway, interview with the author, November 2, 2012.

39. Scafella, ed., and Stoneback, *Hemingway: Essays of Reassessment*, pp. 114–115.

Index

About the Author

Mary Claire Kendall is a writer and columnist based in Washington, DC. Her recent books include *Oasis: Conversion Stories of Hollywood Legends*; *Oasis of Faith: The Souls Behind the Billboard—Barrymore, Cagney, Tracy, Stewart, Guinness & Lemmon*; and *Hemingway's Faith*. As an essayist, she writes a bimonthly column for the online Catholic news and information website *Aleteia*. Her website is maryclairecinema.com.